## ॐ॥ The Romance of Real Life

# ᴙ‖ THE ℛOMANCE
# ᴙ‖ OF REAL LIFE

## Charles Brockden Brown and the
## Origins of American Culture

### Steven Watts

The Johns Hopkins University Press
Baltimore and London

© 1994 The Johns Hopkins University Press
All rights reserved
Printed in the United States of America on acid-free paper

The Johns Hopkins University Press
2715 North Charles Street
Baltimore, Maryland 21218-4319
The Johns Hopkins Press Ltd., London

Library of Congress Cataloging-in-Publication Data will be found at
the end of this book.
A catalog record for this book is available from the British Library.

*Frontispiece:* engraving of Charles Brockden Brown, by I. B. Forrest,
from a miniature by William Dunlap in 1806.

For my parents, Kenneth and Mary Watts,
whose encouragement and expectations
many years ago started all this

The man of the world is entirely covered with a mask; he is so accustomed to disguise, that if at any time he is obliged for a moment to assume his natural character his uneasiness and constraint are palpably obvious. . . . Reality is no part of his concern, he aims at nothing more than appearance.
—Jean-Jacques Rousseau, *Emile*

# Contents

# Acknowledgments

Unlike the economic variety, intellectual and personal debts are a pleasure to acknowledge. A number of fine scholars have generously given of their time to read this manuscript and offer insights, suggestions, and warnings: Philip Barnard, Cathy Davidson, Jay Fliegelman, Norman Grabo, Elizabeth Jane Wall Hinds, and Michael Warner. Occasionally, I even listened to them. Joyce Appleby, Susan Curtis, Robert Gross, James Henretta, and Jackson Lears—superb historians all—have read or heard portions of my argument and made very constructive criticisms over the last several years. Charles E. Bennett kindly assisted me in obtaining several crucial Charles Brockden Brown documents.

Several institutions also deserve many thanks. The Humanities Research Center at the University of Texas made available photocopies of a number of Brown's personal letters, as did the Bowdoin College Library. The University of Missouri has played an important role in supporting this project. Its Faculty Research Council generously provided summer research funds, while a number of my colleagues in the History Department—especially Jonathan Sperber, Kerby Miller, Richard Bienvenu, John Bullion, Gerry Clarfield, and Robert Collins—provided a supportive environment in the last stages of the book's completion. The Johns Hopkins University Press, with its usual combination of good-natured efficiency and high professional standards, has eased the book toward completion. Robert Brugger, Maria E. denBoer, and Kimberly Johnson made the process a pleasurable one.

Patti Sokolich Watts has earned my greatest gratitude. She took time away from her own career as a teacher and soul singer to help out on many fronts—as an occasional typist, a discerning critic and editor, a patient listener, a culinary master. Along with Chaucer, Bart, Buzz, Eleanor, Bianca, George, Ambra, and May, she made life a little easier out on Creasy Springs Road.

# Introduction

The writing of biography can be a humbling experience. For the historian, examination of the single person beckons as a way to get beneath the hazy generalizations and overarching conclusions that characterize the craft. This genre makes visceral connection to an actual human being and real experience seem possible. One digs out a mass of evidence on a solitary life, contemplates the direction and rhythm of its development, and draws conclusions, comfortable in the likelihood that at least *this* person's encounters with history can be grasped and understood.

Then, uneasiness strikes. After climbing inside a subject's head and formulating confident conclusions, the scholar can stumble across small details that jolt complacency. It might be, as in this case, the offhanded discovery that one's subject was nearsighted throughout most of his life— he did not become aware of this impediment until adulthood, when he tried on a friend's spectacles and instantly realized his fuzzy, distorted vision of the world—or that he hated the "irksome and unwelcome sound" of his own last name.[1] Such details, while not crucial in and of themselves, remind us that much in the human experience remains unrecoverable. The implications of this fact are sobering, even terrifying. If we cannot fully fathom even one individual's encounter with the past, is it not pretentious, or worse, to proclaim patterns of historical change and their meanings for vast groups of people?

Recent cultural theory, however, provides something of a refuge from such fears. A complete and "accurate" rendering of individual perception, motivation, and action, much recent theory suggests, is less important than our ideological heritage of liberalism insists and more elusive than our scholarly heritage of empiricism realizes. A variety of approaches— structuralism, poststructuralism, Marxism, modernization, Freudianism, "the new historicism"—all tend to converge in at least one sense. They hold that the individual must be seen not so much as a determining free agent, but rather as a kind of contested emotional and intellectual battle-ground for a wide variety of cultural discourses. While certainly able to choose among many ideas and modes of expression according to proclivity and belief, the single person's choices are not completely free and unlimit-ed. Restricted options are available in a culture, and reaching beyond them can be painful, incoherent, or impossible. As Raymond Williams once put it in a compelling metaphor, cultural life is like driving a car. Motoring about in an automobile fosters the illusion of "movement, choice of direc-tion, the pursuit of self-determined private purposes." Yet, in fact, "traffic flows and their regulation are clearly a social order of a determined kind" as engineers, planners, and government bodies have constructed the routes one can take according to a certain economic, social, and cultural logic. The same holds true for one's "choice" of values and behavior. Modern bi-ography, heeding such lessons, must explore both the possibilities and lim-itations of the individual life. It should attempt not an unattainable recov-ery of complete and freely chosen individual experience, but rather a reconstruction of the complex discursive, ideological, and emotional roles that a historical figure has been able to play.[2]

Charles Brockden Brown, the early American novelist and critic, offers fascinating possibilities for just such an analysis. Both his private and pub-lic life, and the way in which they intertwined, promise to tell us much about the era of far-reaching historical change in which he lived. Research for my broad reinterpretation of the early American republic, *The Republic Reborn: War and the Making of Liberal America, 1790-1820* (1987), first brought Brown to my attention. This book attempted to chart the transi-tion from republicanism to liberalism in the dominant culture of post-Revolutionary America, and to gauge the attraction to armed violence generated by that transformation. Brown emerged as a *dramatis persona* for the study in a brief biographical sketch. A fascination with his career re-fused to go away, however. While my limited treatment of certain themes in his life and writings proved satisfactory, even richer possibilities seemed to exist. Several biographies had been written, but they were outdated.[3] Numerous monographs and articles had appeared in the scholarly litera-ture, but most of them offered literary analyses of a relatively narrow sort.[4] Much of this writer's significance seemed to lay in a broader area that was little explored: his relationship to a society and culture undergoing massive changes in the late eighteenth and early nineteenth centuries.

In particular, several issues demanded further study, and most of them stemmed from the persistence of a stereotyped image. Traditionally,

Brown has been granted heroic, pioneer status as the United States' first serious author, and his outpouring of flamboyant Gothic fiction in the 1790s has provoked considerable critical interest. Yet the inability of the "Father of the American Novel" to sell books and survive as a professional writer has provoked much weeping and gnashing of teeth. His unhappy situation seemed to offer an early indictment of the same provincial culture that would later alienate great artists like Herman Melville, Henry James, and T. S. Eliot. In other words, Brown has taken shape as the first of a romantic type: the brilliant, provocative author rejected by an acquisitive American society with its utilitarian ethic and crass materialism. As with most stereotypes, however, a glimmer of truth lies smothered by a landslide of assumptions. Certain unanswered questions linger uncomfortably. What exactly did the concepts "professional author" and "failure" mean in the context of the late eighteenth century? What was the historical meaning of Brown's bizarre, emotional, Gothic fiction with its perverse focus on abnormal psychology? How did the author's notoriously explosive private life intersect with his public writing? What was the relationship of Brown's entire corpus of writings—political pamphlets, short stories, didactic essays, geographical commentary, cultural criticism—to the four novels of the late 1790s on which his reputation rests? These queries eventually lead to the largest issue of all. As many scholars have demonstrated in recent years, the era spanning the breakdown of centuries-old medieval tradition and the full-blown emergence of modern industrial capitalism offered enormous instability and flux, not least of all in the domain of literature. What was Brown's connection, if any, to the powerful currents of historical change remaking the early modern West?[5]

Such questions call for a "cultural biography," which is defined best, perhaps, by what it is *not*. It avoids the hoary "life and times" approach of the traditional historian, which assumes too much about each partner in this analytical construct. It also rejects the "intellectual biography" model, which frequently degenerates into a treatment of isolated, formal, and abstract ideas with little concern for their material and social connections. Finally, and rather obviously, such a study takes issue with the current postmodern dismissal of biography, in which the importance of the single life has disintegrated under an onslaught of epistemes, language codes, and intertextuality. With the postmodern linguistic invasion— here "words speak people rather than the other way around"—the author has become an inevitable casualty. Unfortunately, however, this language compulsion often silences the very human voices that speak it. It has created, literally, a disembodied view of words and their meanings.

This study aims to reconstruct historically the life and writings of Charles Brockden Brown in terms of their cultural connection. This involves an updated treatment of Brown's entire career and corpus of work. *The Romance of Real Life* examines in detail his early and later writings, both of which have been passed over lightly by literary scholars. By looking at these neglected chronological areas more closely, a new perspective emerges on the well-known novels from the late 1790s. Moreover, a new synthetic look at genre as well as chronology has proved revealing. A close reading of *all* Brown's writings—fiction and nonfiction, essays and editorials, public manifestos and private missives—uncovers broader connections between literature and society, longer trajectories of intellectual development, and more coherent patterns of development in his life.

Several larger principles have guided the analysis. First, the profound transformations of American society and culture in the decades of the early republic provide an essential context for understanding this writer and his efforts. As historians have demonstrated in recent years, the rapid expansion of the market in the post-Revolutionary era radically altered social and economic relationships. The accompanying shift from republicanism to liberalism in American civic life triggered equally important changes in thinking about authority, citizenship, and individual agency. Yet the import and nature of this broad transformation were not clear to those caught in the midst of it. Both public and private life seemed murky, protean, fluid. Struggles to "construct" new meanings in social, political, and personal life underlined the ambiguity and liminality of American culture in this period. This sea change had a powerful impact on literary endeavor, and Brown's life and writings cannot be understood apart from it.[6]

Second, I have tried to analyze Brown's writings in terms of an interplay of text, context, and self, with each factor recognized as mutually shaping the others. A sensitivity to the "social history of ideas," where both the form and content of language remain rooted in the material experience of real life, seems essential to a more comprehensive historical reconstruction. This approach, however, should not be seen as reductionist. However great the sins of disembodied literary analysis, they are not purged by devotion to an equally crude base-and-superstructure model. An ideological criticism that focuses on the interplay among several factors—socioeconomic structures, cultural values, political formations, psychological resonances—constitutes an attractive alternative. Thus, my analysis of Brown and his ideas strives to be neither idealist nor materialist, but dialectical. It explores his work in terms of "discourse," where writing is understood as a kind of cultural conversation, a process of give and take between writer and audience where meanings are never inherent but shaped by participants according to their values and experiences. Viewing Brown and his literary efforts in this fashion not only reconnects them to their social roots, but allows us to appreciate some of the powerful consequences of fiction writing itself in an age of revolution.[7]

Finally, a concern with political and cultural power and the way it is shaped, achieved, and internalized has guided my interpretation. Here the theory of "cultural hegemony" has provided one inspiration, with its notion that a "dominant culture" achieves dominion over "residual" and "emergent" cultures by virtue of successfully prescribing the parameters of discourse. The Frankfurt School, with its blending of Marx and Freud, has proved equally useful. Looking at the dynamics of authority and how it is internalized, this theoretical tradition suggests that the development of dominant social formations also creates cognate psychological types.[8] In more concrete terms, this book explores the process of cultural hegemony by looking at the links between "imaginative" expression and market change. Here it converges with other recent scholarship in exploring the relationship of literary production to a market society in which values and meanings have become increasingly commodified.[9]

While a modern biography of Charles Brockden Brown may be desirable on its own terms, a historicized rendering of his life and writings promises even richer rewards. Seeing this early national author as a case study of emerging market discourse defines the central goal of *The Romance of Real Life*: to explain how a particularly articulate and sensitive individual confronted, wrestled with, and ultimately helped articulate the emergence of a liberal culture in early modern America.

Brown's obsession with exploring the public and private vagaries of individual agency, his attempts to formulate meaningful notions of work and profit, and his search for cohesive social relationships all reveal his engagement with emerging liberalism. As Brown also suggests, however, the world of liberal individualism was fraught with ambiguities and contradictions. For Americans at the dawn of the nineteenth century, "free" agency appeared both liberating and frightening, offering new kinds of opportunity and imposing new kinds of restrictions. In such a light, for instance, Brown's famous Gothic novels of the late 1790s emerge as explorations of this dilemma. His experiences and reflections reinforce the commingled exhilaration and anguish within this new liberal "structure of feeling."[10]

This general orientation has produced a broad, two-pronged argument. *The Romance of Real Life* contends, first, that Charles Brockden Brown embodied many of the social and psychological pressures resulting from the wrenching development of market relations in the post-Revolutionary decades. In both his private life and public writings, he delineated a fragmented personality type as the ultimate expression of a liberal capitalist society increasingly separated by economic interests, gender expectations, moral values, and political organization. Second, the argument holds that Brown, partly by way of compensation, became an exemplary and pivotal figure in the articulation of an American "culture" in the early years of nationhood. The long-term thrust of his writings and personal life clearly pointed toward a bourgeois creed of genteel self-control. As Brown matured, he struggled to separate and elevate "culture" from the vicissitudes of social life. The civilizing force of culture, he hoped, would bind together the fragmentations of both liberal capitalist society and the restless individuals who inhabited it.[11]

The structure of this book embeds the argument. The opening chapter, in order to sketch a background for Brown's efforts, outlines the peculiar situation of literature in the rapidly developing market society of post-Revolutionary America. An examination of his earliest fiction—this writing is utterly self-absorbed in its crude social criticism—follows. Then, an examination of Brown's major novels from the 1790s reveals a rich interplay of literary and ideological themes. Finally, a treatment of his nonfictional writing and social criticism in the first decade of the nineteenth century illuminates the culminating stage of his encounter with bourgeois liberalism. An analysis of this intellectual's emotional state and evolving social thought weaves in and out of the narrative throughout.

The figure ultimately emerging from these pages goes far beyond the old, restrictive stereotype of literary pioneer and heroic failure. Brown, in fact, played a much more interesting role in the early history of the American republic. He helped shape the fascinating process by which America's modern, liberal civilization came into being. He may not have done so through towering influence—after all, his books' lagging sales eventually drove him from professional authorship—but his work teaches a more subtle lesson. His literary struggles and cultural formulations from 1790 to 1810 embodied many of the dynamics and travails of a historical transformation in the early American republic. Charles Brockden Brown's story is a rich one. Illuminating the origins of America's bourgeois civilization, his tale discloses as well some of its dirty little secrets.

# ⚜‖ The Romance of Real Life

# ONE

# ☸‖ The Novel and the Market
# in the Early Republic

As a young man in late eighteenth-century Philadelphia, Charles Brockden Brown loved to take long, solitary walks. A sickly childhood had prompted concerned parents and teachers to prescribe a regimen of more exercise and less study for the boy, and he began a routine of daily journeys on foot. As one observer noted, "so great were the benefits he received, that he continued his pedestrian exercises ever after." Although sometimes losing himself in abstraction and dreaming on these "solitary rambles," Brown also was invigorated by the physical activity and "his mind was constantly on the alert," according to family members. As the son of a Quaker merchant and land conveyancer, the youth undoubtedly wandered the streets near his family's South Second Street home or those near his father's office in the rear of St. Paul's church. This area lay in the heart of the booming commercial district of post-Revolutionary Philadelphia, a scant few hundred feet from the busy docks along a two-mile stretch of the Delaware River. Brown must often have viewed the ships filled with sugar and rum from the West Indies, indigo and rice from South Carolina, and mackerel and cod from New England lining the wharfs. When he ventured into the nearby countryside, young Brown also must have seen wagons rolling into the Philadelphia port from Delaware Valley farms, loaded with wheat and other foodstuffs bound for European markets. The influence of this enterprising milieu became evident in the mature Brown, as eventually he was drawn into the world of ledger sheets and commodities—first as the manager of several journalistic enterprises, then as a partner with his brothers in a mercantile company, and finally as an aspiring commercial lawyer.[1]

However much Brown loved his daily sojourns on foot, he relished even more the act of writing. In fact, writing transcended mere enjoyment and instruction to become something of an obsession for the young Philadelphian. As an adolescent schoolboy he scribbled poetry and essays; later, as a law student, he would stay up late into the night composing journal entries, letters, and fiction. By age twenty, Brown described his writing fervor as a "magician" and "enchanter" so powerful that it threatened to lure him "a greater distance from the tract of common sense than I am at present desirous of being." Then, in the mid-1790s, this literary compulsion exploded in a burst of creativity. By the turn of the century the youthful author would publish some six novels, numerous shorter pieces of fiction, and dozens of literary essays and book reviews. In the early 1800s he would become not only editor of three influential journals but also a political polemicist, translator, and historical novelist. Brown emerged as probably the leading literary figure in the early American republic. In his own words, writing dominated his life as both an expression of "soaring passion and intellectual energy" and a method to "enchain the attention and ravish the souls of those who study and reflect."[2]

These twin images—the solitary individual traversing the streets of an expanding commercial city and the emotive and pioneering writer struggling with ideas and sentiments, pen and paper—broadly suggest the enormously fluid and formative period that framed the career of Charles Brockden Brown. More particularly, they reveal in tantalizing fashion two massive trends at work in the post-Revolutionary republic. First, the young man wandering about Philadelphia in the 1780s and 1790s was witnessing part of a remarkable socioeconomic transformation. The decades between independence from Great Britain and the Panic of 1819 framed the consolidation of a market economy and market society in the United States. The ascendancy of "liberal capitalism," as this process has been defined, entangled growing numbers of citizens in complex webs of commodification and profit seeking that enshrined the competing individual as a social ideal.[3] Second, Brown's frenetic writing activity clearly illustrated the gradual, simultaneous emergence of an American culture during the same period. In concert with the burgeoning efforts of other literati and artists, his novels, essays, and magazines served to usher in a distinctively American mode of cultural discourse and also to help formulate the modern notion of culture itself—an elevated, aesthetic search for beauty and truth separated from the tawdry material concerns of a utilitarian society.[4]

Thus, an aspiring young author in the late eighteenth century faced a situation of enormous change and uncertainty. Historical development had raised important issues but resolved them only slowly and partially. The social and economic landscape was shifting in significant ways, while political perceptions of authority, obligation, and citizenship were assuming new forms. At the same time, pressure mounted from a number of directions for the reformulation of cultural values and moral commitments in the new context of market endeavor. For writers, this emergence of a "liberal America" brought in its wake troubling questions about the meaning and nature of intellectual activity, and about the meaning and nature of selfhood. The Revolution and its aftermath had shaped a new arena for literature and letters in the young American republic. Its parameters, however, became visible only gradually in light of several broad and complex trends.

I

In the three or four decades after the War for Independence, a social and economic revolution of massive proportions slowly gathered momentum to transform American life. The severing of political ties with Great Britain, it seemed, had intensified an erosion of long-standing restraints on the scope of individual action. Traditional colonial ideals of paternalism in social organization, moral economy and mercantilism in economic activity, and a virtuous republicanism in public affairs began to wither under the intense heat of a historical "release of energy." Trends that had been only dimly evident earlier in the eighteenth century—geographic mobility, challenges to social deference, the search for profit in the marketplace, popular political participation—flourished and intermingled in the hothouse atmosphere of the early republic. Benjamin Franklin, a prophet before his time in the mid-1700s with his message of personal ambition, thrift, investment, and utilitarian work, became by the 1790s the prototype of the American citizen in the early republic.[5]

Several dramatic developments gave glimpses of this shift. By the mid-1790s, with British imperial restraints abolished, Americans had begun to flood into the trans-Appalachian west. Kentucky and Tennessee entered the republic as states before the turn of the century and Ohio followed shortly thereafter. The Louisiana Purchase of 1803 extended the young nation's territorial claims across the North American continent to the Rocky Mountains, and over the next decade and a half practically all territory east of the Mississippi River became part of the United States. If the explosion of land-hungry, ambitious American expansion into the interior offered one sign of profound change, the unprecedented overseas commercial boom of 1793–1808 constituted another. With the advent of the Napoleonic Wars on the Continent during these years, the economic energy and resources of the combatants—not only England and France but also their numerous allies—increasingly flowed into military channels. Beginning in the early 1790s and lasting some fifteen years, the imposition of blockades and naval warfare by the hostile fleets drastically impeded normal commercial routes and carriers. American merchants took full advantage of the situation. Moving quickly into this vacuum in the Atlantic, Mediterranean, South American, and West Indies markets, U.S. ships became the leading commercial carriers and re-exporters in the Western world by the turn of the century. An unprecedented flow of wealth flooded the young republic and raised the general level of prosperity, promoted an entrepreneurial spirit, and created large accumulations of capital for further reinvestment by wealthy merchants. In this business bonanza figures like Stephen Girard of Philadelphia, Robert Oliver of Baltimore, and John Jacob Astor of New York City became millionaires. They also became living symbols of an emerging new world of profit, commodities, and personal ambition in this expanding and energetic society.[6]

Other subtle but far-reaching trends further cemented such economic development in the early republic. Growing European demand for foodstuffs, for example, encouraged the commercialization of agriculture in a great commodity-producing belt stretching from Virginia northward to New York. The old "household economy" of colonial America began a precipitous decline as regional markets spread their tentacles outward from eastern port cities ever farther into the interior. Moreover, after 1790 the steady development of both "household" and "extensive" manufactures slowly systematized the broad social thrust toward efficiency, productivity, and profit. This broad, multifaceted commercialization of American life prompted a "business revolution" that gave rise to swelling incorporation, complex bookkeeping techniques, and growing numbers of banks, insurance companies, and commission houses in the decades after American independence had been won. Overall, these changing patterns of economic endeavor comprised the consolidation of a market economy in the early American republic.[7]

The political culture of the young nation also reverberated and shifted in concert with this rapid market development. In the older world of eighteenth-century politics, an ideology of "republicanism" had shaped political discourse and practice. According to this tradition several principles guided and defined political life. "Civic virtue," or the notion of subordinating personal self-interest to the greater good of the commonwealth, comprised perhaps the highest ideal of republican citizenship. A widespread commitment to "independence"—the ability to be self-sustaining economically and hence to avoid a corrupting social and political dependence on the wealthy—also provided a key support for a republican edifice. Finally, an organic vision of society in which common farmers and laborers deferred to the political leadership of an educated, prosperous aristocracy of talent helped animate republican politics. This ideal polity, of course, never existed in pristine form. Nonetheless, the idealization of civic values and a concomitant, constant fear of their corruption helped apotheosize republicanism in eighteenth-century American life and fuel the revolt against Great Britain.[8]

Within a decade of independence, however, older categories of American republicanism were becoming ambiguous, even inchoate under the pressures of historical change. A "contagion of liberty," for instance, emerged from the turmoil of the Revolution to gradually overwhelm the restraints of deferential politics. This ethic of popular participation, in concert with geographical expansion over the Appalachians and swelling market involvement, created by the late 1700s a destructive tension within republican political culture. This struggle of "virtue and commerce," as one historian described it, pitted an older ideal of self-sacrifice and civic community against a growing instinct for individual ambition, advancement, and expression. Thus, by the 1790s—a decade that put political flesh on the skeletal framework constructed by the Constitution—a new kind of politics had emerged with the well-known clashes of Jeffersonians and Federalists. Modes of economic growth increasingly defined the agenda for debate while party competition provided the means. And a pluralist mind-set, which held that the sifting of many private interests *created* the public good, increasingly shaped its discourse. A republican model of politics, in other words, subtly became a liberal one in the early national period as "independence" gave way to "self-interest." In this mercurial atmosphere a market politics was born.[9]

Perhaps even more significant than shifting political and social structures, however, was an underlying transformation of cultural values and assumptions. To use the terminology of recent cultural analysis, the American *mentalité* steadily assumed a different shape and color in the decades after the Revolutionary struggle. In concert with sweeping social and economic changes, traditional cultural definitions of human perception, volition, and acceptable boundaries of behavior began to take on unfamiliar new meanings. At a broad social level, what one historian has termed a "vigorous spirit of enterprise" seemed to emerge in late eighteenth-century America. Rising from the wreckage of colonial paternalism, with its traditional reliance on the authority of ministers and magistrates, courthouse and church, an invigorating sense of ambition detonated an explosion of entrepreneurialism in the economic arena, massive geographical movement in the social one, and participation in the political one. The crumbling of deferential restraints encouraged a growing attachment to the advancement and profit accruing to achieved status.[10]

If ambition became the tonic for a social "crisis of authority" by the late eighteenth century, a related epistemological crisis at elite levels of culture raised other difficulties. The demise of patriarchal authority in early modern Anglo-American culture affected political, theological, literary, and pedagogical endeavor as well as social relationships. Questions of how we know and learn, of how we understand and internalize morality became paramount issues in an age of growing personal independence and increasing self-sufficiency. By the mid to late 1700s, for example, many American intellectuals were wrestling with the implications of John Locke's "sensationalist" psychology. Best expressed in his famous *Essay Concerning Human Understanding* (1690), this theory posited the mind as a tabula rasa and contended that knowledge was based on the individual processing of sensory perceptions, not on innate ideas. Even the Enlightenment itself, that great eighteenth-century upheaval in the Western life of the mind, could be largely traced to a demise of traditional frameworks of intellectual authority. As Immanuel Kant had briskly announced in his definitive essay, *What Is Enlightenment?* (1784), "Enlightenment is man's emergence from his self-imposed nonage. Nonage is the inability to use one's own understanding without another's guidance. . . . 'Have the courage to use your own understanding,' is therefore the motto of the enlightenment."[11]

From this swirling maelstrom of ambition and sensation, mobility and self-reliance, gradually emerged a broad thrust toward individualism in the culture of the early American republic. It became clearly evident in several ways. Post-1790 secular advice literature, for example, gained greatly in popularity as it promoted an ethic of self-made success. With titles such as *The Way to Grow Rich, The Youth's Guide to Wisdom . . . for the Rising Generation,* and *An Instructive History of Industry and Sloth*, these didactic tracts promoted a social creed of hard work, thrift, shrewd investment, and social advancement. The pursuit of self-interest became the centerpiece of this emerging liberal ideology. The sacrifice of personal advantage to the commonwealth, a long-standing republican ideal, slowly receded before the notion that personal enterprise created productivity and prosperity and thereby *produced* the public good. As a newspaper essayist enthusiastically explained,

> While the physical and intellectual powers of man are left free to employ them-selves as the judgement of their possessor may direct, everything valuable finds its proper level and its due value. . . . An active industry and lively competition constantly tend to equalize, and consequently to distribute among the greatest numbers the good things of this life. . . . The condition of every individual as well as that of the nation is in a progressive state.[12]

Such paeans to individual striving also contained a careful cultural modifier. Unrestrained ambition, as countless writers and speakers re-minded citizens of the young republic, contained the seeds of vicious com-petition and, ultimately, social anarchy. Thus affirmations of self-interest were almost invariably accompanied by warnings about the necessity for instinctual repression and self-control. The Second Great Awakening, for example, served as one vehicle transporting this double cultural message outward into society. Welling up by the late 1790s, this massive movement of evangelical Protestantism would spread its influence throughout the re-public over the next four decades. "Moral free agency," a notion eloquently and emotionally enunciated by Charles Grandison Finney, Lyman Beech-er, and countless less famous ministers, lay at the heart of the revival im-pulse. Individual sinners had a God-given choice—in terms of volition this was not unlike the situation of individuals in the marketplace—regarding their moral destiny. They could repent, seek Christ's blessing, and pursue salvation or they could continue sinning and slide into damna-tion. A genuine decision for salvation, as preachers and moralists sternly noted, also involved a self-denial of sensual indulgences and passion. For followers of the evangelical Protestant crusade, virtuous individualism meant a repudiation of the temptations of liquor, violent anger, and illicit pleasures of the flesh.[13]

Scottish Moral Philosophy, like the revivals, promoted an ethic of indi-vidual expression and restraint but did so in the more elevated realms of education and moral theory. Reacting to the potential ethical and episte-mological chaos of Lockean sensationalism—after all, the impulses of physical sensation seemingly ignored the confines of religion and moral codes, and it even eroded certainty of association between appearance and reality—Scottish thinkers like Adam Ferguson and David Reid rather des-

perately insisted on the existence of an innate moral sense. Implanted by
God and subject to cultivation through reason and science, this supposed
faculty allowed, even demanded, that the individual nurture and follow the
dictates of conscience. By the late 1700s this "common sense" philosophy
had begun to filter down into every aspect of American culture. Comprising a "Didactic Enlightenment," it became the bedrock of American pedagogy and moralism for nearly a century. As the culmination of a myriad of
developments, common sense doctrine signaled the central cultural development of the early American republic: the emergence of a bourgeois
creed of self-control. With an important double meaning, this culture simultaneously asserted the freedom of self-control over one's own destiny
and demanded the restraint of self-control over one's passions.[14]

### II

The gradual decline of republican, paternal traditions and the convergence of Protestant moralism, capitalist acquisitiveness, and possessive individualism around the dawn of the nineteenth century had significant implications for aspiring American writers. This liminal market culture, with
its commingled liberations and restrictions, offered uncertain guidelines
for the pursuit of literature. Ambiguity seemed to rule the day.

On the one hand, political independence from Great Britain had sown
the seeds of cultural nationalism. From a self-defined cultural backwater
before the Revolution, the late eighteenth-century republic increasingly
appeared to many visionary enthusiasts as a potential "American Athens."
Vibrant achievements in arts and letters seemed a likely accompaniment to
the establishment of virtuous and enlightened republican government. As
Philip Freneau and Hugh Henry Brackenridge predicted in their 1771
poem, "The Rising Glory of America," this new society would have its
own Homers and Miltons and its own achievements "not less in fame than
Greece and Rome of old."

On the other hand, this sense of cultural opportunity gave way to frequent bouts with despair. For aspiring authors and literati, the period from
1790 to 1820 was one of wrenching tension. Writers seemed caught between the millstones of a dying republican culture and a rapidly maturing
liberal one. Artistic endeavor had always been somewhat suspect in republican thought, primarily because of its long-standing association with aristocratic patronage and sensual indulgence. These qualities, in the eyes of
many theorists, tended toward the "corruption" of the civic virtue and rational moderation at the heart of republicanism. At the same time, the

artist also faced a difficult situation with emerging liberal values. In the context of an ambitious society of individualist and materialist striving, artists felt tremendous pressures to commodify their work. A spreading market ethos demanded that authors conceptualize their creations as products in a competitive arena, that they respond to a social calculus of supply and demand. A deep-seated ambivalence about marketplace success versus creative integrity took root and grew within many authors. Thus, American men of letters confronted a perilous situation of shifting contexts and meanings in the late 1700s. Large, abstract issues concerning the worth, mission, and definition of artistic work proved terribly burdensome and perhaps even intractable.[15]

A number of practical problems weighed equally heavily. For literary aspirants, the paramount difficulty in a growing culture of capitalism was immediate material survival. Aristocratic patronage, the mainstay of traditional European culture, was both unavailable and unacceptable in a republic. Other models, like the gentleman scholar of colonial tradition or the dilettante artist of elitist societies, seemed ill-suited to the creation of a vital and rational culture. What proved most appealing was the historically new role of professional writer, a figure who wrote to live and lived to write. This type of author, whose specialized function partly reflected the rationalizations of market life, persisted and prospered by wits and popularity. The thorny problem for such a writer, of course, was the connection to one's audience. On one level this directly involved writer and reader in the cash matrix of buying and selling. Beyond that, however, producers and consumers of creative writing in the early republic became enmeshed in more tangled relationships. As literary scholars have made clear in recent years, authorship was shifting toward professionalization at the same time that the reading audience was transforming dramatically. By the late 1700s literacy and education were spreading rapidly through the middling ranks of American society. Moreover, changing reading standards—the growing popularity of journalism, didactic tracts, and sentimental stories— were molding the taste of a growing bourgeois public. Writers faced the prospect of pleasing a rising middle-class audience increasingly attuned to a social ethic of self-made individualism and a cultural creed of sentimental self-control.[16]

From this highly charged and volatile cultural atmosphere arose a storm of troubled literary responses. Writers of the early republic, in both their formal work and their reflections on it, evinced an attitude that was part optimism, part anguished confusion, and part alienation. The "Hartford

Wits" and "Augustans" of New England, for instance, presented one kind
of response in the late 1700s and the early 1800s. Rising from the Calvinist, socially deferential traditions of the "Standing Order" in Connecticut
and the bulwark of Boston culture, such authors as Timothy Dwight and
Joel Barlow, Fisher Ames and young John Quincy Adams, shaped a pon-
derous literary classicism directly modeled on the English Augustan era of
Pope and Addison, and more remotely on classical writers of the Roman
Augustan age, such as Virgil and Ovid. Dwight's "Greenfield Hill," Barlow's "Rising Glory of America" and "Columbiad," Ames' "Dangers of
American Liberty," and Adams' "Lectures on Rhetoric and Oratory" unfolded a republican vision of classical symmetry. To their literary eyes
America appeared a polity of organic community, sacrifice to the public
good, and deference to paternal social leadership. Hand in hand with this
cultural optimism, however, went stern, sometimes shrill denunciations of
liberalizing trends toward profit seeking and social mobility in the young
nation. Attacks on "mobocracy," chastisements of money grubbing, and
warnings about the degeneracy of republican standards under such corro-
sive influences became commonplace in this literary tradition. For these
New World Horaces and Swifts, literature became a republican purifica-
tion rite that upheld the old and denounced the new.[17]

At the other extreme, some authors eagerly embraced the ambitious energy of the liberalizing republic and sought to channel it into an appropriate literary mode. "Parson" Mason Weems provided one memorable
case. Combining an enthusiasm for the market ethic with a compulsion to
restrain its more brutal excesses, this clever Virginian emerged by 1800 as
the prototypically "popular" author in early American culture. The basis
for his reputation, of course, was the single best-selling book of the early
republic, *The Life of Washington*. This hagiography, full of fictional tales
about Washington and the cherry tree or Washington throwing the silver
dollar across the Potomac, was first published in 1799 and enjoyed numerous reprintings throughout the nineteenth century. In this text Weems
molded republican patriotism, capitalist social ideology, and Protestant
moralism into a compelling cultural whole. "The Father of His Country"
became the centerpiece of a sentimental success tract, part self-sacrificing
republican hero and part iron-willed self-made man. Weems followed hard
on the heels of this effort with other popular biographies of legendary
Americans (William Penn, Benjamin Franklin, the "Swamp Fox" Francis
Marion) and a steady flow of didactic moral tracts illuminating the evils of

alcohol, gambling, and illicit sex. Moreover, as a commission bookseller and roving minister, the Virginian scoured the roads and communities of the young republic for over two decades personally hawking his cultural wares. For figures like Parson Weems, the literary marketplace created vast opportunities for the writer as schemer, moralist, and popular wordsmith.[18]

Between the alienated Augustans and the literary entrepreneurs, however, stood a substantial group of profoundly ambivalent authors who struggled to come to terms with their shifting cultural milieu. Noah Webster, the New England essayist, polemicist, and lexicographer, combined a fierce social traditionalism with a spirit of nationalist cultural innovation. From the late 1780s through the early 1800s he produced dozens of essays defending paternalism and elite political control in the new republic. At the same time he labored prodigiously to compile his famous *Webster's Dictionary*, a self-conscious attempt to break away from British restraints and to create an American language through the spelling and definition of words themselves. Hugh Henry Brackenridge offered another variation. This self-made Pennsylvanian journalist, jurist, and author achieved a literary reputation with the gigantic picaresque tale *Modern Chivalry*. Originally serialized in newspapers from 1793 to 1815, this extended story humorously skewered both the stultifying traditionalism of republicanism (represented by the stodgy character Captain Farrago) and the dangerous ambition of liberalizing values (represented by the licentious Teague O'Regan).

Other authors, like the benevolent satirists Washington Irving and James Kirke Paulding, followed parallel paths. In works like Irving's *Salmagundi*, and Paulding's *Diverting History of John Bull and Brother Jonathan*, American values and manners were subjected to both illumination and ridicule. While sympathizing with the openness and opportunity characteristic of the changing young republic, Irving and Paulding delighted in taking jovial swipes at American materialism, provincial complacency, and unscrupulous ambition. *Salmagundi*, for example, once described with great glee the manipulative qualities necessary for social advancement in this fluid society: "To be concise, our great men are those who are most expert at crawling on all fours, and have the happiest facility in dragging and winding themselves along in the dirt like the very reptiles." For figures like Webster, Brackenridge, and Irving, the early American cultural landscape simultaneously offered inviting terrain for exploration and uncertain, sometimes even treacherous, footing.[19]

Above and beyond this array of writers rose two overarching developments that gradually began to transform the literary culture of the new republic nearly beyond recognition. First, the proliferation of American newspaper publishing by the late 1700s slowly redefined the context of literary discourse. Second, the unprecedented stream of novels pouring forth after the Revolution not only enlarged the pool of available texts but also carved out a new sensibility for large portions of a growing reading public. The changes wrought by these trends were perceptible. In colonial America, the world of literature and belles lettres had been a small one. Few texts circulated, and they did so almost exclusively within the domain of educated gentlemen. Reading was a genteel, cultivated, masculine activity of ministers and merchants, gentry farmers and professional men. Among the lower classes literacy remained at low or rudimentary levels, especially in the South. The classics, poetry, essays on law and morality, political rhetoric, and especially sermons comprised the currency of serious literary discussion. This pervasion of sacred themes, combined with a self-conscious awareness of London's cultural dominance, made colonial literature intensely provincial and religious. The growing popularity of newspapers and novels by the late 1700s, however, created a veritable "reading revolution" that began to overturn many traditional expectations and assumptions. Evidence for the dramatic development of popular readership appeared everywhere.[20]

Before the Revolution, it has been estimated that newspapers in America numbered fewer than 100. By 1800 there were 230, and ten years later the total had climbed to 376, publishing some 22 million copies annually. Americans had become, in the words of one commentator, "a nation of newspaper readers," and indeed these aggregate figures surpassed those of any other nation. This explosion of newspapers was accompanied by a similar burst of growth for magazines and journals. The three decades after the Revolution saw the appearance of scores of monthly and quarterly periodicals like Francis Hopkinson's and Mathew Carey's *Columbian Magazine*, Hugh Henry Brackenridge's *United States Magazine*, and Joseph Dennie's *Port-Folio*. In varying degrees these magazines presented a potpourri of offerings. They ranged from learned essays to popular book reviews, pirated European articles to native American poetry, natural history to travel narratives, moral tracts to technological reports. The growing popularity of journalism in the early republic, of course, partly reflected a participatory ethic stemming from the Revolutionary struggle. This trend did more, however, than merely popularize and widen networks of public writing and reading. The vogue of journalism also assaulted the traditional literary authority of educated elites in several ways. It displaced the sophisticated art of rhetoric with cruder styles of expression, replaced a genteel code of conversation and contemplation with an ethic of accessibility and commodification, and substituted interest seeking for truth seeking, sensationalism for aesthetics. In early national America, the tremendous growth of journalism was part of a broad "crisis of authority" in the realm of culture.[21]

In many ways the appearance of a new genre—the American novel—generated an even greater cultural impact. Shortly after the end of the Revolution, an increasing array of novels began to assault the reading public, with striking results. Middle- and lower-class readers, especially women, began to devour accessible, cheap editions of fiction with avid enthusiasm. The fluid and engaging prose, vivid depictions of individual characters and social settings, and sentimental moral didacticism of the novel made it enormously attractive both to an educated readership weaned on religious and political discourse and to a barely literate readership having little previous engagement at all with books. The growing popularity of fiction helped promote what one scholar has termed a "democratization of the written word" in this transformative period. The earlier decades of the eighteenth century, of course, had seen European imports like Daniel Defoe's *Robinson Crusoe*, Oliver Goldsmith's *The Vicar of Wakefield*, Samuel Richardson's *Pamela*, and Jean-Jacques Rousseau's *Emile* garner the lion's share of readership. By the end of the century, however, native products like Susanna Rowson's *Charlotte Temple* (1791), Royall Tyler's *The Algerian Captive* (1797), Hannah Webster Foster's *The Coquette* (1797), Enos Hitchcock's *Memoirs of the Bloomsgrove Family* (1790), and William Hill Brown's *The Power of Sympathy* (1789) were generating considerable appeal as well. With such growth during the era of the early republic, the novel was well on its way to becoming "the chapbook of nineteenth century America," providing common readers unprecedented access to the written word.[22]

Beyond mere entertainment and popular sales figures, however, the novel had a striking effect on American social and cultural life. Like the ripples from a stone tossed into a calm lake, its influence spread outward in sweeping concentric circles to alter the shape of values, perceptions, and

assumptions in the young republic. In an era of consolidating liberal capitalism, the novel seemed to express the instincts of a new society struggling for maturity. In fact, modern theorists who agree on little else concur
that the novel was a powerful expression of ascending bourgeois culture in
early modern Western life. Mikhail Bakhtin, for instance, argued that the
novel empowered individual readers to judge and assess social situations
and character in unprecedented ways. As a fluid literary form for a fluid
world of competition, mobility, and individualism, the novel "has no
canon of its own. It is, by nature, not canonic. It is plasticity itself. It is a
genre that is ever questing, ever examining itself and subjecting its established forms to review." Lionel Trilling suggested that the novel expressed
the individualist and pluralist sensibility of modern life. As he noted, "For
our time the most effective agent of the moral imagination has been the
novel of the last two hundred years. . . . It taught us, as no other genre ever
did, the extent of human vanity and the value of this vanity." For early
twentieth century thinker Georg Lukacs, the novel was simply *the* genre of
modern bourgeois life. It expressed, as no other form quite did, the intellectual, spiritual, and psychological conditions of modern capitalist
culture.[23]

Within this broad consensus about its bourgeois affiliation, however,
the emergence of the novel has prompted somewhat discordant assessments. In particular, questions about how and why it became central to
bourgeois culture, about the exact nature of the connection between novelistic expression and the vagaries of a market society have evoked rather
different answers from students of this developing literary form. In the
realm of early Anglo-American fiction in particular, two schools of thought
have predominated.

First, a tradition prevailing since at least the 1950s has held that the vast
social transformations remaking early modern England set the stage for
the emergence of this new genre. The overturning of traditional feudal
economic relationships, the ascendancy of a growing and educated middle
class, the emergence of an ethic of individualism, and the rejection of
"universals" in intellectual life nourished the growth of the novel. According to one scholar, both the novel and its "philosophical realism"—it posited that truth is discovered by the individuals through their senses—

> must be seen as parallel manifestations of a larger change—the vast transforma-
> tion of Western civilization since the Renaissance which has replaced the uni-
> fied world picture of the Middle Ages with another very different one—one

which presents us, essentially, with a developing but unplanned aggregate of particular individuals having particular experiences at particular times and at particular places.

Several features of the novel clearly reflected this new cultural orientation. Its "formal realism"—a narrative presentation of life that self-consciously renders details and particularities of characters and their actions—moved literary attention away from legends, types, and universals to specific people and situations. This focus on personal interaction, private experience, and concrete social relations tended to promote secularization by eroding the religious matrix of human volition. Its overall evocation of the individual tended to ratify the agenda of market society by simply demonstrating the assumption that "society must value every individual highly enough to consider him the proper subject of its serious literature." In this view then, the novel emerged as the logical vehicle for modern liberal capitalism because it carried into public consciousness the picture of "a whole society mainly governed by the idea of every individual's intrinsic independence both from other individuals and from that multifarious allegiance to past modes of thought and action denoted by the word 'tradition.' "[24]

More recently, an alternative interpretive picture has emerged. In one sense, there is agreement that the novel was an important agent of social transformation. The first American novels appearing from the 1780s to 1820, newer scholarship has agreed, were an integral part of a widespread crisis of authority in the early modern West. In the young republic, where this situation became especially evident, the crisis involved political revolt against Great Britain, a steady undermining of patriarchal social authority, and an unprecedented commercialization of economic endeavor. Even more pertinent, it involved a popular "reading revolution" in American culture, which invaded the traditional "gentleman's sphere" of literary discourse and public discussion. It is at this point, however, that interpretations diverge. Some scholars insist that the novel played a critical role in the heady atmosphere of the post-Revolutionary republic by appealing to the least privileged in American society—women, the lower classes, the barely literate. Fictional texts were denounced consistently during the eighteenth century by ministers, educators, political figures, and the culturally powerful as immoral, socially anarchic, and intellectually contemptible. By extending literary participation to socially marginal readers with Gothic tales, picaresque adventures, and sentimental stories the novel offered "a means of access to social and political events from which many readers . . . would have been otherwise excluded in hierarchical colonial culture." In this view, the novel in its various forms comprised a socially defiant and politically subversive genre for a young and restless audience. So if the first interpretation portrays an accommodating literary form closely attuned to emerging bourgeois capitalism, the second position depicts a democratizing one that subverted the imposition of privilege, social authority, and power.[25]

These two broad views of the emerging novel—an older one stressing "accommodation" and a newer one "resistance"—may not be as mutually exclusive, or even as divergent, as they initially appear. A different theoretical context, that of "cultural hegemony," suggests a way to explain the novel's power and also to reconcile different interpretations of this new fictional form. As defined and elaborated by a number of thinkers, particularly Raymond Williams, this theory suggests that the dominant values, perceptions, and ideology of a given society are not simply imposed by brute political power or social authority, but instead become compelling through a process of cultural definition and legitimation. Authoritative social groups, in other words, promote their own status and worldview by successfully prescribing the conventional wisdom of society, defining its criteria of success, and staking out acceptable boundaries of discourse. As Williams and others carefully note, however, it would be a mistake to envision a simple, crude situation of ruling-class domination with ideas taking the place of guns in the hands of the powerful. In fact, cultural hegemony constitutes an ongoing, dialectical series of events in which "dominant" values and perceptions constantly confront, evade, or integrate the dissent of both traditional "residual" cultures and avant-garde "emergent" ones. Cultural hegemony is as much a "process" as a structure.[26]

From this theoretical angle of vision, the first appearance of American novels in the late 1700s takes on a more coherent significance. Much evidence suggests that fictional texts played a key role in the hegemonic shift toward liberal capitalism in the era 1790–1820. The novel itself, as a fresh genre that helped define cultural discourse in this transformative age, uniquely explored and articulated the fluid new market relationships of a liberalizing society. The fact that it incorporated elements of accommodation and of resistance to the rising new order merely reveals the complexity, at times even ambiguity, of the process itself.

Through its language, form, and sensibility the early American novel indeed performed a complicated, multidimensional role in the drama of ascending capitalist culture. Four functions in particular stand out. First, in a number of ways novelistic narratives cogently expressed the instincts and nuances of life in a marketplace milieu. In part, this involved both a "formal realism" that particularized character, temporality, environment, and causation and an underlying "philosophical realism" that promoted the internalization of knowledge. The novel also moved forward along these lines as one of the great vehicles of "antipatriarchal ideology." Undermining the traditional social emphasis on paternal authority, precept, and static community, these new texts promoted an ethic of private character, nurture and growth, affection and education. Moreover, the novel appeared as the first great popularizer of issues raised by the sensationalist psychology of the Lockean and Scottish traditions. Both in the subjects it treated (a central character's struggles to come to terms with his or her social milieu) and in its own narrative strategies (the use of imaginative writing to create an emotional impact on the reader), this genre dramatically illustrated the effect of sensation on individual understanding and action. In a larger structural sense, the novel also emerged as the literature of the marketplace by virtue of its precipitating role in the great transition from "oral" to "print" tradition in the popular consciousness of the early modern West. Unlike speech, the written word does not depend on the immediate presence of others. Hence the novel's surging popularity helped erode personal community interaction while promoting a cultural dynamic based on solitude, impersonal exchange, and silent thought. Thus, in all of these ways—ideological, psychological, technological—the novel took shape as a chronicle of liberal life exploring the vagaries of individual existence: perception, volition, and achievement. Nothing better illustrates this fact than the appellations of the first novels to circulate in eighteenth-century America. Almost without fail they offered the name or description of an individual character as the title: *Robinson Crusoe*, *Pamela*, *Clarissa* with the earliest English imports, then *Charlotte Temple*, *Wieland*, *The Coquette*, *The Algerian Captive* for slightly later indigenous American efforts.[27]

The novel's second major function in the ascendancy of American liberal capitalism appeared dialectically connected to the first. These early fictions proclaimed the individualism of marketplace life, but then moved quickly to restrain its excesses. Novels constantly sounded the alarm about the dangers of unregulated self-interest degenerating into licentiousness, shallow materialism, and social chaos. Such dangers threatened liberal society from within, and authors frequently manipulated plots and employed moral didacticism to delineate the necessity of personal self-control. In a society in which traditional authority was vanishing, responsibility for

governance and stability reverted to the individual and fiction became a
popular signboard for this cultural imperative. Sentimental novels particularly served this cultural purpose. Popular works like *Charlotte Temple* and
*The Power of Sympathy* illustrated for late eighteenth-century American
audiences the moral and social dangers of self-indulgence. In each book
overwrought scenarios of passion, seduction, and guilt culminated in social
disarray and personal disgrace. Such sentimental texts, as scholars have
pointed out, frequently deployed socially displaced figures like orphans,
adventurers, or prostitutes as protagonists. By either showing their destruction or integrating them into a larger community, these narratives
tried to harness a "socially unstabilized energy" that threatened society.
Gothic novels often moved in a parallel direction by depicting individuals
whose aberrant processing of the physical world led them into dissipation
and doom. In other words, these early sentimental and Gothic novels performed a social function by responding to the central problem of sensationalist psychology: the fact that individual sensation could corrupt as
well as educate made the practice of inner moral regulation a crucial necessity. Writers of the first American fiction, by offering their texts as paeans
to self-control, played a critical role in popularizing a bourgeois discourse
of genteel self-restraint.[28]

Third, novelistic expression of this period emerged as a powerful but
highly diffuse conduit for dissent. On the one hand, various forms of the
early American novel clearly criticized social and political tenets of the ascending liberal order. "Picaresque" tales like *Modern Chivalry*, for example,
explicitly lampooned the unscrupulous ambition of men on the make.
Gothic texts like *The Asylum; or Alonzo and Melissa* challenged confident
liberal individualism by showing isolated characters confronting the brutality of the modern world as well as the hidden monsters of human nature. Even sentimental novels such as Hannah Webster Foster's *The Coquette* partially subverted an ethic of male competition and authority by
rendering the female sphere significant and counterposing the moral superiority of its affectionate and benevolent values. At the same time, however, these fictional efforts worked indirectly, perhaps even unconsciously, to
diffuse and neutralize dissent. By sublimating social distress and public
criticism into the language and structure of the novel, writers steered them
into a relatively harmless channel. A potential discourse of political perception and power became depoliticized as it was translated into a literary
discourse of imaginative, privatized communication. Collective issues of
social class, gender relations, and cultural authority translated into dramas

of individual confrontation and adjustment, and over the whole there descended a didactic or sentimental blanket that provided the reassuring warmth of human decency and conflict resolution. As cultural vehicles for social dissent, most fiction of this era ultimately followed an evasive, upwardly spiraling trajectory of genteel optimism. Gathering elements of discontent with liberalizing change, novels transported them into a rarified atmosphere of abstraction far removed from the social and political sources from which they sprang.[29]

Finally, the young republic's first novels functioned as important agents of class formation and cohesion in an era of social transformation. Reaching out to a wider reading audience as republican, paternal traditions were succumbing to the ethic of market individualism, early fiction writers shaped and popularized a body of cultural assumption that defined success, morality, and common sense according to an increasingly competitive milieu. In terms of process, the novel performed an inclusionary role here by joining in common discourse not only prosperous and powerful entrepreneurial groups but also women, educated workers and provincials, the barely literate, and other previously excluded social types. This latter group of marginal figures in the late 1700s and early 1800s became the biggest consumers of early novels, a genre that was to become a bulwark of Victorian gentility by the mid-nineteenth century. In terms of ideology, fictional texts reinforced this process. Although dismissed and disparaged as morally corrupting by ministers, educators, and moralists with its first appearance in the eighteenth century, the novel rather quickly emerged as an effective instrument of "rationalist pedagogy." Reflecting a preoccupation with self-controlled individualism, these fictions explored the achievement of rational self-sufficiency, and explained both how to bolster virtue amidst the corruptions of experience and how to consolidate personal authority in a fluid social environment. By the early 1800s growing numbers of Americans would agree, in the words of one scholar, that the novel served an important pedagogical purpose by morally uniting readers:

> for in the first place, a just and powerful picture of human life in which the connection between vice and misery, and between facility and virtue is vividly portrayed, is the most solid and useful reading that a moral and social being . . . can read; and in the second place, the most trivial and trite of these performances are, to readers of certain ages and intellects, the only books which they will read. If they were not thus employed, they could be employed in a way still more trivial or pernicious.

This rationalist pedagogy of the novel not only promoted rational self-sufficiency but also strengthened other pillars of bourgeois life. The early novel was preoccupied with the genteel, middle-class family, for instance, because marriage in bourgeois society comprised "a means by which society attempts to bring into harmonious alignment patterns of passion and patterns of property. . . . [It] is the all-subsuming, all organizing, all-containing contract."[30]

In these salient ways, then—as an expression of market individualism, as a restraint on self-indulgence, as a ventilator for dissent, as a catalyst for class coherence—the early American novel helped create values and sensibility that permeated nineteenth-century bourgeois culture. These fictions were much more than a collection of intertextual sign-systems. They were part of an active process of cultural and class formation that was part and parcel of the American shift toward liberal capitalism from 1790 to 1820.

III

America's first novels ultimately probed to a deeper level as they explored the murky, subterranean tunnels of early capitalist culture. With literary lanterns of narrative, characterization, and social description held aloft, authors fleetingly illuminated the dark psychological corners and deep internal tensions of a restless society of self-made men. Analyzing the submerged social and psychological constructions of liberal America with varying levels of awareness, novels gradually brought to the surface issues that were both revealing and subversive. In one sense, these fictions suggested that the rationalizing, "scientific" aura of the market model—the competition of self-interests mechanically produces the public good—was in fact a kind of haze that obscured a system fraught with irrationalities, confusions, and alienations. In another sense, they divulged that beneath the confident, assertive individualism of the spreading liberal legend there often existed an isolated, fragmented creature for whom liberation often meant insecurity and fear. Early novels especially reflected such volatile psychosocial dynamics through their connection with two cultural traumas of early liberal society: a "crisis of representation" and a "crisis of self."[31]

An inchoate yet pervasive crisis of representation accompanied the rise of market society in early modern Anglo-America. This defined the permanent sense of transition that seemed to mark social existence within an ascending structure of competition, mobility, and profit seeking. For struggling individuals life had come to resemble, in the words of one scholar, "an infinite series of thresholds, a profusion of potential passages . . . running alongside experience." In a climate of contingency the traditional symbols, and definitions that had anchored personal perception in a cultural harbor of shared understanding now seemed increasingly cut adrift and dispersed. This liquid cultural world, where meanings were there for the making, was clearly reflected in an equally fluid new literary form. In a variety of ways, the novel embodied, grappled with, or desperately refuted the fragmented representations of a mercurial market culture.[32]

The novel genre itself arose from the instabilities of seventeenth-century English life. Amidst the rapid commercialization, political revolution, and religious turmoil of the tumultuous 1600s, the earliest narrative fictions came into existence to formulate and explain unfamiliar problems regarding the nature of "truth" and "virtue." These crucial texts mediated emerging cultural problems of signification which one scholar has posed in these terms: "What kind of authority or evidence is required of narrative to permit it to signify truth to its readers? What kind of social existence or behavior signifies an individual's virtue to others?" In trying to answer such questions and thereby stabilize notions of character, morality, and social institutions, however, the early novel paradoxically depended on deception. Its tales and characters may have resembled real life and real people, but they did not actually constitute those things. The novelist muddied the distinction between imagination and reality by in fact practicing a kind of literary artifice—shaping, inventing, selecting, omitting to create an *illusion* of reality.[33]

Such cultural conundrums appeared in other dimensions of the early novel as well. Adopting a "keyhole view of life," authors peered into the domain of private experience to exploit it for literary purposes. Getting inside both the houses and the heads of their characters, novelists nurtured among readers the notion that private life was the most genuine and the most valid part of existence. Yet once again paradoxes mounted. The presentation of minute-by-minute details of personal experience in a public forum actually violated the integrity of privacy. At the same time, by using illusion to illuminate inner life these texts promoted the deception "that what is fundamentally an unreal flattery of the reader's dreams appears to be the literal truth." As one literary critic has noted wryly, this novelistic obsession with imagination, illusion, artifice—especially in light of its ostensible commitment to "realism"—created a literary situation where "what does not exist is felt to be more attractive than what does." Caught up in

the broad, murky crisis of representation of nascent bourgeois culture, early American novels thus took shape as highly equivocal factual fictions. As
cultural journals of growing social and epistemological fluidity, they comprised a "liminoid genre . . . enacting the liminal experience of the bound-
aryless market."[34]

The novel dug even deeper to unearth a related quandary of developing
market culture: a crisis of self that threatened to explode an exuberant individualism even as it was sweeping over post-Revolutionary America.
This problem appeared in many guises. In an expanding republic increasingly given over to the pursuit of ambition, the paramount social dilemma
addressed duplicity: On what basis can anyone be trusted so that life will
not degenerate into a war of all against all? A parallel cultural dilemma involved representation and understanding: On what basis can common perceptions and values be established so that personal experience will not
wither into solipsism? Yet another dilemma, this one political in nature,
concerned authority and cohesion: On what basis can expressions of self-
interest be harmonized so as to make government a virtuous instrument of
the commonweal? At the convergence of these massive predicaments arose
a deep-seated psychological dilemma that would perplex liberal man perhaps most of all: Who and what am I? With demands for individual
achievement escalating at the very historical moment when traditional social and cultural supports were crumbling, enormous pressures for definition and performance threatened the very coherence of the autonomous
self. These threats to the self appeared mainly in two forms.[35]

First, the pressing issue of "identity" promoted psychological disarray in
liberal society. At an elevated level of discourse and culture, for example,
philosophers from the late 1600s on had been engaged in a major debate
about the nature of individual identity in the postfeudal West. The issue
appeared deceptively simple: What constituted identity and was it the
same for everyone? Some thinkers, such as John Locke and George Berkeley, contended that all individuals had an intuitive knowledge of their own
existence. By the mid-1700s, however, a skeptical David Hume had looked
inward and found only private perception, thereby concluding that selfhood really existed only in the imagination. Around the same time Scottish common sense philosopher Thomas Reid added a more desperate
note to the discussion by insisting that every individual could be secure in
his or her identity as part of the "natural order of things." At a more popular level of culture—here evidence appeared in genres like advice literature,

moralizing sermons, and newspaper essays—metaphysical discussion descended rapidly to earth to confront a trauma of social psychology. In an ambitious liberal society in which individuals were increasingly cut adrift from geographical place, community values, and ties of mutual obligation, how could isolated individuals essentially create and anchor a stable, consistent self? Early Anglo-American novels were immersed in these problematic issues of individual identity. Not just titles offering an individual character's name but frequent use of first-person narrative suggested the novelistic preoccupation with exploration and revelation of personal identity. In a certain fashion, fiction writers tried to escape the snare of mere subjective existence by literally "objectifying" people, thereby securing and solidifying their identity, as physical words on a page.[36]

In addition to problems of identity, a second psychological threat emerged from exhausting demands for social performance. In a society in which achievement and status increasingly depended on buying and selling in the marketplace, success for the liberal individual involved not only objective calculations of risk and gain but also subjective calculations of personal interaction in this transactionary world. The growing market *mentalité* of early capitalist culture commanded a commodification of self in which one became "a speculative fiction of joint manufacture: a venture, a text, a performance in which all spectators, investors, and consumers were invited, albeit obliquely, to subscribe." In other words, the calculus of individual attainment produced social equations based on role playing and masks. This nascent trend had attracted the notice of even the earliest analysts of liberalizing change. Thomas Hobbes, for instance, had written in his mid-seventeenth-century *Leviathan* of the predominance of "artificial persons" in modern society. Removed from nature and self-manufactured, their every act was a studied representation of themselves or of others. A century later Adam Smith embroidered upon this notion in *The Theory of Moral Sentiments* and *The Wealth of Nations* by presupposing that modern individuals constantly calculate both economic and psychological returns in their relations with others. In so doing they negotiate, shape, and sell themselves according to the claims of a commodified world. Novels, as an emerging literary form in the eighteenth century, helped provide a stage for the appearance of this elusive, performative self. "Seduction" novels like William Hill Brown's *Power of Sympathy*, for example, focused on the masks of duplicity used by defilers of virtue. "Picaresque" narratives like Royall Tyler's *The Algerian Captive* depicted footloose, marginal individuals confronting a society of kaleidoscopic settings and situations to which they responded by altering, often in chameleon-like fashion, their values and sensibility. Such characters on the novelistic stage represented a burgeoning social type in liberalizing America rather different from the rocklike autonomous self. These masked figures comprised an unsettled and unfirm "serial self, not a cumulative self—that is to say, a self composed in, of, and for successive performances."[37]

Ultimately, pressures generated by the frantic search for identity and the demands for continuous social performance produced not only a dramatic psychological tendency toward fragmentation within the liberal individual, but a psychological model of personality. Donning a series of self-manipulative disguises while desperately seeking social connection, the autonomous self constantly seemed to dissolve into a volatile, internally divided, and unintegrated state. With unprecedented pressures for individual success and self-control growing by 1800—in combination with social changes that separated individuals from one another, from traditions, and from frameworks of authority—the personality structure of liberal man seemed to splinter into warring elements. The ultimate result was, ironically, a psychological structure based on incoherence. As Frankfurt School critic Max Horkheimer has argued, the development of modern capitalist culture has created a cognate psychological type: the "personae." The personae, as a kind of pluralistic self, represented to the outside world "a set of masks rather than a coherent, integrated personality."[38]

As the "modal personality type" of capitalist society, this figure made many vivid appearances in the earliest Anglo-American novels. This genre, for example, usually focused on an exhaustive examination of human character. The influence of a heretofore obscure psychic life was asserted against the claims of society as the novel juxtaposed "the relative power and validity of inner vs. outer reality." Moreover, much early fiction—Gothic tales and seduction stories loom largest here—graphically illustrated the dark, hidden dimensions of selfhood which sporadically burst forth to create consternation and chaos in the public world. Many early novels became in part a kind of collective cultural diary of painful struggles with identity, performance, and internal fragmentaion by newly isolated and internally riven liberal individuals.[39]

Thus, the novel played a fascinating and multifaceted role in the shaping of capitalist culture in America. It promoted the consolidation of liberal hegemony not only in class and cultural terms, but in psychological terms as well. By constructing and disseminating what Raymond Williams has aptly called "structures of feeling," American fictional texts helped establish the growing dominance of bourgeois values by the late 1700s and early 1800s. They did so in part, of course, by promoting values of individualism, material ambition, self-control, and privatization. In a deeper, more complex, and ultimately more powerful way, however, the early American novel became an active agent in the process of cultural hegemony by defining key parameters of discourse itself in a bourgeois society. Under its auspices literature steadily narrowed into a specialized category of "imaginative" writing, an abstraction to be ratified by taste and criticism. A notion of "culture" emerged from the writing, reading, and content of novels as the embodiment of creative, intellectual, and moral activity set above the materialism and utilitarianism of daily social life; it became a symbolic abstraction for a whole type of human experience increasingly rationalized out of market society. Finally, narrative fiction defined the "self" as a self-created entity, malleable yet elusive, an autonomous pillar of strength nonetheless threatened by internal stresses and fractures. The novel, in other words, played a major role from 1790 to 1820 in creating American liberal society, the liberal culture that sustained it, and the "liberal ego" that inhabited it.[40]

IV

Charles Brockden Brown launched his career in these choppy cultural waters. Born and bred in an urban commercial milieu, he wrestled with the demands of a growing market society from his earliest days until his death. Politically inclined, he followed a convulsive ideological evolution from youthful utopian radical to stodgy middle-age conservative. Given to an intensely agitated private life, he suffered from a recurring crisis of identity and a struggle with meaningful vocation that lasted nearly his entire life.

It was in the literary arena, however, that Brown sustained his greatest involvement with the forces of liberalizing change. His earliest fictional forays explored the traumas of personal liberation in a revolutionary age. His famous Gothic novels of the 1790s delved deeply into questions of social obligation and human motivation as their outlandishly theatrical style belied their probing sensibility. His turn toward historical fiction, sentimental romance, and social criticism in late life presented a final confrontation with bourgeois values and perceptions. Throughout this cycle of literary endeavor, however, Brown consistently engaged questions raised by the emergence of liberal capitalism: What exactly was the nature of free agency, the basis of social cohesion, the meaning of labor, the obligations of citizenship in a market society? His literary and ideological answers were sometimes inconsistent, often convoluted, and usually inconclusive. The struggle itself, however, proved to be both fascinating and highly complex. The tale demands a gradual and nuanced telling, one that must begin with Charles Brockden Brown's earliest days in Philadelphia.

TWO

# ▩‖ The Lawyer and the Rhapsodist

Some one hundred years after arriving in the New World, the Brown family had established a quiet and moderately prosperous enclave for itself. Part of the Quaker migration to North America in the mid-seventeenth century, they had settled originally in New Jersey and northern Pennsylvania before putting down roots in the city of Philadelphia. When Charles Brockden Brown was born on January 17, 1771, his father, Elijah Brown, Sr., made a comfortable living running a small mercantile business. As the Revolutionary struggle with Britain escalated over the next several years, however, Elijah's Quaker faith led him to refuse to bear arms. This action prompted persecution of his family and plunder of his business by zealous non-Quaker patriots. So he quietly turned to an equally lucrative career as a real estate conveyancer and landbroker. Charles' mother, Mary Armitt, was the daughter of a prosperous, prestigious Quaker merchant family that originally had migrated with William Penn. Thus, the future writer, along with three older brothers and one younger sister and brother, grew up firmly ensconced in what eighteenth-century observers often called the "middling orders"—the broad array of laboring groups suspended in the social order midway between aristocratic luxury and struggling poverty. There, hard work, upright character, and material comfort were natural expectations, as Charles would discover to his dismay some years later.[1]

The Brown clan did not exactly fit the standard Quaker mold. While attached to the pious, plain living and philanthropy characteristic of the Society of Friends, the family's interests and activities extended far beyond these traditions. Elijah Brown, Sr., for instance, maintained a lively correspondence with friends and relatives in England and recorded in his journal extracts from newspapers in London, Ireland, Paris, Spain, and New York. Moreover, he read widely in the contemporary literature of politics, science, and philosophy and copied extracts from radical tracts like William Godwin's *Political Justice* and Mary Wollstonecraft's *Historical and Moral View of the Origin and Progress of the French Revolution*. One of Charles' older brothers, Elijah, Jr., became a merchant of cosmopolitan taste who traveled and sampled widely among the artistic treasures—the opera, cathedrals, art galleries, the theater—that he found in Europe. All of the male Brown children received a classical and literary education usually reserved for the offspring of wealthy Philadelphia merchant "Grandees." Charles' family might be described as "Quaker modernists": Friends who melded traditional moral and religious values with an impulse toward modest worldly success, social reform, technological innovation, and "useful" personal enterprise. For such Quakers, religion became a justification for promoting business and science, building canals and banks, constructing hospitals and prisons, ending slavery and disseminating Bibles.[2]

Within this conscientious yet progressive atmosphere young Charles experienced a rather singular childhood. While his brothers enjoyed robust health and slowly carved out business and commercial careers for themselves among the Philadelphia merchant classes, the younger son suffered from a sickly constitution and exhibited quite different inclinations. From a very young age Charles was infatuated with books. Pampered and sheltered by concerned parents, subject to numerous ailments, yet precociously intelligent, he avoided the games and amusements of other children to bury himself in texts of history, geography, and literature. His parents reported that while barely out of infancy the boy "required nothing but a book to divert him" and that after school they often would find him in the parlor "mounted on a table, and deeply engaged in the consultation of a map suspended on the side of the wall." Such bookish habits apparently fostered an overweening arrogance. In 1781, around the age of ten, young Brown became intensely indignant when a visitor to his father called him "boy." Charles angrily asked his father, "Why does he call me boy . . . ? Does he not know that it is neither size nor age, but understanding that makes the man? I could ask him a hundred questions none of which he could answer."[3]

The studious, delicate child began his formal education at age eleven by entering the Friends' Latin School. There he came under the tutelage of Robert Proud, a highly respected teacher of ancient languages and future author of *The History of Pennsylvania*. Over the next four years Brown absorbed Latin and a smattering of Greek, studied the Bible and the classics, acquired a working knowledge of French, developed a fondness for rhetoric, and began to formulate his own method of shorthand. At the urging of Proud and his parents, who were worried that obsessional study was further eroding his health, the boy also began a regimen of daily walks in the outdoors. Nearer to his heart, however, were several literary projects. By age twelve he had composed a poem entitled "The Pleasures of Solitude," a didactic polemic chastising drinking and smoking called "The Grape and Tobacco Plant," and a number of brief, juvenile essays on practical morality, business, and Christmas. Around his sixteenth year, and inspired by his love of Shakespeare, Milton, and Cicero, Brown concocted a grand scheme for three epic poems on the early history of the New World: one on Columbus' voyage of discovery, one on Pizarro's expedition to Peru, and one on Cortez's conquest of Mexico.[4]

The clearest indicator of the boy's omnivorous intellectual appetite, however, appeared shortly after his departure from the Latin School. In 1787 he helped found with eight other friends the "Belles-Lettres Club," an organization of young men devoted to the exchange of ideas and the advancement of knowledge. Brown was selected to give the keynote address, and he somewhat breathlessly revealed the massive topic for his speech in a journal entry: "The relations, dependencies, and connections of several parts of knowledge." Full of confidence and saturated with the Enlightenment's faith in human capacity, he insisted in his speech that "Reason is the authority which exerts over obedience." For young Brown it was a reason tempered with "the invigorating influence of the fancy." As they prepared to step upon "the theatre of life, supported only by our own talents and address," youthful Americans must realize that "the whole circle of human knowledge is indeed bound together by a strong and indissoluble chain" emanating from the human mind. For the orator, intellectual advancement meant exploration of both the "provinces of imagination and reason," and using language—"the one happy faculty [by which] man is capable of giving form to spirit"—to convey the results. In a rhetorical flight of enthusiasm, the young speaker described the ideal intellectual, and probably betrayed an idealized self-image as well: "He gives his imagination full liberty to range without control through the whole circle of human knowledge, in the belief that whatever calls for the execution of his mental faculties is already within his reach, and may reasonably be appropriated to his own use." For Brown, the goal was clear if rather immodest: to know everything, and to integrate it into a coherent system.[5]

By late adolescence, this youthful Quaker intellectual approached the first crucial juncture in his life. In the bustling commercial atmosphere of late-eighteenth-century Philadelphia, the male child of a respectable merchant family was expected to make a career decision as he left childhood for the adult world. Around age sixteen Charles Brockden Brown began to feel the pressure. His natural proclivities led to the world of letters, and in his late teens a small stream of literary creations began to trickle from his pen. Brown's earliest attraction was to poetry, and in 1787 he described himself in verse: "His unskilled hand had touched the lyre, And he felt filled with Celestial Fire." Over the next couple of years he composed poems like "Epistle the First," a set of verses devoted to his merchant brother James, who would "the joys of Poesy with Business blend." Nature poems like "In Praise of Schuykill" lauded the natural beauties of his native region, while love poems such as "To Estrina" lauded the virtues of a young female acquaintance. A versified epitaph for Benjamin Franklin in 1788 revealed the young poet's hero worship of a man "Whose soul for the want of due room, Has left us to range in the skies."[6]

The writing of fiction, however, rather quickly emerged to overshadow Brown's other modes of composition. In the late 1780s he quite self-consciously began to keep a journal to develop his skills and sensibility as a writer. Rather fancifully entitling his efforts "The Journal of a Visionary," Brown explained to a friend that, given his aspirations as a writer, "I thought it incumbent upon me to form some regular and analytical system which should furnish the materials of reflection and which should serve as my lode star." The journal contained a wide variety of items: bits and pieces of stories, observations on ideas and people, a long explication of a utopian commonwealth, religious meditations, and many pages of architectural drawings. Such musings helped lay the foundation for several more serious efforts. In 1788 Brown produced a short piece of fiction entitled "The Story of Cooke," a gloomy and moralistic tale describing a drunken Irish immigrant who terrorizes his wife and three daughters. In the same year he wrote a dark, melodramatic, and rather stilted narrative called "The Story of Julius." This effort detailed the life of a noble young man to illustrate "the triumph of virtue over the most lawless and impetuous passions, of duty over inclination." Admitting his great identification with the heroic young protagonist, Brown revealed to a correspondent the autobiographical character of the tale:

I was . . . much delighted with the prospect of describing the meditations of a youth of the deepest penetration and most vigorous imagination (who had studied books and conversed with mankind) on the sublimest subjects that can engage the human faculties, on the uses, bounds, and relations of the Sciences and on the nature and capacity of the soul. I easily foresaw that this would furnish opportunity for forming, explaining, and digesting my own opinions.

Finally, at the same time Brown composed an ambitious but uncompleted series of letters between himself and a mysterious young woman named "Henrietta." This long, fictional exchange was to have been the basis for an epistolary novel.[7]

These first forays into fictional prose writing emerged partly from the young author's enthusiastic immersion in the eighteenth-century world of letters. In the late 1780s and early 1790s Brown paid frequent homage to his literary influences. In his fledgling speech to the Belles-Lettres Club he cited the authority of Dr. Hugh Blair, the influential Scottish writer on aesthetics who insisted that "A man of correct taste is one who is never imposed on by counterfeit beauties; who carries always in his mind that standard of good taste which he employs in judging everything." Brown also informed friends that his "Journal" meditations were prompted by the French philosophes, particularly d'Alembert's introduction to the *Encyclopedie* and Diderot's "analysis of the branches of human knowledge." The young Philadelphian's greatest intellectual inspiration came from two pioneering novelists of the age: Jean-Jacques Rousseau and Samuel Richardson. In the summer of 1788 Brown first read the Frenchman's *Nouvelle Heloise* and rapturously described it as a book of "impassioned pages and transcendent excellence" and a "model of pathetic eloquence." This novel would inspire Brown's "Henrietta Letters," the protagonists of which he described as "not less ardent and sincere and virtuous and delicate than St. Preux and Heloise . . . [from] the vivid fictions of Rousseau." Richardson, author of novels like *Pamela* and *Clarissa*, also galvanized the aspiring American writer with his deeply moralistic tales of virtue rewarded. "I esteem him," the adoring novice burst out in a letter, "inferior to none that ever lived, as a teacher of virtue and the friend of mankind, but the founder of the Christian Religion." Contemplating these literary giants led Brown to conclude that "genius," rather than mere perserverance, was the key to powerful and effective writing. He reminded himself that each author must "determine exactly what is suited to their strength of intellect

and make a single mode of composition their peculiar study." Brown began
a determined search for his own unique species of genius.[8]

Just as his literary talents began to flower, however, the young author's
parents moved to prune back his efforts. While respectful of literary endeavor, they were skeptical of writing as a career. Mindful of their other
sons' promising mercantile positions, and upholders of the Quaker tradition of useful labor, Elijah and Mary began to push their sickly but intellectually exuberant boy in a more practical direction. Thus, in 1789 Charles
began a three-year stint reading law in the office of Alexander Wilcocks, a
highly respected barrister and city recorder for Philadelphia. Brown bent
to the task of studying Blackstone's legal commentary and spent hours
copying a variety of legal papers—deeds, rents, contracts, wills. He also
joined with other young law students to form a legal society and accompanying "moot court," a forum that allowed him to present several grave legal
"decisions." This engagement with the law was a reluctant one. Unable to
abandon the field, he privately complained of its restrictions. For Brown,
legal study was so intellectually narrowing that it prompted this acerbic
comment: "I should rather think that he can only derive pleasure, and con-
sequently improvement, from the study of laws, who knows and wishes to
know nothing else." Moreover, legal practice appeared merely a means to
wealth. "Our intellectual ore is apparently of no value but as it is capable of
being transmuted into gold," he wrote of lawyers, "and learning and eloquence are desirable only as the means of more expeditiously filling our
coffers."[9]

This unhappy situation gradually generated internal tensions. As the
months wore on, Brown grew increasingly bitter in his criticism of the law,
terming it "rubbish" and denouncing its "endless tautologies, its imperti-
nent circuities, its lying assertions and hateful artifices." The fictional delights and enlightened sensibility of Richardson and Rousseau contrasted
pleasantly to the logic-chopping and crabbed style of Coke and Blackstone, who appeared mere remnants of "barbarous antiquity, polluted with
the rust of ages, and patched by the stupidity of modern workmen into
new deformity." Brown's growing alienation slowly pushed him into a kind
of schizoid existence. His days became one long, tedious round of legal
study and transcription, leaving him "listless and melancholy," while in
the evening he threw himself with abandon into literary pursuits. He filled
his journal with long and often self-absorbed ruminations, concocted
grandiose writing schemes, and engaged in long, written exchanges with
various correspondents. Brown's life became so divided between law and

literature that it astonished his first biographer, Paul Allen. On practically any given page of the journal one found "dry, grave and judicial" legal writing followed closely by a "poetical effusion as much distinguished by its wild and eccentric brilliance as the other composition was for its plain sobriety and gravity of style." These early journals made it difficult to believe that "so much eccentricity, and so much irregularity were the productions of one man . . . to all appearances, two persons are present."[10]

To complicate matters even further, Brown's late adolescence predictably saw the first stirrings of sexuality. Already facing family and career pressures, the young man also began to display intense emotional and libidinous energy. He fell in and out of love with great rapidity. In 1789, for example, he grew enamored of Dolly Payne, a young woman to whom he dedicated these heartfelt lines:

> But when thy gentle self appears in view,
> > Like rosy Venus, absent from her sphere
> Flames that inactive slept revive anew
> > My breast alternate grows with hope and fear.

Miss Payne was succeeded in the early 1790s by Debby Ferris, whom Brown showered with extravagant letters and love poems describing her as "my guide into the temple of virtue . . . up to the everlasting gates of Heaven!" A few years later he would become infatuated with Susan Potts and eventually plan to marry her. None of these relationships matured, probably because of parental interference. Brown's mother and father disapproved of their children's marriage to non-Quakers—none of these young women belonged to the Society of Friends—and evidence suggests that they moved to squelch these attachments. As in the case of career choice, young Brown grew resentful of parental pressure and wrote a somewhat melancholy poem on marriage in the early 1790s:

> Let the girl be not widow, nor wanton, nor shrew
> But all are far better than no girl for you.
> If your parents say yes, where your fancy says nay,
> Never haggle but let the old folks have their way.[11]

Brown's surging sexuality also encompassed intense friendships with two fellow students—William Woods Wilkins and Joseph Bringhurst, Jr. The trio maintained close personal ties and a fervid correspondence until the mid-1790s. Even granting the extravagance of language common to eighteenth-century letter writing, many of Brown's letters to these young male friends exhibited a definite sexual charge. For example, in May 1792 a highly emotional missive to Bringhurst contained these passages:

> My Bringhurst! Suffer me to call thee by thy tenderest appellations. My heart is open to divine and softening impressions. I am soul all over. . . . And what, thinkest thou, occasioned this delightful revolution? I caught a momentary glimpse of my correspondent. I saw him buried in profound and tranquil sleep. . . . He looks upon me with regard. He dreams of me. . . . Let me cherish thee, in the same rapture which thou breathest, a refuge from despair, a cure for madness and an antidote to grief. . . . I see nothing but myself and thee.

In other letters, Brown described his attachment to Wilkins as "like the lightning of love" and frankly admitted that "I am absolutely enamored of him." "If I love my friend, I shall often tell him so on occasion, perhaps when such a declaration is not absolutely necessary," he told Wilkins on another occasion. "I will willingly become a pupil to you and be taught, by my amorous friend, the art and mystery of a Lover."[12]

Whatever their object, Brown's "passions," as he came to call them, became an obsessive concern by the early 1790s. The young man agonized over his physical and emotional urges, engaging in outbursts of confession and repentance. "I have never for a moment been free from the dominion of passions, turbulent and headstrong passions," he despaired at one point. "These passions may, indeed, have sometimes tended to good, as they have much more frequently to evil, but whatever was their tendency they were equally irresistible." In one of his earliest fictional efforts, Brown fantasized about a young woman and a sexual liaison "of yielding beauty, of melting love, of meeting bosoms and unutterable ecstasy," but then chastised himself for these "lawless imaginations"; they had him "plunging deeper into guilt in proportion as I endeavor to disengage myself." This emotional turmoil fed a growing anxiety over success in the world of letters. Brown worried that his ardor was dissipating the discipline and sustained effort necessary to writing, noting that he had scarcely formed a "plan of study . . . before passions, violent absorbing passions, interfered, equally detrimental to study in their gratification and disappointment." As an attempt to control this emotional enthusiasm, he tried to subject himself to a disciplined regimen of nightly writing, keeping to his desk transcribing letters, committing thoughts to his journal, and refining his style. Such efforts, he hoped, would eventually subsume his self-styled "native indolence."[13]

Not surprisingly, Brown's mother and father became agents of repression, in terms of both sexuality and literature, as they moved to thwart what they saw as the self-indulgence of their brilliant but undisciplined son. Elijah and Mary had pressured their son away from writing and into a respectable legal career, and had interfered with several of his female dalliances on the grounds of religion. Beneath these overt authority struggles, however, lay another cluster of disturbing family issues. Although the evidence remains sketchy, Mary Brown appears to have exercised a domineering influence over her son, serving as a fount of parental advice and an agent of authority. Well into adulthood, Charles still appeared excessively concerned with pleasing her.

Moreover, his father appears to have been deeply committed to a hierarchical view of the world that ran contrary to the liberalizing trends of post-Revolutionary America and to his son's ambition. This clash reflected, at least in part, a widespread struggle to redefine authority in eighteenth-century America. An older model of paternalism—seen in the influence of writings like Sir Robert Filmer's *Patriarcha*—offered the father-child relationship as a metaphor for obligation and dependence in public and private life. By the time of the American Revolution, however, paternalism was under assault from several directions. Lockean pedagogical notions about the "contractual" family, literary advocacy of "affection" and "example" rather than duty and deference, political attacks on monarchical authority—all of these shaped an "antipatriarchal ideology" that influenced both the new American republic and the youthful American writer. According to one student of the Brown family, the elder Brown upheld paternal tradition: "Believing in a world hierarchy, Elijah saw social position as fixed and pointing to God. . . . Contentment with one's station was the moral application of this eighteenth-century philosophy." Not only did the younger Brown rebel against his demanding father, but his permissive early upbringing muddied the waters further. Although his parents attempted to discipline Charles as an adolescent, they had pampered and spoiled him as a child. Brown's close friend William Dunlap became convinced that the young man's erratic, agitated personality could be traced to his boyhood, when sickliness and precocity led to parental overindulgence. By late adolescence, these emotional cross-currents led Charles to hint darkly at family unhappiness. In the "Henrietta" epistle, for instance, he refused to discuss family matters and "domestic incidents" with his female love interest because "the pain would outweigh the pleasure of attending to the narrative, and no instruction would be derived from the melancholy tale."[14]

From this welter of pressures emerged a full-blown crisis for Charles
Brockden Brown as he arrived at the threshold of manhood. Beginning in
the late 1780s and intensifying until around 1794, the young intellectual entered an extended period of severe emotional turmoil. His future career
seemingly a shambles because of a loathing for the law and the dampening
of his literary ambitions, his family relations tainted by strain and resent-
ment, and his sexual urges frustrated by half-hearted repressions, Brown
struggled with a darkening vision of the world and himself. This crisis, as
it ran its course, gradually unfolded a number of complex and interrelated
dimensions: a bitter critique of American social values, a series of gender
formulations based on a rather desperate cultural logic, an escalating series
of harsh demands for self-control, and a self-destructive agonizing over
identity and performance. By the early 1790s the young man's friends and
family had just cause for alarm.

Brown's emotional struggles became especially evident in three highly
informative series of writings. First, a long sequence of letters to his close
friend Joseph Bringhurst, Jr.—the correspondence eventually totaled several dozen pages on Brown's part alone—contained lengthy, self-revealing
confessional monologues. Second, the fictional "Henrietta Letters" depicted their young author in a highly charged emotional and cultural dialogue
with himself. Finally, "The Rhapsodist" literary essays, Brown's first significant publication, presented a clear sublimation of personal issues and
social preoccupations into a literary form. In each of these three efforts, an
intermingling of private and public, literary and social, psychological and
cultural emerged as a benchmark of Brown's expression.

The young writer's long correspondence with Joseph Bringhurst Jr., a
close companion from his earliest days in the Friends' Latin School, apparently began in early 1792. At that time Brown was about to make a momentous decision to leave Alexander Wilcock's office and drop his legal
study entirely. By 1793 he would employ himself for a time as a master in
the Friends' Grammar School, all the while concocting literary projects
and meandering restlessly between the homes of friends and family in
Philadelphia and New York City. Bringhurst, also a young man of letters
and fellow member of the Belles-Lettres Club, was busy in Philadelphia
shaping a career as a businessman. Brown began sending a steady stream
of letters to Bringhurst's residences on Union Street and Front Street—
forty-six of those letters have survived—which would flow unabated for
some five years. In these epistles their troubled author unburdened himself.[15]

An overriding theme in Brown's epistles to Bringhurst was an almost frantic pursuit of knowledge. He constantly referred to his hunger to know "the history of nations, and of individuals, of life and manners." The scope of his ambition was vast and inclusive, as he impatiently told his correspondent: "Everything that relates to man is of importance in the study of human nature. Every art and science. Every scheme of the understanding or operation of the senses." As usual, Brown was driven by a desire to integrate all branches of knowledge because an understanding of their relationship "appears to me absolutely indispensable to a rational enquirer." As a dutiful child of the Enlightenment, however, the young intellectual carefully disassociated knowledge from mere tradition or unthinking faith. He was absolutely sure of one thing: wisdom would come only "in proportion as I gain access to truth . . . , in proportion as my understanding is uniformly, steadfastly, and powerfully illumined by its beams; and in proportion as my actions conform to the deliberate judgements of my understanding."[16]

This elevated discourse masked a deeper concern in Brown's psyche: the personal meaning of intellectual pursuit. In a long, self-reflexive letter of 1793, for instance, he explored the relative weights of "diligence" and "genius" in the search for moral and intellectual excellence. Brown contended that while application would certainly lead to improvement, it would be limited because of human inequality. It seemed clear that "genius is indispensable to some pursuits; that genius is the gift of nature; that it is a gift entirely withholden from some." Brown often seemed sure that he possessed such genius. Most youths were so indifferent to knowledge and moral cultivation that to find an elevated one would be as surprising as "an Elephant soberly passing along the streets of my native city." In contrast, the young writer deemed himself to be quite special. Expressing contempt for most of his acquaintances, he admitted that "I imagined myself infinitely superior to my juvenile associates." In spite of this arrogance, Brown was perceptive enough to honestly assess his own motives as a combination of genuine love of learning and desire for distinction. While the possession of knowledge was "inexpressibly delightful" in and of itself, he granted that "reputation . . . when attained, [is] by no means unacceptable."[17]

Brown's concern with the individual pursuit of knowledge and virtue, however, also radiated outward into the realm of social commentary. His many letters from the early 1790s reveal the pain, disapproval, and ambivalence resulting from his encounters with a volatile, expanding American society. Growing up in the booming commercial atmosphere of Philadelphia, where the structures and sensibilities of the marketplace were remaking traditional social arrangements in the post-Revolutionary decades, this young man struggled with the emerging model of striving individualism. In one of his early philosophical journal entries in 1787, Brown observed in rather exasperated fashion that "Man may be considered as one, and alone; or he may be considered as a member of a community, and connected with others." With his own career quandary looming in the background, such ambiguity colored his correspondence with Bringhurst. Brown frequently insisted that as one made a pathway through the world, the applause and support of others must remain strictly secondary to "an anxious desire to obtain the approbation of our own heart." He also lamented that "man cannot become master of his destiny. He cannot, indeed, control the course of events. It were absurd and presumptuous to make that an object of his wishes." Brown's ambivalence grew even more pronounced as he considered the inherent artifice in social relations among ambitious individuals. He grew convinced that "of all the virtues, mankind is most universally deficient in sincerity." Nor did the youthful writer shy away from self-analysis on this point, acknowledging to Bringhurst that in his dealings with others "a mask became so habitual to me that I scarcely remember how I was induced to lay it aside, and to appear before my friend in my native character."[18]

Brown's social critique also took more concrete forms. Stung by personal experience, he set up lawyers as convenient targets for bitter denunciations of a morally vacant scramble for wealth and status. In an American society where material success overshadowed all else, the attorney became a figure of "dull, unvarying temper" whom "chance, not merit, has awakened to fame." In a bitter burst of doggerel written around 1792, Brown vented his contempt for social-climbing attorneys:

> Low at those feet where wealth and power gives laws,
>     Let others prostitute their venal strain;
> And air-blown piles of undeserv'd applause,
>     Build for the weak, the wicked, and the vain.

The young critic did not stop with lawyers. In his wanderings in the countryside outside Philadelphia, he encountered many farmers who seemed as uncivilized and greedy as any barrister. No defender of the yeoman, Brown described a group where "*avarice* is their predominant passion on which

every other principle of action is based, and they are universally sunk in ignorance and brutality." Back in an urban setting, merchants and speculators in the market environment of Philadelphia likewise earned severe criticism for their morally suspect practices and money grubbing. As Brown
put it rather sharply in 1789, he could not disavow "the despicable idea I
have always entertained of the character of a 'Retailer.' "[19]

Even more striking in the letters to Bringhurst, however, was the author's obsessive preoccupation with self. Brown unfolded in these missives
a nearly endless analysis of his own motives, nature, talents, and prospects.
It burst out of every letter, often theatrically, always revealingly. Brown
told his correspondent in late 1792 that "I will set you an example of sincerity, and tell you in what light, were I a spectator, I think I should appear
to myself." He more than fulfilled the promise. On the one hand, the
young intellectual rather arrogantly defended his special character: "Excellence of my kind is singular, and I cannot discover my disadvantage in being noted as singularly excellent on any account." Brown was also given to
playing the tortured artist, frequently advertising a love of solitude and
contemplation. On the other hand, however, and more frequently in this
period he engaged in gloomy self-deprecation and self-pity. Granting a
tendency toward "fits of disconsolateness," Brown admitted to Bringhurst
that his supposed excellence was merely a conceit and that he could be
happy as long as the "delusion lasts, but surely miserable when it is at an
end." He often went to even greater lengths of self-abasement. In July
1793, for instance, Brown insisted that he felt only contempt for himself:

> None of my hopes have been fulfilled, and . . . nearly all my apprehensions have
> been realized. . . . I am not happy. It is useless to deny . . . the disapprobation of
> my own conscience. . . . I am . . . yet a poor and miserable reprobate. Whose
> bitter portion is anger from those he loves and scorn from those he reveres. . . .
> Sunk into the lowest abyss of self-contempt and weighed down by early and ex-
> treme mortifications.

Such extreme self-criticism eventually led the young man to frighten
Bringhurst and other friends with talk of suicide, as he admitted: "I once
was determined to destroy myself" since "there, at this moment, creeps not
upon the surface of the earth a wretch more miserable."[20]

In part, such theatrical displays of self-loathing were pathetic calls for
reassurance from a young man caught up in an agonized struggle to enter
the adult world. They also revealed a kind of internal fragmentation re-

sulting from a struggle with career choice, marriage, and a coherent sense
of self. Problems of identity formation, of course, probably persist as part
of the human life cycle in some way. Scholars have suggested, however,
that the exigencies of developing liberal society greatly intensified them.
"Adolescence," for instance, as a stage of transition from childhood to
adulthood, was itself a postmedieval concept that seems to have been identified only in the eighteenth century. With a market society increasingly
posing choice as the key to destiny, with Lockean pedagogy stressing the
formation of personal autonomy, with the Enlightenment enshrining individual understanding and rationality as an emergence from infantile
"nonage," educated and ambitious young men faced newly intensified pressures by the late 1700s. A splintering of the psyche could result, and this
image often came into full view with Brown.

"To comprehend one's own character is sufficiently hard," he once confessed to Bringhurst. In a nearly hysterical letter in May 1792 he admitted
he was utterly unable to comprehend his own proclivities. "I am no longer
master of myself—I weep involuntarily," he wrote frantically. "I am no
more—I must relinquish my pen and fly from myself." Later the same year
in another letter, Brown revealed even more clearly the picture of a divided
self. Within the space of a few paragraphs, he informed Bringhurst of his
misery and frequent thoughts about suicide and then turned 180 degrees to
state that "in my opinion, no one of the same age that ever lived has seen,
has read, has written, has reflected more than myself." Brown then provided a dramatic snapshot of his own fragmented identity:

> How often have I smiled on considering within myself: how difficult a person
> am I from him whom those with whom I associate, suppose me to be. How im-
> perfectly is my real character represented by my countenance, my manner or my
> dress. How little do they know of him with whom they imagine themselves
> perfectly acquainted.[21]

This self-described masked figure, by Brown's own account, waged a
constant battle with passion. Joseph Bringhurst read numerous missives
insisting that happiness can be found only "in the arms of love." He also
saw frequent recitations of guilt as his young correspondent confessed affairs where he had been both "seducer" and "seduced." As Brown observed
on several occasions, his passions were so strong that they seriously undermined his intellectual aspirations. He had engaged in the systematic study
of "grammar, rhetoric, and poetry," he wrote in 1792, when the "deity of
LOVE" presented herself and "I began to riot in those intoxicating draughts

which the divinity presented to my lips." At that point, he noted sorrow-fully, his projects were "thrown aside and entirely neglected."[22]

Brown's internal fragmentation especially came to light in what would become a lifelong preoccupation: dream life and states of altered consciousness. In late adolescence he began to exhibit an attraction to the dream state as an alternative to everyday life. During one unhappy period in 1792, he complained to Bringhurst that "the privilege of dreaming to any agreeable or useful purpose is denied me, and I am forced to be contented with insipid realities . . . which the wand of wakeful Imagination can call into existence." In that same year Brown related to Bringhurst a long, highly symbolic dream in which both of them played central roles. In the young writer's fantasy, the two friends were in a landscape out of Edmund Spenser's *The Faerie Queene*, wandering as religious pilgrims looking for the temple of some divinity. In Brown's words, "all our happiness depended on the success of our journey." After a long and arduous trip, they came upon an imposing stream laying between them and the temple. After much doubt and delay, Bringhurst lifted Brown in his arms and carried him safely across. At the very moment of success, however, a gigantic knight clad in black armor astride a black horse rushed down upon them, snatched up Brown, and carried him off. At that point Bringhurst, overcome with despair, prepared to hurl himself into the river when his mother appeared to pull him back to safety. At that point Brown "awoke in much distress and horror."[23]

While the precise meaning of the dream is open to interpretation, several issues appeared clearly in it. At an unconscious level it seems to reflect Brown's troubled "journey" to success, a "wild, unknown, and dangerous" travail that had left him wandering and uncertain. Moreover, his companion carrying him across the river suggests a serious questioning of the individualist ethos of self-reliance. And the river itself—water traditionally symbolizes life, organic vitality, and sensuality in Western myth and artistic imagery—pointedly appears as a barrier in the dream, a reflection of Brown's struggle with his passions as an obstacle to worldly success. The dream's culminating episode embodies the dreamer's nascent gender anxieties, where men appear as aggressive "black knights" and women as rescuing, nurturing creatures. Overarching this cluster of psychosocial tensions, of course, was Brown's magnetic attraction to the dream state itself, which he described here almost reverently as "an intercourse with invisible agents." This fascination with his own hidden layers of consciousness even seemed to culminate in a species of death wish. As Brown observed at the end of his dream narrative, while his mother still lived never "shall I voluntarily cease to exist." In other words, for this troubled adolescent suicide seemed to promise the ultimate but forbidden dream.[24]

If the Bringhurst letters provided young Brown an extended stay in the confessional booth, his "Henrietta Letters" comprised a kind of literary diary of the fragmented self. There his internal psychic voices engaged in a fascinating dialogue of contrary emotions and ideas. Apparently written in 1792 and 1793, this long series of letters was presented as actual correspondence between Brown and a young woman with whom he had fallen in love. More recently, however, scholars have demonstrated their fictional status as an aborted epistolary novel modeled on Rousseau's *Heloise*. What fascinates in this text is neither the plot (which is nearly nonexistent) nor the language (which is inflated and stilted) nor the formal ideas (which are highly derivative from Rousseau and Richardson) but rather the cultural and psychological dynamics. The literary discourse of "Henrietta" clearly suggests a process of self-definition, with Brown composing both male and female voices in a dialogue of competing impulses.[25]

The structure of the "Henrietta" manuscript takes a simple and straightforward form. It consists of an extended exchange of letters between "C.B.B.," a youthful gentleman, and "Henrietta," the female object of his affections. While the young man lavishes love, hopes for marriage, and adoration on the young woman, she responds with admonitions to control his passion. Throughout the text there weaves long, highly sentimental discussions of an array of issues in late eighteenth-century culture: education, marriage, equality between the sexes, languages, and political principles. The narrative has virtually no plot or action, and eventually it is aborted. It simply stops before even telling the reader if the two protagonists ever marry.

On several counts this rather frustrating and unsatisfying text reveals more than the author ever intended. First, Brown's fictional exchange with himself discloses a persistent struggle for self-control. For instance, following one of C.B.B.'s passionate declarations of physical love, Henrietta rebukes him: "How would you be induced to write in that inexcusably licentious manner? I read it with indignation. . . . For surely he whose deportment is regulated not by reason or prudence but by violent and domineering passion . . . is in ruins." The young correspondent can only reply that the beauties of her "animating mind" are matched by "the graces of thy person." Brown asks, "Am I not a man? And would you punish me for faults which are inseparable from my nature?" Such internal conflict surfaced frequently in Brown's late adolescent experiences. In published poetry he annunciated "the sacred task, to love as sexless beings," while in private letters he burst out, "what is a being without passion? What is that cold, sapless, and inanimate virtue founded only on principle, and not on sentiment?"[26]

This internal contest for self-control led Brown to postulate clear gender definitions of human impulse in the "Henrietta Letters." In Freudian terms, the female representative Henrietta takes shape as a kind of Superego figure while C.B.B. appears as an embodiment of the Id. The young woman is typically described as an "angel," a model of "purity" that inspires her suitor with "a boundless desire of rising to the same extraordinary pitch of mental and moral excellence." On the other hand, she describes C.B.B. as a creature whose "wild, impetuous, and ungovernable passions" must be guarded against. The clashing juxtaposition of these instincts presents the libidinous C.B.B. embracing Henrietta and showering her with kisses while she cries, "My friend! forbear!" Brown records the victory of the Superego: "It was impossible not to obey you. I unloosed you from my arms, . . . bathed your hand with my tears of remorse and sorrow and supplicated your forgiveness."[27]

Such formulations eventually prompted the young author—this would become especially significant for Brown's developing grasp of his own role as a writer—to identify "culture" as the domain of women. The "Henrietta" manuscript constantly portrays its female protagonist in fervent pursuit of knowledge in languages, literature, and philosophy. Expressing her admiration for the Richardsonian heroine Clarissa Harlowe, Henrietta proclaims, "Why should women be outstripped by men in literary pursuits? For is not female curiosity insatiable, and what other passion is requisite to render learned labor successful?" Brown, writing in the guise of C.B.B., goes even further. Male intellectual capacities, he insists, naturally flow into mathematics, military science, and the law while females are attracted inherently to "the sedentary and domestic avocations" of poetry, moral reflection, and literature. As he reassures Henrietta regarding her love of poetry and romance, "you are destined by your maker not only to rival but to outstrip your masculine competitors in all the excellencies of heart and understanding."[28]

This dissonant dialogue among Brown's internal voices—male and female, libidinous and repressive, willful and genteel—ultimately produces a persistent and disturbing presence in the "Henrietta Letters": the fluid, fragmented self. One glimpse appears from the fictional pen of Henrietta as she recounts her first impressions of C.B.B. as a fleeting visage who "haunted my imagination." Arresting her attention as he stopped to glance in her window before disappearing, the young man would intrude obsessively into her dreams as a mutable, protean figure: "I saw you under a thousand different shapes. At one time methought you came to visit me in a magnificent equippage . . . ; at another time that you put on a mean disguise and became a servant of the gardener. . . . Afterwards I thought you overleapt the garden wall by midnight and suddenly appeared before me."

At another point Henrietta describes her suitor as such an "inexplicable, unintelligible creature" that "it has taught me hereafter to place no confidence in external appearances." Writing as C.B.B., young Brockden Brown replies in a highly schizoid manner. Insisting on his absolute abhorrence of pretenses and disguises, he claims always to have "acted and spoken with sincerity from the strongest and [most] invincible motives." Just a few sentences later, however, he confesses, "I own I do not thoroughly comprehend my own motives." With such images in the "Henrietta Letters" any sense of firm identity or stable sense of self seems to have vanished.[29]

In the autumn of 1789 Brown's first substantial publication, a quartet of essays entitled "The Rhapsodist," appeared. Offered in the pages of Philadelphia's *The Universal Asylum and Columbian Magazine*, these short pieces were likely a portion of his early notebook "The Journal of a Visionary." They constituted a benchmark in the young man's development both as a writer and as a human being. The essays presented their author as a literary observer who utilized both reason and fancy to explore "the sentiments suggested by the moment in artless and unpremeditated language." As a clear product of the turmoil of Brown's private and public life in this era, however, "The Rhapsodist" also took shape as an exercise in sublimation. It provided an intriguing self-portrait as the young artist struggled to claim a social comprehension of place, a cultural means of expression, and a psychological sense of self. As Brown frankly admitted, the rhapsodist would employ "that caution and decency becoming one who is painting his own character."[30]

From the outset young Brown made clear his central theme in defining this persona: the question of individual sincerity and deception. At the beginning of the first "Rhapsodist" essay, he passionately affirmed the "sincerity of my character" and promised to write only what is "strictly true." Brown then made the following bold and highly revealing statement:

I speak seriously when I affirm that no situation whatsoever will justify a man in uttering a falsehood. I have, therefore, rigidly exacted the truth from myself, even in a case where the world is willing to be deceived. . . . Truth is with me the test of every man's character. . . . Wherever I perceive the least inclination to deceive, I suspect a growing depravity of soul. . . . But I am not alone sagacious in discovering the faults of others. I am also careful to regulate my own conduct by this immutable standard.

Uneasy in a liberalizing social milieu of competitive individualism, and agitated by vocational and personal pressures, the young intellectual self-consciously presented himself to the public as a sincere, even artless moral writer. The rhapsodist, he promised, "will write as he speaks, and converse with his reader not as an author, but as a man."[31]

Brown, however, quickly added an important addendum to this self-definition. The genuineness and sincerity of the rhapsodist, he insisted, could only flow from a condition of isolation. The author claimed at one time to have written in solitude on "the solitary banks of the Ohio," but now in Philadelphia he was forced to retire to the deepest recesses of his garden or bedchamber to escape the clamor of society. When alone, Brown claimed, he could indulge flights of fancy and "solicit an acquaintance with the beings of an higher order." Thus, an important cultural juxtaposition—the sensitive, imaginative, artistic imperial self versus the mundane, utilitarian, constricting demands of society—began to take shape in his earliest writing. A rhapsodist, he wrote, yearns to

be left to the enjoyment of himself, and to the freedom of his own thoughts. It is only when alone that he exerts his faculties with rigour, and exults in the consciousness of his own existence. . . . In spite of my pretensions to unlimited sovereignty over my own person and actions. In spite of my strong original propensity to silence and reserve, I am, in some measure, compelled to pay obedience, tho' grudgingly, to the laws of society.

In a sentence heavy with cultural, economic, and psychological layers of meaning, Brown claimed as his goal to "withdraw himself entirely from the commerce of the world."[32]

Such brave proclamations of romantic individualism in "The Rhapsodist" essays ultimately turned even further inward. Once again Brown betrayed a magnetic attraction to the pull of the dream state and unconsciousness. The rhapsodist's lively imagination carried him far beyond the

world's mundane materiality, he argued, so that "there is scarcely a piece of
unanimated matter existing in the universe. His presence inspires being,
instinct and reason into every object, real or imagined." As Brown added a
bit later, the rhapsodist "loves to converse with beings of his own creation,
and every personage and every scene, is described with a pencil dipt in the
colours of imagination." This proclivity led the young writer to describe
the hurly-burly of Philadelphia urban life in terms of a fantasy, as "the
lively representation of a dream." It prompted him to relate the contents of
a long, messianic vision in which, as an "imaginary hero," thousands of
spectators pay tribute to his genius. Ultimately, this preoccupation with
fantasy helped foster the young writer's growing tendency to define,
separate, and elevate the realm of "imagination" away from the day-to-day
utilitarian realm of social existence. For Brown, the aspiring man of letters,
work life and creative life seldom intersected. Thus, it must be, as he
conceived it in these essays, that "the life of the rhapsodist is literally a
dream."[33]

With "The Rhapsodist" essays the earliest stage of Brown's life reached
a highly schizoid culmination. On the one hand, by early manhood his literary definitions and goals had begun to crystallize into a coherent intellectual foundation for his career. At the same time the young writer's personal definition and selfhood had fallen into increasing incoherence and
disarray. The contrast, and tension, between these elements, was growing
acute by the early 1790s.

As a writer, Brown had developed remarkably in early life. With a flurry of half-formed juvenile efforts, the young author had begun to shape a
pronounced literary sensibility. The writing of fiction, he concluded,
should focus on the domestic experience of people—"the personal character of individuals, their visages, their dress, their accent, their language,
their habits, manners and opinion, their *personal behavior*." The novel
could present unmatched insights into the "human heart." Even skilled
writing, however, could only partly capture "the influence of the passion"
and the "strange events in our own domestic experience." As Brown put it
directly in the "Henrietta Letters," "Fiction, however published and elaborate, could never yet surpass reality." Literary explorations of real life and
moral issues, however, could benefit equally both the author and the reader. The culture of books—both writing and reading—seemed useful inso-
far as it provided "a text to which your imagination must furnish a supple-
ment. . . . The ideas of others are of no importance and utility but as you
render them by meditation your own . . . the products of your own labor,

or the offspring of your own imagination." For Brown, this belief shaped a kind of authorial solipsism where spontaneity of expression was essential. Regarding his ideas and words, "whichsoever first offer themselves are instantly adopted" and any revision or rewriting was anathema as "the dress of borrowed or artificial sentiments." The fledgling novelist, in the language and sensibility of liberal individualism, staked out his literary claim early in life: "I deliver the suggestions of my heart, I speak in my native character."[34]

Behind this apparent intellectual coherence, however, Brown's sense of self had shattered into psychological fragments. Poised on the brink of manhood, the young writer faced an intense and persistent emotional crisis. Dramatically claiming that "I utterly despise myself," Brown stared into an "abyss of ignominy and abasement into which I am sunk by my own reflections." By the early 1790s his gloomy self-absorption had helped create a personal fantasy world contructed of, in Brown's own words, "air built structures of a wild, undisciplined, untractable imagination." Making false claims about traveling in Europe, fabricating wild tales about an early marriage and his wife's premature death, and deliberately confusing his own woes with those of his fictional characters, the young author, according to the admonitions of his friend Dr. Elihu Smith, too often wandered "in a world of your own creation." Brown himself recognized these imaginative journeys as both dangerous and liberating. On the one hand, they allowed him to be "rescued from the tedious or distressful present, by the aid of an excursive imagination," an instinct that would feed his writing. On the other hand, however, Brown agonized over whether "a visionary has not now become a lunatic, whether the objects around me be phantoms or realities, whether my reason be not overpowered by imagination."[35]

This volatile mix of professional, public integration and private, psychological disintegration might seem to comprise a full-blown "identity crisis," as one scholar has termed it.[36] Brown's situation actually had roots extending much deeper and ramifications spreading much wider. From the specific historical matrix of a transforming market society in the early American republic, several intense pressures—career choice, expression of sexual passion, parental authority—had emerged to entangle this sensitive young intellectual. Struggling with the liberal model of individual success, Brown had gradually begun to shape his literary efforts as an expression of this social milieu. For Brown, the public man, writing became an expression of pure individual imagination, removed from and elevated above the sordid material world of profit seeking. Defenders of culture, he insisted, must flee society and "seek . . . a visionary happiness in a world of their own creation." At the same time, the deeply troubled private man, cut loose from the moorings of social identity and strained by the external demands for success, grew splintered and formless. Brown recognized in himself, at some layer of consciousness, a fragmented and fluid self:

> No one more widely differs in his sentiments and dispositions from others than at different periods from himself. . . . We vary according to the variations of the scene and the hour, and . . . the particular circumstances in which we shall then be placed. Man . . . is always either returning from a certain point or leaving it behind him.[37]

Charles Brockden Brown's early life crisis, however, was but the first act in a lifelong drama of the market and the self. Unhappy in the social world and anchorless in the private realm, he appeared trapped in a scene where external and internal struggles entangled one another. The writing of literature, as a complex act of cultural mediation, offered one way out. So, too, did Brown's alienation, which gradually began to flow outward into a social critique. As he had observed in the "Henrietta Letters," a penchant for concealing motives and counterfeiting conviction had made it obvious that "of all the virtues mankind is the most universally deficient in sincerity." By the mid-1790s this sentiment would trigger Brown's developing literary assault on the social relations and cultural values of the liberalizing American republic.

# THREE

# ❦‖ The Young Artist as
# Social Visionary

In the last quarter of the eighteenth century, Philadelphia was the most vibrant and cosmopolitan area in the United States.
The largest American city in this period, it also stood at the juncture of
several important trends in the infant republic. Politically, the city had
been the birthplace of the American nation. Philadelphia had housed the
wartime Continental Congresses, seen the proclamation of the Declaration of Independence, and served as the nerve center of the revolutionary
struggle against Great Britain. In the summer of 1787 its inhabitants had
witnessed the gathering of the great convention in the Old State House
that produced the new federal Constitution. Then, in 1790, as the nation's
capital, the city became the forum for increasingly controversial and bitter
political debate. By the end of George Washington's administration in
1796, the republican political culture of America's Revolutionary age had
divided into two quarreling camps. With an emerging party system of
competing Federalists and Jeffersonian Republicans—divided over issues
of economic development, government power, and popular virtue—
Philadelphia became a hotbed of political intrigue, electoral organization,
and ideological disputation.[1]

However great its political role, the economic influence of this Pennsylvania port city loomed equally large. In the two decades after the onset of
the American Revolution, Philadelphia's merchant class stood at the fore-
front of a rapidly expanding market revolution that was transforming the
economic landscape of the entire Atlantic world. The city's evolution followed two routes. First, from 1776 to the mid-1790s, Philadelphia's merchants and entrepreneurs made it the most dynamic port in all of North
America. It became a critical juncture for import and export trade in the

growing web of Atlantic commerce that created ties with the West Indies, Bordeaux, Barcelona, and eventually London. A burgeoning "spirit of enterprise," in the words of one scholar, helped foster the China trade, commercial banking, the tobacco trade, and securities speculation among busy Philadelphia overseas merchants. Second, this eastern Pennsylvania city also became the center of a growing regional market structure at home. Beginning in the early 1790s Philadelphia became the commercial hub for domestic manufactures, market-oriented agriculture, and primitive coal mining and iron production—and this trend became even more dramatic in the early nineteenth century. This explosion of economic enterprise in the Philadelphia area helped clear the ground for a massive surge in overseas trade during the Napoleonic Wars, and also for the later and more gradual industrialization of the Delaware Valley.[2]

With such an environment of intense political and economic transformation, it seemed only natural that Philadelphia's cultural life also came to full flower in the late eighteenth century. By the early 1790s the city had emerged as the center of intellectual activity in the young republic. Its American Philosophical Society, for example, served as the leading organization for American scientists and became the chief medium for exchange of scientific communication with European scholars. Moreover, painters such as Charles Willson Peale, Gilbert Stuart, and John Trumbull spent considerable time in the Quaker city. Public exhibitions and discussion of such artistic endeavors eventually led to the establishment of the "Pennsylvania Academy of Fine Arts" in Philadelphia soon after the turn of the century. At the same time, the controversial physician and chemist Benjamin Rush was earning the title "Father of American Psychiatry" for his work at the University of Pennsylvania and the Philadelphia Hospital. The city's community of letters also flourished. Joseph Dennie's *The Portfolio*, combative journalists like William Cobbett and James Duane, the publisher Mathew Carey, and poet Philip Freneau helped create a lively literary atmosphere. Perhaps nothing better symbolized Philadelphia's preeminent cultural position in the 1790s than the construction of the famous and popular "Peale's Museum." With its wildly eclectic exhibition of Revolutionary portraiture, natural history artifacts, musical demonstrations, and geological displays, the museum elicited both popular acclaim and serious intellectual discussion.[3]

In this atmosphere of political, economic, and cultural ferment aspiring author Charles Brockden Brown became intoxicated with the possibilities of writing. Emerging from an adolescence colored by vocational anxiety, emotional upheaval, and intellectual infatuation, the young Philadelphian began to focus on writing, particularly fictional prose, as his contribution to the formation of an American culture. As Brown noted in a letter of 1794, it had become his belief that "the genius of a poet should be sacred to the glory of his country." He threw himself into several literary projects. A grandiose "Philadelphia novel," probably entitled *Ellendale*, engaged him first around 1795-96. Brown then authored *Alcuin: or, the Rights of Women*, a long fictional dialogue in epistolary form, in 1796–97, and a lost novel manuscript "Skywalk" the following year. The latter he publicly advertised as a proud depiction of American uniqueness, a treatment of "our ecclesiastical and political system, our domestic and social maxims." Several brief essays, poems, and stories accompanied these longer efforts.[4]

Brown embodied the excitement and flux of Philadelphia's golden era not only in these first extensive literary productions, but even more dramatically in his dalliance with ideological radicalism. Facing an "age of democratic revolutions" in the late eighteenth-century Western world, this youthful intellectual was swept up in a strong current of challenges to traditional authority. This insurgent spirit appeared in several ways. It became evident in his embrace of the novel itself, an innovative and popular literary form that undermined older, more elitist genres in the realm of belles lettres. It became even more striking, however, in the actual content of Brown's public and private writings in the mid-1790s. There he offered a mélange of subversive themes and ideas—skeptical attacks on traditional Christianity, explorations of inequality in gender relations, speculative schemes of political utopianism. Thus, by 1798, at the conclusion of his early literary career, Brown seemed to personify that boldness and fluidity characteristic of Philadelphia and the American republic in a revolutionary period.

While this youthful writer's intellectual and ideological energies became more focused, however, his deportment fluctuated rather wildly due to certain developments in his private life. On the positive side, Brown's attempts at professional writing benefited enormously from immersion into a network of fellow intellectuals in Philadelphia and New York City. A friendship with Dr. Elihu H. Smith proved critical. In 1790, when Smith came to Philadelphia for a year of medical study with Benjamin Rush at the Pennsylvania Hospital, he and Brown struck up a friendship. When the young physician returned to New York City to open a practice, his Philadelphia friend began a frequent round of visits. Brown gradually became acquainted with Smith's circle of ambitious and curious young intellectuals and professional men. This group—which included historian and minister Samuel Miller, scientist Samuel Latham Mitchill, lawyer James Kent, the barrister and translator William Johnson, and especially the painter, playwright, and theater manager William Dunlap—formed the Friendly Club in 1793 as a forum for discussion of scientific, moral, and political issues. As a regular visitor to the city by the summer of 1794, Brown faithfully attended their meetings. Smith and Dunlap especially encouraged him in his literary ambitions, the latter with a constant stream of private advice and approval, the former with economic assistance in publication. This support was not lost on Brown, who noted that "the influence of my friends and their unexpected and uncommon zeal inspire me with a courage which I should be unable to derive from any other quarter." The discovery of a support group of like-minded intellectuals allowed him an escape from vocational anxieties rooted in his family's expectations.[5]

On the negative side, however, Brown's persistent emotional agitation, even hysteria, retarded his progress as a writer while frustrating even his most ardent friends and supporters. These attention-seeking, despairing outbursts seem to have become an emotional habit by his early twenties. In the mid-1790s he described himself to friends with both distress and opacity as "the child of passion and inconsistency, . . . the slave of hopes no less criminal than fantastic." The young man, in a letter to William Dunlap, demonstrated the depths to which his self-pity could sink: "I am sometimes apt to think that few human beings have drunk so deeply of the cup of self-abhorrence as I have. There is no misery equal to that which flows from this source. I have been for some years in the full fruition of it. Whether it will end but with life I know not."[6]

Such miseries were compounded by Brown's annoying tendency to start and then abandon the literary projects he had described to friends in a grand manner. In 1795 he proudly announced his conception of a great "Philadelphia novel" that would be completed in just six weeks. After several years' labor, however, he typically abandoned the project, having written only fifty pages. Paralyzed by a perception of defective skill and sensibility, he related: "I dropped the pen, and I sunk into silent and solitary meditation." The following year Brown conceived and then aborted two other plans, one for a giant novel called "Alloa" and the other a stage adaptation of Robert Bage's novel *Hermsprong*. Even when completed works did appear sporadically, they were filled with undisciplined, fantastic writing and melancholy reflections. In a long, autobiographical section of the 1793 poem "Devotion: An Epistle," for example, he lamented the studious course of his life as a trek "through the thorny tracts that lead to nothing in the metaphysic wilderness." Other verses reveled in gloom: "Dark, desolate, and void, and dreary is the temple of my soul." Brown's short pieces of fiction in this period also featured characters awash in self-pity and given to bizarre behavior. In "A Series of Original Letters," the protagonist Henry, a law student in Philadelphia, describes himself unhappily: "In this busy and populous place, I am more alone than if I were in a wilderness." In "A Lesson on Sensibility," the youthful character Archibald goes mad from his obsessive attraction to love, a trait fostered by "Romancers and Poets." In Brown's autobiographical words, "A phrenzy at first furious and terrible, subsided into a melancholy, harmless to others but invincibly silent and motionless. . . . He has remained for some years, an example of the fatal effects of addicting the undisciplined mind to books."[7]

This role of anguished artist, which the young writer fell to playing, eventually drew sharp reprimands. After witnessing several of Brown's displays of self-indulgence, for instance, close friend Elihu H. Smith took him to task. In two long letters in May 1796, the physician attempted to rein Brown in emotionally. Both the analysis and the recommendations were highly revealing. Reacting to his young friend's morbid preoccupation with his own difficulties and his veiled threats of self-destruction, Smith confronted Brown:

> Why do you so much delight in mystery? Is it the disease of will? or of habit? Do you, of choice, give to the simplest circumstances the air of fiction . . . [and] enwrap yourself in the mantle of ambiguous meaning, that your pen involuntarily borrows the phraseology of fancy, and by the spell of magic words still diffuses round you the mist of obscuring uncertainty? The man of Truth, Charles! the pupil of Reason has no mysteries. . . . He seeks only to know his duty and perform it, and he has no occasion for disguise.

Fed up with Brown's self-pity, his friend told him frankly, "I am pained to be the useless depository of complaints I cannot understand, of sorrows I cannot assuage."[8]

Having ventured this far, Smith plunged ahead. An inability to control the passions, the doctor stated bluntly, was threatening to destroy Brown's literary talent. "Why is it so? Wherefore are you so vigorous, so firm in thought," he wrote, "and so weak, so vacillating in action?" And when Brown actually completed a piece of writing, Smith complained, emotional licentiousness often garbled its coherence with "imperfect metaphors tumultuously heaped upon each other" and "poetical periphrasis which sometimes puzzle us." In the doctor's words, "the word *simplicity* [needs] to be inserted in capitals in your vocabulary." According to Smith's analysis, however, Brown's ultimate problem lay in a failure to distinguish fantasy from reality. He was so caught up in the novelistic worlds of writers like Rousseau and Richardson that "You began to fancy that these fictions were real; that you had indeed suffered, enjoyed, known, and seen all that you had so long pretended to have experienced; every subsequent event became tinctured with this conviction and accompanied with this diseased apprehension; the habit was formed." As Smith concluded rather brutally, Brown's "self-love" had produced a pattern of unrestrained behavior in which his "actions burst out in all the extravagance, his voice swells with all the emphasis of passion."[9]

This criticism unquestionably wounded Brown, partly because of its censorious tone and partly due to its accuracy. Yet it seemed to have little effect. The young writer's cycle of overwrought emotion and paralyzed self-abasement would continue nearly unabated until his marriage around the turn of the century. At the same time, however, Brown seems to have begun a fitful process of sublimation in the mid-1790s as emotional unheaval and a passionate desire for expression gradually fed a growing stream of writings. This sublimation, converging with the "revolutionary" spirit of late eighteenth-century Philadelphia, helped shape in this novelist a certain kind of literary expression. Brown's work became a vehicle for ideological radicalism. With several forces—the Enlightenment, the novel, Revolutionary republicanism—challenging long-standing patterns of cultural authority, and with a market revolution transforming traditional economic and social life, Brown entered a maelstrom of controversy. He began to attack the tenets of organized Christianity, to question male dominance of women in Western society, and to offer a brand of political and social utopianism. These "radical" writings, occurring midway between his adolescent scribblings and mature novels, served as an intellectual and emotional bridge. In the form of artistic expression, they connected Brown's social encounters with liberalizing change in the American republic and his personal sense of profound unease and psychological fragmentation.[10]

In many ways, Brown's struggle with Christianity drove an entering wedge for other kinds of radical influence. Beginning in the early 1790s he began to dispute the validity of Christian tenets and denigrate their influence on Western culture. Several influences came to bear here: the young writer's struggle to achieve autonomy from his Quaker family, his exposure to the secularizing influence of Enlightenment writers in literature and science, his esteem for utopian social critics and anticlerics like William Godwin. The results first appeared in "Devotion: An Epistle," a long poem likely composed sometime in 1794. Its stanzas included an extensive autobiographical section in which Brown alluded to growing religious skepticism and waning "devotion." Noting his allegiance to "Newtonian banners" in the war with "Prejudice, intrench'd behind the mound of old opinion," he derided the unquestioning believer who

> Of monkish dreams talks loud, and priestly craft;
> Of miracles which none believ'd who saw;
> Of mystic prophecies, a knotted maze
> Inextricate, obscure, inscrutable
> That must be first fulfilled, ere understood;
> Of Fate that made a world, and Fate that rules.[11]

Brown's religious radicalism, however, became more evident in two other forms. First, from 1792 to 1795 he wrote a long series of private letters to Joseph Bringhurst, a close friend and traditional Christian with whom he debated doctrinal and moral issues at great length. Second, his initial attempt at writing a novel called "Ellendale" from 1793 to 1796—the manuscript has survived only in fragmentary form—apparently produced an anti-Christian, utopian narrative propounding a new system of morality. Both of these efforts revealed a young man in the throes of religious rebellion.

Brown's exchanges with Bringhurst clearly exhibited his growing skepticism about Christianity. "I once thought . . . that religious beliefs were desirable, even if it were erroneous," he remarked in 1795. "I am now of a different opinion, and believe that utility must always be coincident to truth." As Brown explained in greater detail in several missives, Christianity failed as a compelling system of morality and spirituality. Its extreme sectarianism—"there are a thousand sects in this world, who call themselves Christian"—resulted in a babble of argument over intricate and technical questions and exclusive claims of veracity. Much Christian doctrine, he continued, was so obscure as to be "incomprehensible" and it affected practical human action only weakly. For Brown, "belief in the divinity of Christ and future retribution" had destroyed human friendship, "created war, and engendered hatred" throughout history.[12]

This broad critical assault narrowed to a consideration of Jesus Christ himself. In many letters to Bringhurst, Brown privately vented his heretical judgments on "the divine Son of Mary." Christ, according to the young intellectual, was a virtuous man who offered to humankind "the highest degree of moral excellence" and he deserved emulation. Brown was unwilling, however, to go much beyond that. He tended, in his own words, toward "reducing Christ to the rank of the Grecian Sages" while his doctrines must be understood and compared with "the creed of Moses, . . . of Mahomet, of Confucious, of Pythagorias or Solon." Brown's Jesus was essentially a great moral philospher, perhaps the first among equals, but one whose moral precepts must rest on "intrinsic evidence" of their virtue and truthfulness rather than on fear of future punishment.[13]

Such logic eventually led the youthful author to the most sacred text of Christianity. In the fashion of numerous Enlightenment-influenced intellectuals in the late eighteenth century, he challenged the Bible's stature as the divinely inspired word of God. This great book, to his mind, presented numerous problems. Its original form had been fashioned in the "obscurities of a foreign language and unintelligible idiom"; its subsequent forms had passed through the hands of numerous "transcribers" with great opportunities "to debase the purity of the text . . . [with] artful interpolations and omissions"; and the whole was rendered obscure by extraneous "metaphysical refinements and mysterious circumstances." Brown extended this critique to more shocking lengths. "If I ask what is the gospel history more than a Romance, will you not be startled?" he inquired of the pious Bringhurst. And if the Bible was indeed a semifictional narrative aiming at moral instruction, should it not be compared with similar, modern literary efforts? Brown answered affirmatively and undoubtedly appalled his correspondent by ranking the Bible lower on this scale than Richardson's *Sir Charles Grandison*:

> Let it not offend your piety that I draw a parallel between an english novel and the evangelical history. . . . Does not my reason compel me to give the preference to the performance of Richardson?
>
> That one is truth and the other fiction is of no importance to one who considers both as moral lessons, or rather it is to fiction that the english work is indebted for its superiority since . . . it is, as a work of invention, more accurate and uniform, and consequently more instructive . . . how much more strongly do the catastrophes of [Grandison's] three inimitable tales incite me to persist in a virtuous course than that of the sacred narrative.

Speaking even more bluntly, Brown further insisted that Richardson was nearly the equal of Jesus. The English novelist was "inferior to none that ever lived, as a teacher of virtue and the friend of mankind, but the founder of the Christian religion."[14]

Brown made these private musings public only in diluted form. In 1793 he embarked on a sporadic three-year effort to complete what he termed his "Philadelphia novel." The intended title of this work, "Ellendale," derived from its setting on a farm along the Schuykill River above the city, but the context apparently flowed from its author's anti-Christian inclinations. While Brown abandoned the project in 1796, in typical fashion, its several surviving fragments offer at least a glimpse of the religious radicalism that motivated it.[15] In two long segments dated August 1793, the author suggested both the epistolary form of the novel and its thematic thrust. In his words, "It would be strange indeed if [in] the future annals of this Western Continent, the stream of power and opinion should not be seen to flow from some new Muse of Nazareth. If they should tell of some new conception of duty, and ambassador to Heaven, some founder of nations and friend of man." Brown embellished this vision of a new religion and messiah in a 1795 letter to William Dunlap, where he acknowledged the intense reading and writing necessary "to render my system of morality perfect in all its parts." In an October 1795 diary entry, Elihu H. Smith discussed the controversial nature of his friend's book. Brown, along with his intellectual comrades, would surely encounter "rancour and misrepresentations" from the forces of "superstitious fury," he predicted. "Storms and tempests hover over our heads, ready to burst, or are gathering in slow and sullen vengeance, to break and overwhelm us with destruction."[16]

One section of the novel—it was not discovered until after Brown's death—was entitled "Harry Wallace." This portion of the "Ellendale" saga told the truncated tale of a figure in Revolutionary Pennsylvania whose life paralleled that of both Jesus and Brown himself. The young protagonist, abandoned shortly after birth, was the illegitimate son of a young woman named "Mary." Left on a doorstep on Christmas morning in 1770—only three weeks before the author's own birth—the child was reared by the prosperous Mr. Ellen on his large farm fifteen miles from Philadelphia. The bright youngster received an education there, became a somewhat frustrated law student, and finally found a respectable career as a land conveyancer. As an adult, Harry fortuitously reunited with his real mother, while traveling in "the neighborhood of Bethlehem and Nazareth," Pennsylvania. Another fragment of the novel was also discovered and reprinted in the early nineteenth century under the title "Adini." Supposedly extracted from the papers of Mr. Ellen and narrated by Harry Wallace, this story focused on Signoir Adini, an enigmatic addition to the Ellendale circle. An immigrant arriving in 1784, he became a tutor to the Ellen children. Although reluctant to discuss his past, Adini, by bits and pieces, partially revealed himself as a utopian revolutionary whose activities remained shrouded in mystery. At one point, he spoke admiringly of Sir Thomas More's *Utopia* and fleetingly disclosed his radical fervor: "The purposes of daily life, philosophy, and reason, demand a reformation. . . . The condition in this respect of that nook called Europe is mournful in one view, hatefully stupid and ludicrously forlorn in another. The whole mass, indeed, wants a thorough shifting . . . [and] the change should come quickly." The Adini story ended abruptly and inconclusively, but it suggested nonetheless Brown's attraction to contemporary currents of social and religious radicalism. Along with his private musings, the sketchy "Ellendale" narrative showed the young author in a confrontation with the authority of Christianity by the mid-1790s.[17]

Brown was no pioneer of religious dissent. His skepticism about Christian doctrine, of course, reflected a widespread trend among Enlightenment intellectuals. From Voltaire to Rousseau, Thomas Paine to William Godwin, Benjamin Franklin to Thomas Jefferson, Western social thinkers in the eighteenth century had been embracing Biblical criticism and challenging the explanatory and moral power of traditional religion. In another area, however, Brown ventured beyond all but the most daring intellectual contemporaries. By the mid-1790s the aspiring Philadelphia writer began to question the entire structure of gender relationships in the society of the Atlantic world. In part, this stemmed from a fascination with female status, proclivities, and talents which persisted throughout his career. More broadly, his inquiries into social definitions and structures based on gender brought into question male domination of Western cultural tradition.

His own personal and problematic encounters with women provided an influential backdrop for this investigation. Brown's adolescent attraction to young females had become entangled with two serious issues: his parents' demands for engagement with a girl of Quaker affiliation, and his own repeatedly frustrated attempts to gain self-control over his passions and his destiny. Thus, in 1794 his unrequited ardor for non-Quaker Debby Ferris led him to construct an ideal of platonic, passionless relations between the sexes in his long poem "Devotion: An Epistle." Pure love, he described, "boasts participation with divine existences; soul thralldom; reason leagu'd with reason." A few years later, his extended relationship with Susan Potts—again, she was not of the Friends' faith—prompted parallel reflections in a series of "Stella" poems. There excessive idealism gave way to despair. Brown brooded over his perception that women and love represented a blockade to his ambitions and career hopes.

As lonely o'er my little fire,
    I sit and muse, and dream of fame.
My hopes on Fancy's wing aspire,
    To wealth, and rank, and sounding name.
But ah! the little traitor Love
    Unbidden mingles in the theme;
The fixed resolve dares disapprove,
    And stile the vision but a dream.

These troubled attempts to comprehend male-female interaction reflected young Brown's bewilderment in dealing with his sexuality, his desire for escape from the generational authority of his parents, and his attempt to control emotion in the interests of personal cohesion and career advancement.[18]

If such private experiences laid the emotional groundwork for Brown's interest in the status of the sexes, public immersion in America's "age of revolution" prompted him intellectually. As recent scholarship has shown, the traditional eighteenth-century woman's role consisted of a troika of responsibilities: wife, mother, and household mistress. Ensconced in a hierarchical structure of paternal authority, females occupied a secondary social status where their destiny was to marry, have children, maintain the domicile, and free men for their public roles as heads of households and citizens. By the late 1700s, however, the influence of the American Revolution had begun to undermine this arrangement. Under twin influences— women's active participation in the political struggle with England and the pervasiveness of republican ideology—the social role of women became overtly politicized. The notion of "republican motherhood" began to take shape, in which women assumed a quasi-public role as molders and shapers of a virtuous citizenry.[19]

Brown reflected this Revolutionary atmosphere of flux in certain of his 1790s writings on women, and it emerged most strikingly in a liberationist theme. In the "Henrietta Letters," for instance, the author claimed to yearn for "the sacrifice of masculine privilege—hateful, arrogant pernicious privilege." As he further explained to his female correspondent, "I never conceived that the minds of women were naturally inferior to those of men. I have always indeed strenuously maintained that you are originally foremost in the scale of being, and it is easy to produce examples which show that you are capable of outdoing us both in vice and virtue." Brown expressed similar sentiments in a 1792 review of Mary Wollstonecraft's controversial *A Vindication of the Rights of Women*. This radical tract, which eloquently denounced domestic restraints on women and called for their free and equal participation in the public realm, received his cautious endorsement. Writing in a 1792 number of the Philadelphia *Ladies Magazine*, he noted that Wollstonecraft's "wide variety of reflections, solid and entertaining" had given him "great pleasure." And while Brown could not "wholly agree with our fair authoress in all the points she contends for," he ultimately pronounced himself "much pleased with her work."[20]

In another sense, however, this young intellectual's efforts to interpret the Revolution for American women proved more problematic. Like many other republicans of his generation, Brown struggled to shape a civic role for women without removing them from their "natural" domestic setting. This often resulted in a redefinition of republican "virtue" as the particular product of female moral efforts in the household. In a 1792 essay, for instance, he argued that while men were created to protect women, the female's moral superiority "will teach our sex politeness and affability, will render us worthy members of society; will eradicate rough behavior . . . ; will render us cheerful and happy . . . ; will keep us from having any intercourse with the lower class of their sex." In line with this portrait of civilizing, middle-class females, Brown went on to suggest that men should seek wives based not on riches or passion, but on "the beauties of her mind" and moral "merit." Overall, he elevated women to a position of intellectual and literary superiority. In his words, "it is the province of *female excellence alone*, with the beams of intellectual light, which illuminates the paths of literature."[21]

Much of this rethinking of gender categories came together in one of Brown's earliest and most fascinating literary efforts. In the spring of 1798 *Alcuin; A Dialogue* became the first of his major works to appear in print. With the first section published as a book in New York by his friend Elihu H. Smith, it almost simultaneously began serial publication in the Philadelphia *Weekly Magazine*. The text offered one of the most extensive, probing, and insightful discussions of female status and rights in late eighteenth-century America. Cast in terms of a long conversation between Alcuin, a Philadelphia schoolteacher, and Mrs. Carter, an educated and thoughtful advocate of women's rights, the work obviously derived inspiration from contemporary debates among writers like Wollstonecraft and her husband William Godwin, educational theorist Benjamin Rush, and reformer Judith Sargent Murray. In fact, the controversial character of the first half of *Alcuin* probably caused Brown, in concert with his cautious intellectual supporters, to suppress publication of the second half of the book. The entire text would not appear in print until 1815, some five years after his death.[22]

Brown structured the book as a week-long dialogue consisting of several serious conversations between a male and a female. In the first half of the text, Alcuin—the name comes from the leading humanist scholar and educator at the emperor Charlemagne's court—showed himself to be a receptive but somewhat reluctant supporter of female rights. His foil, Mrs. Carter, a widowed acquaintance who kept house for her brother, appeared as an eloquent critic of female subservience in the new American republic. Readers of *Alcuin* generally have interpreted the text in one of two opposing ways. One critical reading sees the text as a radical statement in behalf of women's rights, with Brown as a late eighteenth-century pioneer for female liberation. On the opposing side, others view the book as a conservative pronouncement on the "woman question," with the author openly examining the issues but then rejecting the agenda of Wollstonecraft and her allies.[23]

On the face of it, *Alcuin* presents abundant evidence for both positions. In the first section of the book, Alcuin clashed with Mrs. Carter over the present and future status of American women. For her, the liberty of the American Revolution rang hollow for female inhabitants of the republic. Under this "charming system of equality and independence," not only women but the young, the poor, and Blacks were disenfranchised and classified "with dogs and swine." As Mrs. Carter pointed out, by marrying a woman lost all right to separate property and became subject to the absolute will of her husband. Under this despotic system, the sexes were forced to view one another in wholly opposite ways: a male attitude of "reserve and artifice," a female one of "adulation and affected humility." Mrs. Carter heatedly insisted, however, that both men and women were "rational beings, and as such, the same principles of truth and equity must be applicable to both." Alcuin responded with a mixture of sympathy and paternal condescension. On the one hand, he admitted that male intellectual superiority was a medieval prejudice and that environmental deprivation had robbed women of the opportunity for knowledge in science, politics, and elevated literature. He quickly added, however, that "strength" often legitimately determined male or female tasks. Alcuin also disputed whether republican society would be advanced by recognizing "no condition to a voter but that he be a thing in human shape, not lunatic, and capable of locomotion." His ultimate point was a moral one. For Alcuin, it was clear that while men were superior in "power and property," they also excelled in "vice and folly." Female superiority lay in "feelings" and "senses"—a result of their insulation from public brutality—and in those qualities resided a potential for civilizing control over male society.[24]

In the second half of the narrative, Alcuin the reluctant reformer and Mrs. Carter the enthusiastic radical seemed to switch roles. In a conversation that resumed a week later, Alcuin claimed to have visited a utopian "paradise of women" where absolute equality between the sexes held sway. Holding to an ethic of "utility," this society demanded a sharing of work, intellectual activity, and material fruits regardless of gender and without the constraints of marriage. Mrs. Carter recoiled in horror. She claimed that her criticisms had implied no such "speculative systems," for they eroded "the deepest foundations of civil society."[25]

Thus Alcuin, rather confusingly, makes it possible to see Brown as either radical or conservative on the question of female status, both because of the book's dialogic quality and its protagonists' shifting opinions. A possible solution to this problem, as some scholars have suggested, is to recognize that the book represents Brown's own confused struggle for values and commitments in a highly volatile and transformative age.[26] While this notion certainly has some merit, a more compelling possibility lies elsewhere. Brown's consideration of gender did not appear in isolation. Instead, as he revealed in the text of *Alcuin*, it collided with and collapsed into equally fundamental considerations of social class and market-defined work. The result was a complex socioeconomic perspective on the whole question of radicalism and women's social position. *Alcuin* was more revolutionary in some ways, but less revolutionary in others, than it appeared at first glance.

Brown gave a hint of concurrent social concerns early in the narrative. Alcuin, in describing his entrance into the salon of the well-to-do Carter family, pointedly noted his lowly social position. "I looked at my unpowdered locks, my worsted stockings, and my pewter buckles. I bethought me of my embarrassed air and my uncouth gate," he reported. Such vulgar commonality, according to the author, presented a jarring contrast to the social graces and "superciliousness of wealth and talents" of his upper-class hosts. This portrait of class divergence became even clearer as Alcuin offhandedly recounted in conversation his obnoxious landlady and noisy neighborhood, his low-paying job that left him shabby and poor, and his constant ill health.[27]

Alcuin's personal concerns, however, translated into a social critique. Debating with Mrs. Carter, he clearly countered her gender-based argument with an analysis rooted in social class:

> If a certain part of every community must be condemned to servile and mechanical professions, it matters not of what sex they may be. If the benefits of leisure and science be, of necessity, the portion of a few, why should we be anxious to which sex the preference is given? . . . The state of the ignorant, servile, and laborious is entitled to compassion and relief, not because they are women, nor because they are men, but simply because they are rational.

Moreover, in meeting Mrs. Carter's indignant demands that women should be allowed to become merchants, bankers, physicians, and lawyers, Alcuin proclaimed that he had "little respect . . . for any profession whatever." Professional figures were driven by gain, he insisted, and they disregarded honesty because "whatever it be, it is not the road to wealth." In general, the public masculine world was one of toil, roughness of manner, intellectual stagnation, greed, and want, and women entered it only at their peril.[28]

This conceptual clash of class and gender became even more pointed in the second part of *Alcuin*. Alcuin returned to Mrs. Carter's salon several days later, claiming to have visited a utopian "paradise of women." In this revolutionary society, he reported, gender relations had been reformulated as part of a broader system of labor and social reform. In this utopia, labor and skill were donated for "the common benefit" as work was "divided among many" according to their propensity and choice. So, too, the fruits of labor were distributed according to need. This division of labor avoided the "monstrous conception" of apportionment by gender. It was a certainty that human work degenerated "into painful and unwholesome drudgery, by being confined to a sex." This vision of primitive socialism emerged as a central theme in *Alcuin*:

> Perhaps that precept of justice is practicable, which requires that each man should take his share of the labour, and enjoy his portion of the rest: that the

tasks now assigned to a few, might be divided among the whole; and what now degenerates into ceaseless and brutalizing toil might, by an equitable distribution, be changed into agreeable and useful exercise.

So, for the wide-eyed reformer of the second part of *Alcuin*, equality between the sexes could only be achieved within the context of a revolutionary reform of marketplace work.[29]

Mrs. Carter's reaction to Alcuin's vision proved equally fascinating and revealing. Horrified by its radical sweep, she hastily retreated and retrenched. Her promotion of women's rights, she insisted, did not extend into an attack on the foundations of civil society. The "paradise of women," in Mrs. Carter's eyes, represented a kind of wild, speculative philosophy characterized by "specious but fatal illusions." Most serious was its implicit undermining of the institution of marriage. Alcuin's utopia advanced such an extreme ethos of liberty that matrimony would be impossible to maintain due to an unavoidable "guidance of a sensual impulse." While Mrs. Carter opposed marriage as practiced, she carefully noted that she did not oppose it in principle. Brown's female protagonist revealed her Lockean liberal agenda: free choice, access to property, rational individual liberty. Marriage needed restructuring because it rendered "the female a slave to the man" and thereby restricted free agency. It demanded reform because it left women "destitute of property." The solution to these problems lay in "an unlimited power of divorce" that promoted "unbiased and enlightened choice" for the figures involved. In other words, Alcuin's ethereal socialist utopia clashed with Mrs. Carter's liberal reformism and her ethic of possessive individualism.[30]

Thus, Alcuin's exploration of women's rights reached an ideological and emotional impasse. For Brown's protagonists, one advocating a collectivist blueprint and the other a liberal individualist blueprint, consensus over the construction of a just society for women proved nearly impossible. They could agree only that liberalized divorce was theoretically desirable but practically problematic, and that liberated "sensuality" was morally reprehensible and socially dangerous.[31] Moreover, the text's early lines of demarcation had become extremely blurred by the conclusion of the dialogue. Was Mrs. Carter really more radical than Alcuin? Which viewpoint, if either, did the somewhat mysterious author endorse? This uncertainty, however, ultimately confirmed one clear point. Brown's struggle with issues of female equality could not be separated from his larger confrontation with an emerging liberal society in America. The treatment of female liberation comprised but one piece in his larger mosaic of radical challenges to the logic and constraints of market individualism.

Brown's questioning of both Christian and male authority ultimately paved the way for an even broader crusade in the mid-1790s. The young writer proffered, if sporadically and rather unsystematically, a persistent political utopianism throughout much of the decade. William Dunlap, for instance, examined Brown's papers after his death and was struck by the numerous "plans and scraps of Eutopias" which sought "to improve and secure human happiness." In private letters the Philadelphian also frequently mused upon a cherished goal of "confirming the confidence of men in a system of morality that would sustain social amiability, destroy material deprivation, and promote intellectual contemplation." Brown's written work provided more evidence of this inclination. The narrator in his "Adini" story, for example, was taken from Sir Thomas More's *Utopia*. Another of his earliest characters observed pointedly,

> There must be one condition of society that approaches nearer than any other to the standard of rectitude and happiness. For this it is our duty to search; and, having found it, endeavor to reduce every other condition to this desirable mean. . . . Human beings, it is to be hoped, are destined to a better condition on this stage, or some other, than is now alotted them.[32]

In part, Brown's utopian instincts in early manhood flowed from his uneasiness with a growing ethic of market individualism. Confronted by the liberalizing American republic in the 1790s, he often reacted by criticizing its citizens' unrestrained ambition and money grubbing. The very settlement of North America, he observed in a *Monthly Magazine* book review, had arisen from "the most sordid passions incident to man": ambition, greed, materialism, adventurism. In a fictional short story, again for magazine publication, Brown recounted the tale of a West Indies immigrant family to further chastise his restless fellow Americans. For Brown, the travails of this family, who had lost their possessions and property in the revolution on St. Domingo, offered a cautionary lesson to the ambitious. Their ability to maintain a zeal for life amidst their struggle for survival demonstrated that it was "our duty to make the best of our condition; to snatch the good that is within our reach, and to nourish no repinings on account of what is unattainable."[33]

Brown's critique of a society on the make, however, went beyond the realm of moral platitudes. The appearance of "The Man at Home" stories in thirteen installments in Philadelphia's *Weekly Magazine* highlighted

their author's deep concern with debt, fraud, poverty, money, and other issues rooted in momentous market growth. Published from February to
April 1798, these efforts—fiction, part essay—offered Brown's typical rambling plot. The stories focused on a sixty-year-old gentleman who wrote
from a secluded chamber. Obsessed by an old locked trunk left in the
room by a previous occupant, he finally pried it open and eventually discovered a dusty manuscript hidden beneath a false bottom. There he
found a picturesque tale of a Frenchman, his daughter, and their adventures during the American Revolution. This rather desultory and anticli-
mactic plot-line proved deceptive. It was merely a story within a story.[34]

The narrator's own tale was the real one and his isolation, it turns out,
was a result of his hiding from creditors. Having endorsed the notes of an
old friend and business partner, he had been driven out of retirement and
into hiding when the acquaintance went bankrupt and his own fortune
was insufficient to cover the debt. Hounded by a writ of arrest, he had fled
to the home of his washer woman and holed up in an isolated room. There
the narrator had taken to writing, punctuating his fictional sallies with an
often bitter social commentary. Depressed by his plight, he observed that
"Money is power, and may be subservient to ill as well as to good. From
the frailty of humanity, and the misarrangements of society, the injurious
application of this instrument is always most probable." At another point,
immersed among the Philadelphia lower classes, the narrator confessed
that his attitude toward them had become one "of compassion rather than
of scorn." Then, at the end of the essays, he engaged in an extensive mus-
ing on the problem of debt and imprisonment in a commercializing society. The narrator did not question the "sacredness of property." In a society
where increasingly "debts are daily contracted," however, some inevitably
fell victim to foolishness rather than crime. Thus, it seemed apparent that
in a system defined by investment, risk, and profit seeking, effort was required to distinguish between "the insolvency that flows from misfortune
and that which flows from knavery."[35]

In his "Series of Original Letters," appearing in the Philadelphia *Weekly
Magazine* from April to June 1798, Brown expanded this social critique.
Cast as a series of epistles between Henry, an unhappy law student, and
his sister—the autobiographical overtones are evident—these exchanges
wove together a dialogue about the usefulness of the law with a sketchy
tale of a schemer named Beddoes and his prostitute sister. Brown's social
commentary was arresting. Young Henry, for example, anguished over the
pressures of individual career choice and his own unhappiness as a law stu-

dent. "How momentous a thing is the choice of a trade!" he wrote. "How much does it behoove us to deliberate with accuracy and decide with caution!" Moreover, the law itself, as the social and economic glue for a liberal society of contracts, appeared to be a field where "success can be purchased at no price but that of our sincerity and honour; and . . . is universally stigmatized as fraudulent and corrupt." Henry further expounded a variety of guilty class-consciousness. Admitting his contempt as a professional lawyer-in-training for common "servile mechanics," he chastised himself for excessive social pride and ambition. As Henry asked, "Is it dishonourable to labor for one's own subsistence? Who am I that dare to plume myself upon my rank?"[36]

This welter of concerns arising from a liberalizing social milieu—isolated individualism, greed, duplicity, class divisions—helped fuel Brown's utopianism in the mid-1790s. It especially pushed him down a path of visionary reformism blazed by William Godwin, the English political theorist and critic. Godwin had surfaced in the late eighteenth century as one of the most provocative dissenting voices in the Atlantic world. His influential tract, *Political Justice* (1793), first established him, in the words of one historian, as "the most radical theorist of the day." Then, his "reformist novel" *Caleb Williams*—published in England in 1794, then reprinted in Philadelphia the following year—gave fictional expression to his theories. These books revealed Godwin's radicalism to be an assault on medieval hierarchy and superstition which blended two elements: an extreme sense of ethical individualism, and an unrelenting utilitarianism. The essence of humanity, he argued, was the ability to act according to "the unbiased dictate of my own judgement." Social issues could invariably be reduced to simple questions: "How may the peculiar and independent operation of each individual in the social state most effectually be preserved? How may the security each man ought to possess, as to this life, and the employment of his faculties according to the dictates of his own understanding, be most certainly defended from invasion?" In such a context, social institutions could be evaluated only in terms of their rationality and utility. In this Godwinian world of enlightened individual judgment and utilitarian·standards, customs and traditions had little place. Monarchy, social castes, organized religion, and even the state itself promised to disappear in Godwin's individualist "republican Utopia."[37]

Brown's attraction to Godwinian reform was no secret in the 1790s. His long-time friend William Dunlap noted that by mid-decade the young intellectual "was an avowed admirer of Godwin's style, and the effects of that

admiration may be discerned in many of his early compositions." Brown
harshly judged his earliest fictional writings against "the transcendent merits of *Caleb Williams*," and he often urged friends to procure Godwin's political tracts. Elihu H. Smith, perhaps Brown's closest friend and intellectual companion, presented an unhappier view of this influence. In a 1796
letter he chastised the author for his self-indulgence in concocting "mighty
purposes of reformation" that were left half-completed in a realm of fantasy. This lack of intellectual discipline, for Smith, could be traced in part to
one of Brown's infatuations: "*Godwin came & all was light.*"[38]

The Philadelphian's interpretation of Godwin's principles surfaced frequently in his early writings. In private letters he mused on his desire to
implement reform by endeavoring to "enforce on mankind the observance
of their duty, and by demonstrating the connection between their duty and
their happiness." This ethic of individualist morality seasoned many of his
1790s stories and essays with a Godwinian flavor. A "different condition of
society" could be created, Brown speculated, where "our faculties will not
be able to vary from a true direction," where people could abjure popularity to listen for "the applause of our own conscience," and where the individual interacted with his fellow citizens rationally and "dispenses benevolence with singular and obvious utility." Brown's first novels when they
began to burst forth in 1798, were also laced with Godwinian politics,
character-types, and sensibility.[39]

A long and introspective letter to Susan Godolphin, however, provided
perhaps the best evidence of its author's self-image as a utopian reformer
following in the footsteps of his English radical hero. Written on July 2
and 3, 1793, to one of his early love-interests, this epistle contained Brown's
reflections on the moral meaning and social purpose of his literary endeavors. Carefully explaining himself, the young intellectual insisted that individual "disinterestedness" was the the basis for pursuing one's "sense of
duty." Avowing that in his own life "every personal advantage appears as
trivial in comparison with duty," he defined that duty as contributing "all
in our power to augment the picture of human happiness." Such principles
led Brown to conclude that while human development could lead either to
improvement or degeneracy, man's "progressive" tendencies usually triumphed. Thus, it was one's obligation to uncover "the laws which regulate
this progress" and "the causes that produce it." Brown bluntly stated his
utopian creed near the end of the letter: men "are justified in fostering designs which contemplate the most extensive efforts. The happiness of
mankind must be allowed."[40]

Within this broad utopian project, however, Brown went on to define a clear role for the writer-intellectual. As he explained to Miss Godolphin, the author's first duty was to promote man's "natural tendency" to wisdom, justice, and truth by exposing the "foreign and artificial institutions" that hindered progress. Brown quickly added to this Rousseau-like dictum a Godwinian admonition: the author must also follow a utilitarian guideline. "Men are strenuous in their virtue in proportion as they have a powerful conception of the benefits flowing from it," he wrote. "Let me win them to the practice of it by displaying its practical effects." For this idealistic young author, the moral and social liberation of the individual—a goal of the conscientious writer—promised not only human happiness but human harmony.[41]

Thus, by the mid-1790s Charles Brockden Brown had begun to define himself as a writer primarily in terms of utopian moralism. Fired by the ideas of Rousseau and Godwin, he increasingly saw his task as the promotion of social and ethical reform using fiction as his vehicle. A pervasive questioning of religious, gender, and social authority provided the first ideological thrust for these efforts. Yet Brown's task was less clear-cut than it may have seemed. The ambiguous, even muddled quality of his position occasionally crept into the open, especially regarding the issue of individualism. The young intellectual, on the one hand, fervently endorsed the Godwinian ethic of the complete "independent operation of each individual in the social state." On the other hand, he fervently denounced the notion of the individual pursuing his material self-interest in the marketplace. To make the situation even more complex, Brown also demanded "virtuous" conduct—in eighteenth-century discourse this meant the sacrifice of selfish interests to the public good—even while agitating for the moral liberation of the individual and the enshrinement of a utilitarian social code. These problematic positions revealed that Brown's intellectual struggles occurred in a specific historical context: the wrenching and profound transition from a republican to a liberal society in late eighteenth-century America. His agenda for reform embodied much of the fluidity and ambiguity of the age in its attempt to redefine categories, definitions, and principles.

This attempt to come to terms with the emerging liberal republic could be exhilarating, as Brown's passion for writing and reform clearly demonstrated. It also could be frightening and frustrating. In 1792, for instance, as this sensitive young intellectual was just beginning to wrestle with ideological questions, he wrote an essay entitled "On the Nature and Essential

Qualities of Poetry, as Distinguished from the Prose." While much of this magazine piece featured technical literary formulations and flights of metaphysical fancy, near the end it focused on a highly revealing subject. Modern social development, Brown mused, was bringing a refinement of manners and a more comfortable standard of living for many fellow citizens. Yet the cost was heavier than realized.

> Civilization and science have, as it were, minced into finer portions, the feelings of the heart. . . . These larger masses have been broken by the hand of culture into smaller pieces, which are in perpetual currency, and which maintain among us a more equal and constant enjoyment. . . . We may perhaps hope to excel in softness, delicacy, and refinement; but these are feeble graces. The mind soon tires with the perpetual chime of smooth versification, and with the unvaried flow of gentle and unimpassioned sentiment. The bursts of honest nature, the glow of animated feeling, the imagery, the enthusiasm. . . . For these, no appendages of art can be deemed an adequate compensation.[42]

These unintended consequences of social advancement—a fragmentation of experience and sensibility, a loss of vital human passion—at times turned inward to threaten suffocation for this idealistic young writer. Brown's reactions varied. As a utopian he sought to break free by means of a liberating vision of social freedom. As a critic he sought to preserve social coherence and virtue by condemning greed and materialism. In confronting the segmentation and rationalization of a market society in the liberalizing American republic, however, Brown finally found but one method of coping. The act of writing itself became both a means of personal escape and an instrument of social salvation. Entangled in the discourses of Enlightenment intellectual life and the market, Brown became, in his own highly suggestive phrase, a "dealer in fiction."[43] Through the novel he determined to explore the myriad consequences of fragmentation and dissipation while at the same time fulfilling his commitments to viable individual morality and utilitarian reform. With such a volatile ideological and personal agenda in place, the stage was set for one of the most astonishing bursts of creative activity in the history of early American culture.

# FOUR

## ☙‖ The Major Novels (I):
## Fiction and Fragmentation

In the early 1790s Charles Brockden Brown sat down in his Philadelphia apartment to compose a typically self-indulgent letter to a friend. In it he raised an emotional appeal to the muse of literary inspiration:

> Here I am seated at my desk—with pen and writing implements at hand; and shall I not employ them? . . . I beseech thee, kind, propitious, amiable, gracious bountiful divinity, deny not the gift I solicit. . . . Deny me not, I most eloquently entreat thee. . . . The poetical fervor is upon me. The magician . . . is now standing at the threshold of his cell and waving his potent wand at my command. . . . But unless I break his wand or make it motionless and drive the enchanter into his gloomy dwelling I shall be seduced to a greater distance from the tract of common sense than I am at present desirious of being.[1]

This passionate declaration—part entreaty, part cautionary reminder—summarized much of the young man's early career. It revealed an intense compulsion to write, where putting words to paper became a wonderfully enchanting "gift." At the same time it disclosed a lurking fear of writing as a kind of evil magic that lured its practitioners into a dangerous, inescapable realm of fantasy. This tension had shackled Brown's efforts well into the decade, resulting in a literary trail of half-completed manuscripts, aborted projects, and frustrated plans. Not until the end of the century did he break free of these fetters and gave full rein to his "poetical fervor." The results were dramatic.

Between 1798 and 1800, to the astonishment of his friends and probably to himself, Brown overcame his earlier malaise and issued four major novels in a feverish burst of composition. Publication of this quartet of texts comprised the first sustained body of work by an American author, and they seemed to suggest that a serious writer had emerged in the infant republic with the start of a new century. Throughout the spring and summer of 1798 the young man labored on *Wieland; or, the Transformation*, which he apparently finished in September. Then in a frenzied effort he completed *Ormond; or, the Secret Witness* over a six-week period from mid-November to the end of the year. That novel was published in early 1799. Brown then returned to a manuscript he had begun early in the spring of 1798— *Arthur Mevyn; or, Memoirs of the Year 1793*—and finished Part 1 by the end of February 1799. He would complete Part 2 of this novel in early 1800 and publish it later that year. Finally, in the early months of 1799 he completed *Edgar Huntly; or, the Memoirs of a Sleepwalker.* Over the same two-year period Brown also wrote two large novel-fragments, "Memoirs of Carwin the Biloquist" and "Stephen Calvert," both of which were prematurely abandoned and published in magazines several years later.[2]

This creative outburst brought its author more reputation than money. Lagging sales frustrated Brown's hopes for survival as a professional author, and the struggle to market his work to an appropriate audience never succeeded. Nonetheless, these novels of the late 1790s spawned a number of imitations and prompted considerable comment from both American and European critics. The reasons are not a mystery. Brown's four fictional texts hit their readers with a heavy emotional impact. Written in a kind of Americanized Gothic style, these tales presented mysterious, passionate, bizarre stories of psychological turmoil and dark human impulses. They startled the senses with their emotional intensity and darkly dramatic textures. At the same time these novels—this might be anticipated, given their extremely rapid completion—exasperated readers with inconsistent plots, half-developed characters, meandering explanations of motive, and outlandish use of language. Like casks of fine wine cracked prematurely and spilling forth, they both scintillated and disappointed the literary palate. While one could sense immediately what might have been in terms of beauty and power, the texts seemed only partially distilled and half-mature. Impressive but rather raw, *Wieland, Ormond, Arthur Mervyn*, and *Edgar Huntly* often left an unsatisfying aftertaste in the reader's mouth.

Nonetheless, Brown's major literary efforts in the late 1790s marked an important step both in his career and in American cultural development. As a ground-breaking corpus of serious fictional writings, these novels constructed a kind of foundation for American literary effort later in the nineteenth century. Authors like James Fenimore Cooper, Richard Henry

Dana, Edgar Allen Poe, George Lippard, and Nathaniel Hawthorne would acknowledge this with admiring comments. Whatever their flaws, the psychological power and crude emotional urgency of Brown's fictions assured his place as a "founding father" of American letters.[3]

In more personal terms, however, this explosion of writing around 1798 also emerged from an agonized struggle for literary expression and social success. These four texts arose out of a long-standing, complex process of private ferment. They resulted from the convergence of several trends: the author's years-long search for a successful career, his youthful ideological and intellectual commitments, and his unrelenting confrontation with an emerging market society of liberal individualism. Although in quite different ways, Brown's major works all turned on a common cultural/psychological axis: the search for social identity, personal cohesion, and ethical unity by individual protagonists operating in a fluid and morally elusive society of commercializing values.

I

The creative impulse behind Brown's novels of the late 1790s can be glimpsed in the literary formulations and precepts that he began to articulate earlier in the decade. This commentary took a variety of forms— private letters, short fictional pieces, and literary essays—and it provided revealing insights into their author's motivations and half-conscious impulses as a novelist. In 1792, for instance, he published an early reflective essay entitled "On the Nature and Essential Qualities of Poetry, as Distinguished from Prose." There Brown tentatively described a vision of fiction that he would try to realize some half-dozen years later.

The young writer began by rejecting the traditional notion that "imagination," "fiction," "imagery," and "creative fancy" were the exclusive property of poetry while prose was reserved for discussions of history, philosophy, law, and political affairs. In this common view, he noted, poetry was linked with primitive, vitalist forms of society in which life was "full of danger and variety" and "language was bold, and poetically sublime." Thus, men of letters attributed primitive, mythological powers to poetry which "elevate, astonish, and delight the mind." For Brown, however, this distinction was a false one. He insisted that a "poetic character" could also infuse good prose writing, whether it be in "the melody and sweetness in the arrangement of prosaic syllables" or in an "elevation of sentiment, fire of imagination, and regularity of metre." As the youthful intellectual concluded, "For poetry and prose, like two colours, easily distinguishable from each other in their pure, unmixed state, melt into one another by almost imperceptible shades, till the distinction is entirely lost." This determination to write a poetic, emotionally charged prose led Brown to make an important cultural observation regarding social class. The print culture of books, he admitted, was largely the realm of elevated "gentlemen." In contrast, an oral culture of storytelling prevailed among the lower classes, "for common people, who are not much accustomed to books, hardly understand anything they read, unless it be accompanied with the voice." For the aspiring novelist, the conclusion seemed clear. Compelling fiction must reach across this divide to engage a popular audience by embodying "ingenious fables," "striking resemblances," and "the most sensible delight."[4]

The following year Brown attempted another explanation of the writer's mission as he was coming to understand it. In a long July 1793 letter to Susan Godolphin, apparently one of the writer's love interests, he attempted to explain the importance of his intended career. Most writers, he argued, could be defined either as "historians" or "poets." While the "course of nature" was open to view for both, the literary obligations were decidedly different:

> It is the duty of the historian to describe as it is. It is the purview of poetry to imagine a change more or less extensive: to suppose one or more events to have taken place which, however, never happened, and then to pursue the consequences which naturally and inevitably flow from these events. . . . He [the poet] may make his stage . . . a planetary system, fill his scenes with empires and nations . . . and the excellence of the work will entirely depend upon the faithfulness with which he transcribes from the volume of eternal truth and the salutary end which his transcripts tend to promote.

As an aspiring author of poetic fiction, Brown thus proposed not merely to describe reality, but to change it through "sublime visions of imagination" promoting truth and morality.[5]

Over the next few years Brown refined and clarified these literary guidelines. Grappling with structural issues, for example, he considered the various merits of "the epistolary and narrative forms of compositions." The former mode he believed to be intrinsically superior, while the latter seemed more appropriate to his talents. Along the same lines, the young writer disclosed an attraction to realism in fiction, noting his inclination to relate domestic incident, dialogue, and scene "with the most excessive and elaborate minuteness . . . in which no circumstances, however frivolous and inconsiderable, should be omitted." Brown also pondered the question of audience. Most readers of fiction, he admitted rather uneasily, were "idle and thoughtless" people looking for "frivolous sources of amusement." As he put it rather sarcastically, "I do not form prodigious expectations even of one who reads a novel or comedy once a month." Brown did not reject the common reader, however. Instead, he determined to capture that reader's sensibility and instruct his intellect through stories that were fascinating, yet "joined with depth of views into human nature and all the subtleties of reasoning."[6]

Such meditations eventually led the youthful Philadelphian into moral musings on literature. Every writer's burden, he suggested, was to insure that one's work always "should contain something instructing as well as amusing." Vices should be painted in odious colors while "virtues of the most splendid kind [created] in the character of their hero or heroine." But composition, Brown frequently noted, perhaps most benefitted the author. The very act of imaginative writing in which "invention is active to create, and the judgement busy in weighing and shaping its creations" shaped for an author "pleasure in the mere exercise." Writing, he argued, provided an antidote to personal lethargy and despair because "it forces me to think, and a rapid current of ideas washes away a thousand muddy cares and vexatious impediments." Digging even deeper within, Brown unearthed a final link between literary creation and the self: "I must, necessarily, in the wildest of my reveries, exhibit my own character. . . . It may display something to be shunned, or something worthy of imitation." The impulse to interpret himself led the young writer to propose a strong correlation between stages of personal development and stages of social development. Analysis of "the vicissitudes of individuals or of nations from their hour of birth to their hour of extinction" promised to yield great insight into "the mechanisms of human society and the laws of human action."[7]

This jumble of half-formed thoughts and speculations about fiction writing, arising from various contexts, finally achieved coherence near the end of the century. In 1799, amidst his astonishing flurry of novels, Brown published a fascinating and peculiar piece entitled "Walstein's School of History." Appearing in a late summer number of the New York *Monthly Magazine*, the article combined a fictional narrative, a plan for three novels, and an essay on the purpose and scope of fiction. This last dimension remains the most important, because it provided the most coherent expression we have—composed as it was in the very heat of its author's most creative period—of Brown's intent and focus as a novelist.[8]

"Walstein's School" appeared in the form of an essay written by a fictitious German author, Krantz of Gotha. It purported to examine Walstein, a famous professor of history, and the circle of intellectual disciples he had gathered around him. The principles that guided their writing of history earned the greatest attention. As the piece unfolded, it became clear that Walstein was a kind of alter ego for Brown, serving as a mouthpiece for the author's notion of what defined a compelling mode of fiction writing. Rather than separating historical narrative from "poetic" prose, as he had advocated some years earlier, Brown now defended an idealized form of fiction that combined historical fact with creative imagination. This fictionalized history would be didactic and entertaining as it promoted both morality and happiness.

Brown, speaking through the injunctions of Walstein, first established ideological guidelines for literary endeavor. Although mindful of the "uncertainty of history" and the difficulty of explaining motive and uncovering truth, Brown firmly embraced several political positions. First, in the best tradition of republican culture, he condemned Catholicism and "feudal institutions" as the enemy of modern historical progress. Their oppressiveness and superstition, he claimed, had promoted degeneracy by opposing the spread of "learning and commerce." Second, Brown insisted that "human society is powerfully modified by individual members" through their intellectual power and social achievements. This expression of a liberal individualist ethic prompted a third, rather stunning ideological maxim. Social relations, he declared flatly, could be reduced to the twin factors of property and sex:

> Opinions, relative to property, are the immediate source of nearly all the happiness and misery that exist among mankind. If men were guided by justice in the acquisition and disbursement, the brood of private and public evils would be extinguished. . . .
>
> Next to property, the most extensive source of our relations is sex. On the circumstances which produce, and the principles which regulate the union between the sexes, happiness greatly depends.

Few statements better reflected the emerging domination of liberal capitalist culture. By establishing this connection between the calculus of material acquisition and that of libidinous regulation, Brown offered striking recognition of the new "structure of feeling" accompanying a competitive society of striving individuals.[9]

With these ideological tools, the youthful author constructed an authorial role combining social and literary responsibilities. The best method of fiction writing, he asserted in "Walstein's School," combined history and imagination. Real incidents and actors from the stage of history should be intertwined with vivid depictions and artful embellishments flowing from the author's fancy, all designed to "illuminate the understanding, to charm curiosity, and sway the passions." The object of such writing, Brown made clear, was not mere scintillation or amusement but moral instruction. In his words, "the narrative of public events, with a certain license of invention, was the most efficacious of moral instruments." Mere reason and intellectual argument were lifeless instruments of moral enlightenment, but with interesting and detailed stories the "affections are engaged, the reason is won by incessant attacks." History provided numerous examples of virtuous conduct, and the writer, by "displaying a model of right conduct . . . [was] furnishing incitements to imitate that conduct." As Brown approvingly described Walstein's efforts, "He imagined that the exhibition of virtues and talents, forcing its way to sovereign power, and employing that power for the national good, was highly conducive to their [mankind's] happiness."[10]

Brown sharpened these authorial principles to a finer point. In a ringing affirmation, he proclaimed the writer's "intellectual powers" as a great instrument of social justice. By demonstrating the benevolence of virtue and the baneful effects of vice, the skilled wordsmith could "rescue the victims of prejudice and passion from the yoke of domestic tyrants, and shield the powerless from the oppression of power, the poor from the injustice of the rich, and the simple from the stratagems of the cunning." In even stronger terms, Brown insisted that the writer's "genius and virtue may labour for the public good" by influencing "a change of national opinion." This, he claimed, was "the necessary prerequisite of revolutions." Brown's depiction of the writer as reformer partly reflected a liberalizing atmosphere that granted wide scope to individual agency:

> every man occupies a station in society in which he is necessarily active to evil or to good. There is a sphere of dimensions in which the influence of his actions and opinions is felt. The causes that fashion men into instruments of happiness or misery, are numerous, complex, and operate upon a wide surface. . . . Governments and general education cannot be rectified, but individuals may be somewhat fortified against their influence. Right intentions may be instilled into them, and some good may be done by each within his social and domestic province.[11]

Thus, in "Walstein's School," Brown framed an activist vision of the writer directing and molding social morality. Unquestionably influenced by the vast changes transforming the American republic in the late eighteenth century, he saw the author-reformer using his intellect and his pen for good in a fluid society increasingly conducive to individual choice. This ideological rendering of literary purpose would, at least in part, come to fruition with the outburst of novels in the late 1790s although not in pure form. These literary formulations first would have to engage the still erratic and highly emotional state of the writer's personal life.

In 1798—Brown was now age twenty-seven—he remained in many ways entangled in a late adolescent angst of personal turmoil and indecision. Physical infirmities, emotional afflictions, and career frustrations continued to flavor his correspondence. Moreover, he continued to bicker with his family over romance and career. They persisted in pressuring Brown to pursue his legal studies while he resisted in behalf of writing. He pursued liaisons with several young women, while his parents labored to break off his connection with all females who were not Quakers. In July 1798, for instance, the young man bitterly complained to friends about his family's maneuvers to separate him from his current girlfriend, Susan Potts, denouncing "the unjustifiable means . . . employed to separate" him and Miss Potts. In addition to all of this, 1798 brought a severe epidemic of yellow fever to New York City which ravaged the population, including Brown's circle of young intellectuals. Perhaps his closest friend and advisor, Dr. Elihu H. Smith, died of the disease in September. Brown himself was stricken, and friends nursed him briefly in the same house where Smith lay before he fled the city for Perth Amboy, New Jersey. He recuperated fully.[12]

This habitual tumult in Brown's private life contributed to a pattern of psychological agitation. Well into the 1790s his erratic behavior and fits of melancholy elicited frustrated comments from close associates. Shortly before his death, for example, Elihu Smith wearily noted in his diary Brown's habit of abandoning half-finished literary projects: "He starts an idea, pursues it a little way; new ones spring up; he runs a short distance after each; meantime the original one is likely to escape entirely." William Dunlap, in his 1815 biography of the novelist, recorded a litany of corroborating impressions:

Brown acted as if he had no use for money.
Brown was without system in everything.

Brown was negligent of personal appearance, even to slovenliness.
Brown was in mixed company often silent and absent.
Brown was fitful and irregular.

This intense disquietude not only impressed others but even prompted a dispassionate analysis, as opposed to earlier hysterics and emotional theatrics, on the part of the young writer himself. On New Year's Day, 1799, Brown ventilated his troubled private existence in a letter to his brother. The "surface of my life"—his lodging, his friends, his daily activities— probably would be thought "tolerably smooth" by most, he wrote. Yet the mere "external ease and temporary accommodation" provided by food and shelter could never be "sufficient to afford a reasonable being happiness," Brown mused unhappily. This growing awareness of a multifaceted tension in his life—public versus private, superficial versus real, habitual versus meaningful—also showed itself in what would have been Brown's first published novel. *Skywalk*, a fragmentary and finally abandoned manuscript, was announced in a public advertisement of March 1798 with this subtitle: "The Man Unknown to Himself—An American Tale."[13]

By the late 1790s, then, the process of writing had assumed a greater sense of urgency for young Brown. As an exercise in sublimation, fiction writing had become a cathartic, almost magical process that channeled a flood of raw psychological energy. The author confessed to a correspondent, for example, that "a craving to invent" through writing had become a "mental necessity" that was "as necessary to my mind as sustenance to my frame." Writing served as the primary emotional outlet for a young man seeking to define himself in terms of "lofty eloquence, the exhibition of powerful motives, and a sort of audaciousness of character." Brown once again disclosed himself in the advertisement for *Skywalk*, where his public justification for the novel demonstrated a passionate, almost sexual charge: "The world is governed not by the simpleton, but by the man of soaring passion and intellectual energy. By the display of such only can we hope to enchain the attention and ravish the souls of those who study and reflect."[14]

Thus, by 1798 the young Philadelphia intellectual was emerging, albeit rather unsteadily, from an emotional and professional adolescence. Poised on the threshhold of maturity, Brown's frustrated psychological energy, literary commitments, and desire for social success comprised a coiled motivational spring. Its release powered a tremendous outpouring of fiction during the last two years of the century. The two novels generally written

and published first, *Wieland* and *Ormond*, were sensationalist texts that
delved into the abnormal psyches, fluid identities, and passionate motivations of mysterious and isolated individuals. The succeeding pair of tales,
*Arthur Mervyn* and *Edgar Huntly*, continued to explore these concerns, but
provided even more penetrating treatments of social context and personal
fragmentation. All of these fictions, in varied and highly complex ways,
brilliantly illuminated their author's struggle with the promise and privations of liberalizing change.

II

At first glance, *Wieland; or, the Transformation* and *Ormond; or, the Secret
Witness* seem to be an odd pairing for analysis. Among Brown's novels the
former enjoys the most critical respect while the latter suffers probably the
least acclaim. *Wieland* offered a tone of consistent and spectacular dramatic tension; *Ormond* appeared intellectually speculative and morally didactic. The first novel focused on the bizarre actions and psychological motivations of three protagonists; the second presented a small army of
representative characters, each of whom stood rather woodenly for a certain set of ideas. From a purely literary point of view, as a novel *Wieland*
worked and *Ormond* did not. Yet the two books shared a great deal more
than is evident on the surface. Composed and completed within a few
months of each other in 1798, they were Brown's first complete novels to
appear before the public. The books also share a number of thematic,
emotional, and ideological impulses.

First, Brown tendered *Wieland* and *Ormond* in perhaps his purest
Gothic style. Replete with mysterious occurrences and concealed motives,
displaying a dark and brooding tone, and preoccupied with the abnormal
psychology of characters, these books self-consciously attempted to engage
and startle the senses. Appropriately, each concluded with a dramatic
death—suicide in one case, murder in the other—following impassioned
confrontations between the main characters. Second, both novels utilized a
female narrator as a lens for viewing and comprehending the willful, demented male behavior that propels the stories along. This subtle juxtaposition of gender sensibilities both complicated and highlighted Brown's exploration of human motivation and deception. Third, *Wieland* and
*Ormond* doggedly pursued the theme of "sincerity," posing it as an enormously difficult, perhaps paramount, problem in social relations. Finally,
and most important, these two texts provided the earliest and most direct
fictional reflection of Brown's ideological concerns as a young man: reli-

gious delusion in *Wieland*, political radicalism in *Ormond*, and sexual politics in both. Converging as stories of unfettered individual agency gone awry, these novels began an analysis that would become more complex, sensitive, and penetrating in later fictional work.

In *Wieland*, Brown unfolded his concerns in a gripping and highly theatrical style. The plot of the tale derived from an actual occurrence near Tomhannock, New York, where in 1781 an intensely religious farmer, James Yates, went berserk and ritually murdered his wife and four children after hearing the command of religious "voices." The young novelist borrowed this terrible event as the premise for his horrifying story of the fictional Wieland family. Set in the countryside outside Philadelphia, the narrative revolves around Clara and Theodore Wieland, the children of an English-born religious enthusiast whose mysterious death had orphaned them as children. Reared conscientiously and in some affluence by a maiden aunt, the pair reached young adulthood with sound educations and in close friendship with Catherine Pleyel and her brother Henry. Theodore married the former and sired four children, while Clara and the latter came to share an affection that promised matrimony. As the story unfolded, however, Theodore began to hear a mysterious voice that first spoke of innocuous issues, but then began to intrude more seriously into the lives of his friends and family. This strange phenomenon, which elicited much debate over its natural or supernatural origins, was accompanied by the arrival of a stranger, Carwin, an Irish immigrant of disheveled appearance, personal allure, and unknown character, who slowly ingratiated himself into the Wieland circle. He alternately charmed and frightened the small coterie, especially Clara, with his powerful but erratic personality. After a series of traumatic occurrences—Carwin was discovered one night hiding in Clara's bedroom closet; Henry Pleyel accused Carwin and Clara of having a love affair; *everyone* began to hear the whisperings of unknown voices—the tale reached its climax. Theodore, hearing what he believed to be "divine" voices urging him to murder, descended into madness and killed his wife, children, and a young servant girl. In the throes of a homicidal fit, he then confronted Clara and was about to stab her when Carwin appeared. He announced his powers as a "ventriloquist" and commanded young Wieland to halt, at which point the young madman, lapsing momentarily into sanity, killed himself with a penknife. After this horrifying episode of physical carnage and psychological wreckage, the novel drew to a close with Clara's rather desolate meditations, after a three-year absence and recovery, on human understanding and moral duty.[15]

At one level, the meaning and intent of *Wieland* emerged clearly. Brown had related in the prefatory "Advertisement" for the novel that he saw himself as a "moral painter" aiming at "the illustration of some important branches of the moral constitution of man." More precisely, he admitted a keen interest in "the latent springs and occasional perversions of the human mind." In the novel itself, this theme assumed a specific form: a devastating critique of eighteenth-century rationalism based on sensory impressions. From the time of John Locke's famous *Essay Concerning Human Understanding* (1690), most enlightened intellectuals in the Atlantic world had agreed that human beings were the passive recipients of sensory impressions that became the basis for all thought, understanding, and action. With its emphasis on the lack of innate ideas and the ordering of sensory signals as the mind's function, this "sensationalist" psychology placed an enormous stress on human reason. As one of Brown's characters put it, the senses of sight and hearing were "the most explicit and unerring of those which support the fabric of human knowledge."[16]

This entire edifice, however, tottered and crashed under *Wieland*'s fictional assault. From the opening pages a series of delusions, misapprehensions, and irrationalities shredded the neat connection between sensory experience and rational behavior. Brown consistently stressed the difficulty, if not impossibility, of drawing just and truthful inferences from the raw data of the senses. Dangers came from several directions. Deliberate deception by malignant human agency always threatened, as a poem on the novel's title page suggested: "From Virtue's blissful paths away / the double-tongued are sure to stray." Carwin's manipulation of his ventriloquism in *Wieland* graphically illustrated this hazard. The irrational deductions of a diseased mind, manifested in the insane machinations of both the older and younger Wieland, further menaced the vision of calm human rationality. Finally, Brown consistently emphasized the simple inadequacy of human faculties for filtering and interpreting experience. Here Clara Wieland served as the author's proxy. "The will is the tool of the understanding, which must fashion its conclusions on the notice of sense," she noted. "If the senses be depraved it is impossible to calculate the evils that may flow from the consequent deductions of the understanding." So for the young Philadelphia writer, much lay beyond and beneath the human capacity for reason. Once again Clara expressed this disturbing conclusion: "Ideas exist in our minds that can be accounted for by no established laws."[17]

Brown's conscious focus on abnormal psychology and the weaknesses of sensationalist epistemology, of course, have long been recognized as an element in *Wieland*. Less obvious but equally important, however, are several ideological themes that also permeated the text. Expressed at times only half-consciously, this trio of motifs—the destruction of patriarchy, the dangers of religious fanaticism, the fragmentation of individualism—derived only partly from Brown's critique of Lockean epistemology. They also flowed from a social source. In his first novel the author drew on his encounters with, and misgivings about, the fluid society of liberal individualism arising in post-Revolutionary America.

The demise of patriarchal authority, along with its troubling consequences, haunted Brown's first novel. The spectacular death of the elder Wieland—a religious zealot, who dies from spontaneous combustion while praying at his rustic "temple"—not only sets the tone for the tale but stamps an enduring impression on the thoughts and actions of his children. By his death they are orphaned and "left to the guidance of our own understanding, and the casual impressions which society might make upon us." And, as Clara notes ruefully, the novel's ultimate tragedy could be traced to "the force of early impressions, and . . . the immeasurable evils that flow from an erroneous or imperfect discipline." While the patriarch's fiery end preoccupied the daughter, it absolutely obsessed the son. As Clara describes Theodore, "His father's death was always regarded by him as flowing from a direct and supernatural decree. It visited his meditations oftener than it did mine. The traces which it left were more gloomy and permanent. . . . When we sifted his thoughts, they were generally found to have a relation, more or less direct, with this incident."

Here Brown painted a clear picture of social and psychological difficulties—an absence of meaningful authority, an isolated and brooding individualism—coming in the wake of patriarchal decay. In this context it is little wonder that when authority reappeared to Theodore it came misrepresented as a Godly voice, and when individual agency exerted itself strongly it did so as the acts of a madman. Thus, *Wieland* reflected not only Brown's own earlier struggles with his family, but also the larger struggle in post-Revolutionary America with the disturbing consequences of a late eighteenth-century "revolt against patriarchal authority."[18]

If crumbling patriarchal dominion created a vacuum in *Wieland*, the force of religious fanaticism filled it with unfortunate effect. Brown, it seems clear, pursued this theme throughout the text as part of a long-standing critique of Christianity and its influence. As earlier letters exchanged with Joseph Bringhurst demonstrated, the young author questioned the validity and efficacy of Christian doctrine in behalf of rational inquiry. In *Wieland*, he implied that a narrow reliance on revealed religious duty led almost inevitably to dangerous excess. Again, the elder Wieland sets the stage. As a young man he was attracted to the Abigenses—a French Protestant sect widely thought to hold bizarre religious and social views—and embarked for the New World to serve as a missionary among the Indians. Later in life, according to his daughter's description, he grew even more restricted and obsessive in his religious sensibility:

> The empire of religious duty extended itself to his looks, gestures, and phrases. All levities of speech, and negligences of behavior, were proscribed. His air was mournful and contemplative. He laboured to keep alive a sentiment of fear, and a belief of the awe-inspiring presence of the Deity. Ideas foreign to this were sedulously excluded.

When the father's compulsive prayers and clenched-jaw devotions led directly to his death, the burden of religious zealotry shifted heavily to his children.[19]

In part, Theodore and Clara escaped doctrinaire religious training under the lenient tutelage of their aunt. Their education had "no religious standard" based on "the weighing of proofs and the dissection of creeds," but they did imbibe liberal religious sentiments that were "the product of lively feelings, excited by reflection on our own happinesss, and by the grandeur of external nature." The younger male Wieland, however, also inherited his father's extreme inclinations. While Clara remained content to weigh the varying claims of reason and religion in particular cases, Theodore became more and more concerned with "the history of religious opinions" and the grounds of their claims to validity and merit. "Preparation and provision" for the future steadily crowded out his other interests in science and ancient literature until he approached the point of lunacy. Even after murdering his family under the influence of divine "voices," the young man denounced his accusers as "Impious and rash! thus to usurp the prerogatives of your Maker! to set up your bounded views and halting reason, as the measure of truth!" This denunciation of flimsy rationality and defense of divine revelation reached a climax in Theodore's simple justification: "I believed that God was my mover!" For Brown, an unquestioning allegiance to divine revelation over reason threatened destruction in a world where social and moral authority was crumbling, and where the flow of sensory impressions seemed to bring delusion as much as understanding and stability. *Wieland* brilliantly exposed such dangers.[20]

Ultimately Brown's concerns with sensory uncertainty, crumbling patriarchy, and religious illusion converged in *Wieland*'s most pervasive theme: an incoherent, fragmenting sense of individual self. Writing in the late 1790s as the American republic was in the early throes of liberalizing change, and as he was still personally grappling with problems of career choice and success, the young author presented in his first novel a gallery of distressed individuals with splintered identities, self-destructive urges, and precarious destinies. He established this theme early in the text. The spectacular death of the elder Wieland by spontaneous combustion—perhaps the most striking scene in the novel—provided an arresting example of a character literally exploding from internal pressure. This revealing motif of individual disintegration pervaded, perhaps even dominated, the subsequent unfolding of the narrative.[21]

The development of Clara and Theodore Wieland offered variations on the theme. The son diligently pursued a goal of taut self-control, delving into science, literature, and history with grave intensity. Keeping a tight rein on his emotions, he evinced an "air of forethought and sobriety" and his companions "scarcely ever knew him to laugh." Theodore also took shape, however, as a bundle of contradictions. Brooding over his father's death—Clara noted the "obvious resemblance" between them, as "their characters were similar"—he combined a dark fascination with supernaturalism and mysticism with an adulation of Cicero, the classical republican and Stoic moralist of ancient Rome. A member of the landed gentry whose inherited wealth made diligent labor unnecessary, Theodore nonetheless believed that "Power and riches were chiefly to be dreaded on account of their tendency to deprave the possessor. He held them in abhorrence, not only as instruments of misery to others, but to him on whom they were conferred." Although driven by "moral necessity, and calvinistic inspiration," he admitted that "Human life, in his opinion, was made up of changeable elements, and the principles of duty were not easily unfolded." Such contradictory impulses culminated, of course, in Theodore's crazed outburst of homicidal violence after which, in a flash of lucidity, he realized the gruesome deeds committed by "his own misguided hand." He could not resolve his internal confusion, bursting out that "If a devil has deceived me, he came in the habit of an angel. If I erred, it was not my judgement that deceived me, but my senses." Since it was inconceivable that "nature should long sustain this conflict," in Clara's words, her brother finally, violently resolved his horrible inner conflict with a self-inflicted stab to the neck.[22]

Clara's disintegration was less dramatic but more palpable. As the narrative voice in the novel, she faithfully reported the series of strange and horrible incidents that led to her family's demise. Her own mental state and moral sensibility steadily unraveled in the process. She set this tone at the outset when, preparing to tell her tale in an epistolary flashback, she grimly confessed a fatalism that was "perfectly indifferent" both to the future and to a Deity whose guidance over her life "admits of no recall." As the story actually began, however, the young woman revealed her earlier self to have been quite different: gently idealistic, sympathetic toward victims of misfortune, intellectually curious, interested in music and poetry, receptive to religious guidance yet respectful of human reason. Only with the mysterious appearance of unknown "voices" and the stranger Carwin did her calm, assured existence begin to fall apart. Unable to comprehend the accelerating delusion of her senses and rational faculties, Clara began to fear that everything was appearance and illusion. Admitting the increasingly confused quality of her epistolary narrative, she exasperatedly proclaimed, "What but ambiguities, abruptness, and dark transition can be expected from the historian who is, at the same time, the sufferer of disasters?" Her dream life became an agony of nightmares in which she was "tor-mented by phantoms of my own creation" and hovered on the edge of "imbecility." By the denouement of *Wieland*, where her demented brother has pulled back from murdering her and instead ended his own life, Clara's inability to confront and understand experience had become almost complete and her capacity for meaningful action had been destroyed. She stood before Theodore's body utterly devastated, uncomprehending, and suicidal: "This scene of havoc was produced by an illusion of the senses. Be it so: I care not from what source these disasters have flowed. . . . I ask only quick deliverance from life and all the ills that attend it."[23]

While Theodore and Clara illustrated a fragmenting self susceptible to delusion and debilitation, Brown presented another character whose instincts led in a more quietly disturbing direction. Carwin, the mercurial Irish immigrant, provided through his appearances and actions a catalyst for much of *Wieland*'s story. In fact, the author was so taken with his creation that he began writing "Memoirs of Carwin the Biloquist" while the original novel was still in press. He would not publish the "Memoir" until six years later, and then only in magazine installments.[24] In *Wieland*, however, Carwin appeared as a walking embodiment of deception and duplicity. From the time he first appeared at the Wieland household as an acquaintance of Henry Pleyel, his erratic conduct both entranced and confused his hosts. Carwin charmed with his elegant conversation and "mind of the highest order" while he carefully hid his character and beliefs. The contradictions in his personality and appearance—repellent physical features along with animal magnetism, claims of innocence and implication in evil, a thirst for knowledge in concert with the habits of a vagrant trickster—became steadily more striking. By the conclusion of the text, Carwin had become "the double-tongued deceiver" of whom Brown had warned on the title page.

Carwin's deceptions involved several complex and fascinating dimensions. Quite clearly, for example, his strong sexuality generated a pulsating psychological charge throughout the narrative. When he first arrived at the Wieland household asking for a cup of water, Clara was infatuated not with his looks—he was coarse-featured, shaggy, with sallow complexion and large teeth—but with his "eyes lustrously black," a passionate voice "mellifluent and clear," and a "radiance inexpressibly serene and potent." The young woman was so stricken that she burst into tears, and penned a sketch of him that she brooded over for days. This sexual dynamic grew more complicated, however, when it became known that Carwin had been carrying on an affair with Clara's womanservant in the summer-house. And it became positively alarming when Clara later discovered the stranger hiding in her closet with the admitted intent to "have borne away the spoils of your honor." In this fashion a growing awareness of Carwin's intense sexual appetite, usually hidden beneath his civilized demeanor, gradually subverted a naive reliance on both human rationality and human appearance.[25]

In a different sense, however, Carwin's mystery also took on a social cast in the novel. As Brown spun out the narrative in *Wieland*, attempts to penetrate the social masks of the visitor became steadily more central to the tale. Clara expressed her considerable discomfort shortly after Carwin's arrival, noting that "The inscrutableness of his character, and the uncertainty whether his fellowship tended to good or evil, were seldom absent from our minds." As his actions and explanations became murkier and even contradictory, she suspected that "nothing could be discerned through the impenetrable veil of his duplicity." Even Henry Pleyel, Carwin's friend, became highly distrustful of "the ambiguous expression of his countenance," "the cloud which obscured his character," and "the suspicious nature of that concealment which he studied." This growing preoccupation with "genuine" character versus mere "appearance" reflected Brown's long preoccupation with the issue of social trust: On what basis could ambitious, aspiring individuals be relied upon to act forthrightly and scrupulously? In *Wieland*, Carwin provided disturbing answers.[26]

"Ventriloquism"—most critics have seen it merely as a mechanism for Brown's Gothic literary machinations—brilliantly symbolized Carwin's fragmented self and its capacity for deception. The reader gradually learns that the chorus of mysterious "voices" heard by Theodore, Henry, and Clara were the product of Carwin's singular ability to mimic others and throw his voice. He confessed to Clara after Theodore's murderous rampage, in an attempt to absolve himself of guilt in the killings, that "I have handled a tool of wonderful efficacy without malignant intentions, but without caution." Carwin also admitted that he had often abused his talents for verbal manipulation. "Unfortified by principle, subjected to poverty, stimulated by headlong passions," he related, "I made this powerful engine subservient to the supply of my wants, and the gratification of my vanity."[27]

This ability to assume identities, to bewilder the senses of sight and sound, eventually led to a horrifying conclusion. The crazed Theodore, finally grasping that Carwin's "voices" had contributed to his delusion, denounced him as a monster: "If a devil has deceived me, he came in the habit of an angel. . . . Now he personates a human form; then he was invisioned with the lustre of heaven." For Clara, moral responsibility for her family's destruction led directly to the stranger as "the grand deceiver; the author of this black conspiracy; the intelligence that governed in this storm." His delusory powers as a ventriloquist, and his malleable identity, also turned inward and forced Carwin to face his internal turmoil. As his involvement in the Wieland tragedy became clearer, he acknowledged that he was "self-expelled" from a formerly happy group as "I had warred against my peace and my fame . . . [and] the fellowship of vigorous and pure minds." Carwin betrayed this sense of inner fragmentation even more clearly when he was earlier discovered hiding in Clara's bedroom. Admitting his designs to ravish her, he spoke with great intensity about the "voice" that had warned her of his presence (we later learn, of course, that Carwin himself had produced this voice by ventriloquism):

> He is my eternal foe; the baffler of my best concerted schemes. Twice have you been saved by his accursed interposition. But for him I should long ere now have borne away the spoils of your honor. . . . The power that protects you would crumble my sinews, and reduce me to a heap of ashes in a moment, if I were to harbour a thought hostile to your safety.[28]

So Carwin perhaps best illustrated the larger thrust of Charles Brock-den Brown's first novel. As a dealer in illusion, Carwin was a dangerous social figure who survived as a kind of psychological "confidence man." With his chameleon-like talent for constantly changing shape and form, steadily assuming voices and identities, he embodied the "serial self" of a liberalizing culture. Exhibiting the identity diffusion of the personae, Carwin had no hard sense of self. With Theodore's lunacy and suicide, with Clara's collapse into a long-suffering fatalism, he alone survived as a fragmented individual standing in the middle of a scene of social and psychological devastation. Carwin suggested what *Wieland* offered, at various levels of authorial intent, in a larger sense: a devastating picture of social relations and consciousness in late eighteenth-century America. Brown presented a frightening depiction of society crumbling from the collapsing supports of religion and the patriarchal family, of human agency choosing disastrously under the burden of social deceit, of liberated individuals whirling apart under the pressures of sensory delusion. In the last few weeks of 1798 the author would frantically paint the same scene in yet another novel. This time he used a somewhat different palette of colors.

III

Brown's second novel, *Ormond; or, the Secret Witness*, presented a version of the standard eighteenth-century seduction tale. Its structure and sensibility, however, seemed to pull in different directions. The book's plot unfolded a highly melodramatic story of passion, sexuality, and sociopathy. Setting out the standard fare of Gothic storytelling, the novel invited its audience to feast on a banquet of murder and mayhem, mystery and malevolence, rape and suicide, all accompanied with the familiar condiments of foreboding, inscrutability, and gloom. At the same time, however, Brown's text was a rather wooden novel of ideas. Caught up in political and intellectual agitation of the late eighteenth-century Atlantic world, the author constructed his characters as somewhat mechanical representations of clashing ideas and ideologies. The two features prodding the story along—the carrot of melodrama, the stick of didactic intellectualism—ultimately pointed in different directions. Brown lamely attempted to camouflage this dilemma in the book's introduction, where he claimed to be offering "an authentic, and not a fictitious tale" devoid of "artificial or elaborate order" and based on conclusions "which the facts . . . sometimes abundant, and sometimes scanty, would permit." This contrariness in the novel could be attributed partly to the extreme hastiness of its composition. Apparently beginning sometime in October 1798, Brown threw himself into writing with such intensity that he admitted to being "scarcely conscious of the lapse of time" and "thoroughly weary and unfit for a continuance of the same employment in any new shape." Thematic and contextual complexity, more than mere haste, however, explained much of *Ormond*'s frustrating divergences.[29]

The novel's plot was deceptively simple. As narrated by Mrs. Sophia Westwyn Courtland, it focused on the life of close friend Constantia Dudley, a sixteen-year-old girl who had lived a life of hardship, and her encounters with Ormond, an arrogant and aristocratic political radical. Constantia's father had been financially and emotionally ruined by a fraudulent business partner, so his daughter had taken over support of the household by working as a seamstress. Well-educated, independent-minded, and virtuous, Constantia had rejected all suitors and by hard work maintained her family in a genteel but honorable poverty. When an epidemic of yellow fever swept through the city, she protected her father and nursed her friends with admirable benevolence. Constantia gradually became acquianted with Ormond, an extreme rationalist devoted to the building of a utopian society. As their friendship blossomed, he found himself attracted first to the young heroine's moral and intellectual qualities, then to her physical features. As Ormond began to pursue Constantia, he gradually developed a sexual obsession. When the young woman's father was horribly and mysteriously murdered and she prepared to embark for Europe with a patroness, Ormond lost all control. Confronting her and prepared for rape in the novel's climactic scene, he was stabbed and killed by Constantia during a physical struggle.

As *Ormond*'s story line moved toward this climax of virtue defended and evil defeated, it was accompanied by several interposed narratives and character sketches. Several of them focused on female characters: Sophia, a sentimentalist and worldly-wise woman who became Constantia's protector and religious counselor; Helena Cleves, Ormond's mistress, a beautiful and artistic young woman of limited intellect who killed herself from grief when her lover's affections turned elsewhere; and Martinette de Beauvais, Ormond's sister, a widely traveled and vigorous woman whose adventures in revolutionary Europe included military service and political assassination. These characters, like the two protagonists, often seemed to be little more than abstract representations of self-controlled virtue, self-regarding evil, religious character, shallow sensuality, and extreme feminism. The cross-currents and interactions between them, while usually intense, constituted an artificial and stilted debate of ideas more than anything else.

As critics have noted, several obvious influences underpinned Brown's second novel. The eighteenth-century "sentimental romance," for instance, was much in evidence. As tendered by authors like Samuel Richardson in *Pamela* and *Clarissa,* these tales presented highly moralistic treatments (usually revolving around the seduction theme) of sensual temptation, ethical duty, and rational critiques of religion. *Ormond*'s embroidery upon this narrative form was apparent, but so too was its debt to the immensely popular Gothic novels of the late 1700s. Like Ann Radcliffe's *Mysteries of Udolpho* or Matthew Lewis' *The Monk,* it embraced a sensationalist mode of supernatural influences and scheming villains, dark houses and mysterious passageways, secret burials and unhinged characters. Finally, the "novel of purpose," as practiced by radical writers like Robert Bage and particularly William Godwin in *Caleb Williams,* heavily influenced Brown's text. Enamored with their revolutionary challenges to the moral values of society, the young American writer attempted a fictional analysis of whether man could perpetually improve himself by fulfilling his rational capabilities.[30]

This mélange of literary inspirations, however, never fused into a coherent artistic whole in *Ormond.* The various elements too often remained disparate and undeveloped, without a lucid intellectual, political, or moral thrust. Unintendedly, however, like *Wieland* this novel displayed a subtle underlying unity. *Ormond*'s Gothic, sentimental, and radical dimensions all exposed, from various angles of vision, a central problem that had preoccupied Brown throughout much of his early life: the simultaneous possibilities and perversions of liberated human agency in a liberalizing society. His chaotic and hastily drawn sketches of characters' fluid values and moral incertitude reflected the disarray of both the author's own convictions and the social scene they surveyed.

Brown hinted broadly at this thematic obsession early in the text of *Ormond.* The introductory letter that prefaced the novel contained the promise that Constantia Dudley's story would illustrate the "modes of life, the influence of public events upon the character and happiness of individuals in America." This was important, the author emphasized, because the "distinctions of birth, the artificial degrees of esteem or contempt which connect themselves with different professions and ranks" in Europe "are but little known among us." Later in the story, narrator Sophia Westwyn Courtland added a caveat to this portrayal of aspiring American individualism. In this New World republic, she asserted, "all things tended to the same level. Genius, and virtue, and happiness, on these shores, were distinguished by a sort of mediocrity." The context of individual liberation and social leveling opened several interpretive avenues, and characteristically Brown chose a dark and pessimistic one.[31]

Indeed, the opening vignette of *Ormond* clearly mapped the disturbing social boundaries of the novel. As background for Constantia's struggle to survive, the author related the travails of her father, Stephen Dudley. Young Stephen had been trained to be an artist, even traveling in Europe to hone his skills as a painter, until the death of his father forced him to assume the family's "apothecary" business. There the "drudgery of a shop" gradually blunted his sensibility and fostered bitterness. Yearning for "pursuits which exalt and harmonize the feelings," he developed a conviction that "disgrace was annexed to every employment of which the only purpose was gain." Brown heightened this critical view of American commercial life with two narrative additions. First, Stephen Dudley was betrayed and forced into bankruptcy by the fraud of Thomas Craig, a young man whom he had befriended and made his partner. Craig's secret embezzlement drove the old man into poverty, disgrace, and eventual alcoholism. When Dudley went blind later and was unable even to paint, the tragic corruption of art by commerce was complete. Second, as Constantia picked up the burden of financial support, Brown depicted her rejecting several suitors, particularly one named Balfour. This prosperous figure, according to the novel, led a life that was "a model of chasteness and regularity." His failure, however, lay in banality rather than evil. Balfour's devotion to the power of "industry and temperance to confer and maintain wealth" made for a rather single-minded existence. This self-made man valued Constantia for "her admirable economy of time and money and labor, the simplicity of her dress, her evenness of temper." Constantia rejected him on the grounds that "riches were not barren of constraint, and its advantages might be purchased at too dear a rate" (pp. 7–20, 82–83).

Thus, Brown enveloped *Ormond*'s tale in a disquieting bourgeois environment in which commercial fraud, bankruptcy, shallow materialism, and individual greed seemed to prevail. Against this backdrop of social insecurity, he explored several themes that connoted the liberated yet frightening aspects of individual agency. Education, for instance, the activity that prepared one to cope and survive in a competitive world, garnered considerable authorial attention. Here gender considerations surfaced, and "male" and "female" modes of instruction constantly intruded into the narrative.

Constantia circumvented the usual limits of female learning under the inspiration of her father, who "sought to make her, not alluring and voluptuous, but eloquent and wise." Like a young man, she studied Latin and English, history and literature, mathematics and science. By contrast, Helena Cleves, Ormond's mistress and Constantia's friend, followed the usual female standard. She believed that "women are generally limited to what is sensual and ornamental: music and painting, and the Italian and French languages, are bounds which they seldom pass." Helena's "feminine and fascinating quality" consisted of "voluptuous sweetness of temper and mediocrity of understanding." Her education had shaped a mind "inured to the discussion of logical points and the tracing of remote consequences." The author's constant juxtaposition of the two young women—Constantia's preparation allowed her to survive while Helena's led her to suicide—reflected in part a liberated female model previewed in *Alcuin*. It suggested even more strongly Brown's sense that late eighteenth-century society required for *everyone* an education geared less to "female" artistic, expressive, and ornamental adornments and more to "male" qualities of worldly knowledge, individual aspiration, and the rational calculation of costs and benefits (pp. 33, 119–21, 146).

Even more than pedagogy, however, deception provided a major thematic thrust of *Ormond*. Brown stretched this issue in various directions throughout the text, from the explicit social manipulations of the "confidence man" to the more subtle psychological delusions of ambitious individuals. As Sophia shrewdly noted, echoing the youthful author's long-standing concern since his *Rhapsodist* essays,

> To scrutinize and ascertain our own principles are abundantly difficult. To exhibit these principles to the world with absolute sincerity, can scarcely be expected. We are prompted to conceal and to feign by a thousand motives. . . . To comprehend the whole truth, with regard to the character and conduct of another, may be denied to any human being.

A strong fear of deception, of an inability to penetrate the masks hiding the character and motives of others, particularly appeared in the two key players in the novel (p. 111).

Ormond himself, of course, was a study in duplicity. With his mysterious political views, his aristocratic elegance shrouding intense animalistic instincts, and his wondrous capacity for secretly, almost supernaturally penetrating the thoughts of others, this protagonist became a moral chameleon to other characters and to the reader as well: "No one was more impenetrable than Ormond, though no one's real character seemed more easily discerned. . . . [His] appearances were merely calculated to mislead and not to enlighten." If Ormond's deceptions consistently permeated the text, Thomas Craig's jolted it more briefly and spectacularly. When he first appeared in Stephen Dudley's shop, young Craig proclaimed devotion to the self-made success ideal. Determined to make his own way, this English immigrant claimed he had "come to America, in search for the means of independent subsistence." His enormous appetite for wealth and status, however, eventually led to lying, embezzlement, and murder. Craig became the horrifying embodiment of one of Brown's greatest fears: the masked individual for whom greed was a habit and mendacity a ritual.

> There were few men who could refuse their confidence to his open and ingenuous aspect. . . . His temptations to deceive were stronger than what are incident to most other men. Deception was so easy a task, that the difficulty lay, not in infusing false opinions respecting him, but in preventing them from being spontaneously imbibed. He contracted habits of imposture imperceptibly. In proportion as he deviated from the practice of truth, he discerned the necessity of extending and systematizing his efforts, and of aug-menting the original benignity and attractiveness of his looks by studied additions. The further he proceeded, the more difficult it was to return. Experience and habit added daily to his speciousness till at length the world perhaps might have been searched in vain for his competitor. (pp. 116–17, 8, 99)

This unveiling of duplicitous confidence games in American private life prompted Brown to examine an analogue in public life: politics. Here Ormond's enigmatic schemes of radical utopianism cast a dark shadow over the novel. His political principles came into the open slowly, and then only by fits and starts. The young Ormond, it turned out, had been involved with a group of radical "schemers and reasoners" in Berlin "who aimed at the new-modelling of the world, and the subversion of all that has hitherto been conceived elementary and fundamental, in the constitution of man." The "secret efforts" of this clique—Brown invoked here the infamous Bavarian Illuminati—had focused not only on plans for revolution but on a colonizing effort in some unexplored wilderness area of the New World. Although convinced that a "mortal poison pervaded the whole system" and that the "principles of the social machine must be rectified before man can be beneficially active," Ormond remained reticent about his revolutionary plans. He would only assert rather vaguely that the wise man "carefully distinguished between men, in the abstract, and men as they are." Each individual, he argued, "was part of a machine, and as such had not power to withhold his agency." Thus, while benevolence and the "general benefit" should not be totally disregarded, another conclusion was inescapable: "A man may reasonably hope to accomplish his end, when he proposes nothing but his own good: Any other point is inaccessible." This program—highly rationalistic, self-interested, secretive, incendiary— offered a dark variety of liberal politics, one rooted in an individualism twisted toward greed and destruction. Ormond the ideologue carefully concealed his political maxims and kept them "exhibited, or hidden, or shifted, according to his purpose" (pp. 252, 111–12, 112–13).

*Ormond*'s world of false appearances, hidden motives, and deceptive individualism gained additional credence from a pair of authorial habits, one a thematic concern and the other a literary device. Ironically, given Brown's anticlerical leanings, religion infused this story in a highly didactic way. Constantia's susceptibility to Ormond's deceit, he explained, would be largely traced to her indifference toward "the felicity and excellence flowing from religion." Without it, "her principal security and strongest bulwark" against misfortune was missing. Ormond's evil, at the same time, flowed from his active atheism, a "disbelief at once unchangeable and strenuous." Viewing the universe as a physical mechanism with no beginning and no end, he dismissed religion as a contemptible irrationality that he "not only dissented, but abhorred." This depiction of a moral void was reinforced by characterization in the novel. Practically every character in *Ormond* was an orphan. This included not only several minor players, but also Thomas Craig, Sophia, Ormond and his sister, Helena Cleves, and eventually Constantia herself. Moreover, murder (the death of Stephen Dudley and Ormond) and suicide (Helena's, Constantia's threat of it) seemed to carry Brown's vision of individual isolation to its logical, if extreme, conclusion. As one character anguished, "We must lay aside the burden which we cannot sustain. If thought degenerates into a vehicle of pain, what remains but to destroy that vehicle?" (pp. 179, 180, 26).

In such fashion, *Ormond*'s characters could find no solid moral ground, could discover no firm basis for coherent selfhood at the very time their society was releasing individual agency to pursue its own ends. Stripped of family support, religious values, and community commitments, they struggled in vain to find solace in ideology or worldly achievement. The inner anxiety that resulted found expression in one of Brown's most powerful themes in this novel: the collision of rationality and sexuality. Throughout the text these attributes fiercely contended with one another, fighting for control of the character and the narrative. Significantly, neither triumphed but only succeeded in further fragmenting any sense of human cohesion.

In the early sections of *Ormond*, a loyalty to rational principles defined both Constantia and Ormond. The aristocratic young gentleman had "a mind of uncommon energy," and he valued above all else "intellectual energy." Contemptuous of religion and the opinions of others, he interpreted the world according to "the suggestions of his understanding." Mere physical pleasures and love, "in his scale of enjoyments and gratifications . . . were placed at the bottom." Ormond's system and manner of calculating reason, in many ways, were mirrored in the young woman who became his obsession. Constantia's education, as noted earlier, had elevated "serious" rational study and downplayed the traditional female emphasis on the ornamental arts. Her family's social privations only encouraged a hardened self-reliance. Perhaps out of necessity, the young woman became a keen observer of human nature, constantly "examining, comparing, deducing." Wary of being swept off her feet by love, eager to contemplate substantial ideas, her encounters with Ormond became literally a meeting of the minds. Yet rationality ultimately failed both protagonists. Ormond slowly but inexorably abandoned reason for physical lust until he was carried over the precipice into self-destruction. Constantia, for all her determination to rationally penetrate "forms" and discern the validity of "the outward figure to exhibit the internal sentiments," fell victim to terrifying self-delusion. In both cases, it was no accident that sex lay near the center of things (pp. 114–17, 76, 77).

As Brown's second novel unfolded, the erosion of rationality seemed increasingly prompted by a surge of aggressive, even deviant sexuality. Ormond's case was fairly simple: he "contracted a passion" for Constantia, a desire for her "person and affections . . . which it was the dearest purpose of his existence to gain." This affliction pushed Ormond to the point of rape and led Brown to this meditation:

> Several sensations associating themselves in a certain way with our ideas, beget a disease which . . . is a case of more entire subversion and confusion of mind than any other. The victim is callous to the sentiments of honour and shame, insensible to the most palpable distinctions of right and wrong, a systematic opponent of testimony, and obstinate perverter of truth. (pp. 178, 160)

The assault of sexuality on reason was rendered more subtly in the case of *Ormond*'s female characters. Helena Cleves, of course, committed suicide as a result of her inability to hold Ormond with her sensuality and sexual favors. Constantia followed a more indirect path. It seems no accident that as her rational faculties steadily proved less able to illuminate the social and moral atmosphere, she turned to the attractions of female homoeroticism. This theme, although muted because of eighteenth-century convention, ran deep in the novel. Early on, for instance, Constantia became infatuated with Martinette de Beauvais, first hoping that she "would prove worthy of her love," and then later becoming daily "more enamoured of her new acquaintance." This paled, however, in comparison to Constantia's relationship with Sophia Westwyn Courtland. Brown referred frankly to their "romantic passion for each other," and described Constantia's cries—"O! precious inebriation of the heart! O! preeminent love!"—upon meeting Sophia. In one particularly revealing passage, the text presented this sketch of a joyful reunion between the two women after a long separation:

> The succeeding three days were spent in a state of dizziness and intoxication. The ordinary functions of nature were disturbed. The appetite for sleep and for food were confounded and lost, amidst the impetuousities of a master-passion. To look and to talk to each, afforded enchanting occupation for every moment. I [Sophia] would not part from her side, but eat and slept, walked and mused and read, with my own arm locked in hers, and with her breath fanning my cheek.

*Ormond*'s powerful sexual energy—especially with its connotations of loss of control and gender confusion—finally collapsed inward upon itself. With Ormond's murder and Constantia's permanent trauma, it produced an orgy of death, suffering, and chaos. Sex and rationality, equally dangerous and pulling in opposite directions, could only destroy one another in the end (pp. 12, 189, 256, 250).

The burden of *Ormond*, with its inconsistencies and passions, finally came to rest on the shoulders of its three protagonists. Sophia, Constantia, and Ormond, for all their abstract qualities and stilted ideologies, embodied Brown's vision of willful, yet deeply flawed individuals set loose in a mutable world. Sophia, both as narrator and central actor, played a crucial role. The author invested her with qualities of worldly experience, wisdom, and benevolence and she became an attempted savior of her young friend's virtue. Having traveled widely, she was acquainted with much "innovation and imposture" in human behavior. Moreover, with her mother's lunacy and death some years before she had been forced to become "expert in the management of all affairs relative to property . . . [and] obligations

and cares, little suitable to my sex and age." Sophia maintained a strong
sense of Godliness – "I know that all physical and moral agents, are merely
instrumental to the purpose that he wills"—as well as a benevolent desire
to appreciate her fellow human beings and industriously promote their
happiness. Yet this coherent and purposeful woman, even with her moral
strength and narrative power, failed in the end. Sophia's piety and benevolence proved to be a false interpreter of events, and her friend's escape
from the clutches of the rapist Ormond came in spite of, not because of,
her rescue efforts. As she acknowledged in rather subdued fashion at the
novel's end, she could only hope that the story would provide to others "as
much instruction, as the contemplation of the sufferings and vicissitudes
of Constantia Dudley has afforded me" (pp. 252–53, 224, 294).

Indeed, Sophia's impotence faded before the inexorable disintegration
of her close friend. As the narrative of *Ormond* proceeded, Constantia's
fate comprised one long fall from innocence, both in a private and public
sense. In her personal life, the young woman embodied benevolence as she
cared for plague-stricken friends, accepted responsibility for support of her
emotionally crippled father, and tried to aid her friend Helena Cleves.
Moreover, this young woman of "quiet thoughts and steadfast purposes . . .
yielded nothing to caprice or passion." Kindness and self-control, however,
provided no preparation for dealing with the world. As Sophia described
Constantia near the end of the novel,

> The mind of my friend was wavering and unsuspicious. She had lived at a dis-
> tance from scenes, where principles are hourly put to the test of experiment. . . .
> Hence my friend had decided without the sanction of experience, had allowed
> herself to wander into untried paths, and had hearkened to positions pregnant
> with destruction and ignominy.

In the public sphere, Constantia had pursued the goal of industrious individualism. Rejecting the pecuniary dependence of marriage and toiling
alone as a seamstress, "she was at least mistress of the product of her own
labor" and "the profits, though slender, were sure, and she administered
her little property in what manner she pleased." Yet this self-reliance came
to nothing in the young woman's struggle with power and deceit. Con
stantia ultimately became an object in a battle of wills between Sophia and
Ormond, two strong-minded individuals who contended for both her
mind and her body. She collapsed under the pressure, and saved herself
only with a desperate act of violence (pp. 21, 252–53, 84).

Ormond, the driving force of the novel, personified Brown's greatest fear and greatest fascination: the forceful man of genius going beyond all social boundaries, pursuing his own vision, and evincing contempt for all limits. As the young writer had admitted in early 1798, "Great energy employed in the promotion of vicious purposes, constitute a very useful spectacle. Give me a tale of lofty crimes, rather than of honest folly." Ormond gave Brown just such a story.[32]

This aristocratic character arrogantly dismissed the opinions of others, setting little store by their prejudices and sensibilities; "He, everywhere, acted . . . as if he were alone." Ormond rationalized his conduct, however, with a claim of absolute "sincerity" to which "he refused no sacrifice." His "air of ferocity and haughty negligence" flowed from an absolute faith in his own rational judgment and its expression. Ormond's life, in fact, was one long exercise in deceit. From youth he had developed "a remarkable facility in imitating the voice and gestures of others," and he often "assumed a borrowed character and guise" that allowed him to accomplish many designs. Moreover, Ormond demonstrated a peculiar kind of mental telepathy that allowed him to climb secretly into the minds and communications of his acquaintants. Part of his justification for duplicity was utilitarian: since most people "were in the perpetual use of stratagems and artifices, it was allowable, he thought, to wield the same arms." Even more important, as he both recognized and relished, duplicity bestowed power:

> Ormond aspired to nothing more ardently than to hold the reins of opinion—to exercise absolute power over the conduct of others, not by constraining their limbs or by exacting obedience to his authority, but in a way of which his subjects should be scarcely conscious. He desired that his guidance should control their steps, but that his agency, when most effectual, should be the least suspected.[33]

Ormond's relentless desire for individual dominion, however, eventually turned inward to unhinge and splinter his own psyche. He lost the ability even to discern the difference between deceit and integrity in social relations. For Ormond, society quite literally became a stage, and Brown brilliantly described his use of masks and disguises:

> Compared with this the performance of the actor is the sport of children. This profession he was accustomed to treat with merciless ridicule, and no doubt, some of his contempt arose from a secret comparison, between the theatrical species of imitation, and his own. He blended in his own person the functions of poet and actor, and his dramas were not ficticious but real. The end that he

proposed was not the amusement of a playhouse crowd. His were scenes in
which hope and fear exercises a genuine influence.

For this consummate social actor, the playing out of his own desires became the only reality, and by the end of the novel he had become dimly
cognizant of his internal distortions. Confronting Constantia after engi-
neering the murder of her father, and preparing to rape her, he asked with
great agitation, "Catch you not a view of the monsters that are starting
into birth here (and he put his left hand to his forehead). But you cannot."
Ormond may have become aware of his own internal "monsters," but he
had no way to control them. Ultimately, like many of Brown's characters
and many Americans of the era, his center would not hold.[34]

# FIVE

# 🦋‖ The Major Novels (II):
# Deception and Disintegration

Both *Ormond* and *Wieland* reflected Charles Brockden Brown's confrontations with, and entanglements in, a post-Revolutionary society of liberation, flux, opportunity, and danger. Like the first stage of an archeological excavation, however, the Philadelphian's first two novels only identified the project site and uncovered superficial layers that suggested deeper treasures. Their sporadic, uneven treatments of religion, politics, sexual tension, and personal delusion gave way to a more penetrating exploration in his next brace of books. There Brown would expand his excavation in a wider circle to reveal more of the social context of the liberalizing American republic, and at the same time dig deeper into the self to illuminate the hidden mysteries of fragmenting individualism. In his last two major novels, the young author would discover more about his society—and about himself—than he probably ever wanted to know.

I

Late one evening as he returned home in 1793, Dr. Stevens, a respected physician in plague-ridden Philadelphia, was startled by a sight that had become all too familiar. Leaning against the wall a few steps from his porch was the desolate figure of a sick stranger. Dressed with rustic plainness, the handsome young man was lethargic and emaciated, and felt hot to the touch. Overcome by this image of yet another victim of the yellow fever epidemic sweeping through the city, the doctor took the unfortunate youth into his home and nursed him back to health over the next several days. As he recuperated, the visitor began to unfold an astonishing story of his adventures and travails as a country boy come to the big city. On such a dramatic note began *Arthur Mervyn; or, Memoirs of the Year 1793*, Charles

Brockden Brown's third major novel. Published in two parts, the first section appeared in Philadelphia in May 1799 and the second in New York around July 1800. At first glance the text offered a variation on the Franklinesque success story of a young man from the countryside journeying to the city in search of fame and fortune. Yet the "diseased" atmosphere of Philadelphia so permeated and overwhelmed the plot that the novel quickly took on a darker cast. For Brown, the unrelenting yellow fever came to symbolize a pervasive social as well as biological sickness. As he suggested at the outset, the horrors of the plague were "fertile of instruction to the moral observer, to whom they have furnished new displays of the influence of human passions and motives." Those passions and motives, particularly in terms of social context and relations, emerged as the emotional and intellectual center of the novel.[1]

*Arthur Mervyn*'s plot, in typical Brownian fashion, spun a knotted and tangled narrative web. In telling his life story to Dr. Stevens, young Arthur detailed a boyhood in rural Chester County where his adored mother had died, leaving him in the hands of a drunken and abusive father. When the elder Mervyn then married a lascivious servant girl half his age, the outraged son left the farm for the lure of Philadelphia. Upon arriving, however, the young protagonist fell immediately into misfortune. Arthur first lost his clothes and money through a swindle, then was abandoned in a strange house by a young prankster who pretended to befriend him. Penniless and discouraged, the young man was preparing to return home when he made the acquaintance of Thomas Welbeck, who appeared to be a prosperous and influential businessman. Mervyn's life would never be the same.

Welbeck took his new acquaintance under his wing, made the young man his private secretary, and gradually involved him in a series of extraordinary occurrences. Mervyn was first put to work plagiarizing a stolen manuscript. He then discovered that his patron's "daughter," Clemenza, was in fact a young woman whom Welbeck had financially ruined and then forced to become his mistress. Shortly thereafter, the youth witnessed Welbeck's murder of a rival and helped him bury the body in the basement. Arthur also stumbled across $20,000 that Welbeck had embezzled. As the young man gradually ascertained that his employer was no less than a vicious fraud and confidence man, Welbeck disappeared, and Arthur returned to the countryside to work for the Hadwin family. There he became enamored of young Eliza Hadwin, but eventually returned to Philadelphia at the height of the plague to rescue a friend of the Hadwins' and to return money Welbeck had embezzled. Back in the city, the protagonist encountered a number of threatening situations that brought the novel toward its conclusion: Clemenza was rescued from a house of prostitution, Welbeck was found dying in debtor's prison, and Arthur himself fell ill with yellow fever and was nearly buried alive. *Arthur Mervyn* ended as the young man abandoned Eliza, gave up his plans to become a doctor, became engaged to the wealthy heiress Ascha Fielding, and prepared to leave with her for Europe. This enormously complex narrative, filled with numerous subplots, false appearances and identities, and incredible coincidences, ultimately came together around one central theme: the individual's lonely struggle for survival in a shifting, threatening commercial world.

Much of Brown's attention focused on the character of Arthur himself. While *Ormond* and *Wieland* had presented an ensemble of characters operating in static social settings, this novel concentrated on an isolated individual scrambling in a fluid, dangerous social world. Indeed, much of *Arthur Mervyn*'s interest stemmed from the uncertainty of its young protagonist's fluctuating goals and values. A fundamental and recurring question concerned Arthur's sincerity. Brown seemed to make his authorial intentions clear in a February 1799 letter to his brother. "Arthur is intended," he wrote, "as a hero whose virtue, in order to be productive of benefit to others, and felicity to himself, stands in no need of riches." At the same time, the text itself called Arthur's benevolence and self-sacrifice into question. In fact, one of Brown's other characters, a friend of Dr. Stevens, made a harsh accusation: "He suspected that Mervyn was a wily imposter; that he had been trained in the art of fraud, under an accomplished teacher; that the tale which he had told to me, was a tissue of inglorious and plausible lies." Somewhere between these two polar images—Arthur as virtuous hero, Arthur as villainous confidence man—the protagonist's character assumed a complex, malleable, and elusive shape.[2]

The young man's isolation and loneliness provided perhaps the first key to unlocking his inner nature. Arthur lost all organic connection when he left the Chester County farm for Philadelphia—his family had disintegrated, he had abandoned his community, and neither church nor marriage maintained an emotional hold. A short time later, after his father's death, Arthur poignantly described his social condition:

I was now alone in the world, so far as the total want of kindred creates solitude. Not one of my blood, nor even of my name, were to be found in this

quarter of the world. Of my mother's kindred I knew nothing. So far as friendship or service might be claimed from them, to me they had no existence. I was
destitute of all those benefits which flow from kindred, in relation to protection,
advice, or property. My inheritance was nothing. Not a single relic or trinket in
my possession constituted a memorial of my family. . . . The fields which I was
wont to traverse, the room in which I was born, retained no traces of the past.
They were the property and residence of strangers.[3]

This alienation was heightened by Arthur's social suspension between
the countryside and the city. As the novel developed, it became clear that
its protagonist had no clear sense of place, but fluctuated in his loyalties.
At times he condemned urban life for its "depravity and danger" and
claimed that "the city was no place for me." With his old rural life seemingly possessed of "a thousand imaginary charms," he reminisced that "the
trade of plowman was friendly to health, liberty, and pleasure." At other
times, however, he insisted that farm labor offered little attraction while
provincial culture had made him "childishly unlearned and raw; a barn-
door simpleton; a plow-tail, kitchen hearth, turnip-hoeing novice!" Young
Mervyn further confirmed his mixed feelings when he observed that "if
cities are the chosen seats of misery and vice, they are likewise the soil of
all the laudable and strenuous productions of mind." Simultaneously
frightened and exhilarated as he sought firm social footing, Arthur finally
rejected both the country and the city, indeed any kind of social mooring,
in favor of a creed of individual perception. As we faced the world, he
argued,

> our own eyes only could communicate just conceptions of human performance.
> The influence of manners, professions, and social institutions, could be thor-
> oughly known only by direct inspection. . . . [T]heir value could be known, and
> their benefits fully enjoyed only by those who have tried all scenes; who have
> mixed with all classes and ranks; who have partaken of all conditions; and who
> have visited different hemispheres and climates and nations.

This young man sought to encounter the world alone, unencumbered by
social baggage and with a determination to make his own meaning.[4]
    Much of that meaning emerged from a creed of success-seeking indi-
vidualism. This faith, as preached by Mervyn, followed in the footsteps of
Benjamin Franklin with its message of material advancement, moral improvement, and personal independence. Very early in the text, for example,
the young man explained his reluctance to take a job as a clerk or day-

laborer as a matter of controlling his own destiny. In Dr. Stevens' words, "he could not part with the privilege of observing and thinking for himself." Arthur added that wage labor promised "a destiny to which I, who had so long enjoyed the pleasures of independence and command, could not suddenly reconcile myself." This insistence upon charting his own course led the youthful enthusiast to pledge a program of moral self-improvement. It had become his duty, he stated, both to avoid "mischievous or contemptible purposes" and "to cultivate all my virtues and eradicate all my defects." In typical Franklinian fashion, Mervyn also claimed the mantle of social reformer as he denounced the "capricious" distribution of inherited wealth and sought to rectify the cruelty and hardship of the public hospital. At one point in the novel, he brilliantly conveyed the inner resolve at the heart of the self-made man:

> My spirits were high, and I saw nothing in the world before me but sunshine and prosperity. I was conscious that my happiness depended not on the revolutions of nature or the caprice of man. All without was, indeed, vicissitude and uncertainty; but within my bosom was a centre not to be shaken or removed.

This sensibility often prompted Arthur to seek a higher social status, as when he first saw Thomas Welbeck as a means to advancement, or Dr. Stevens as an opportunity to become a doctor. It also prompted a nagging suspicion in the reader of *Arthur Mervyn*: perhaps the protagonist was preeminently a social climber for whom sincerity was a mask and dissembling an art.[5]

This image of Arthur as manipulator and fraud lurked as a recurring subtext in the novel. This seems to have been no accident, since a number of Brown's characters leveled flat charges of dishonesty against the young man. Wortley, a friend of Dr. Stevens who had been defrauded by Welbeck, hated young Mervyn as a "young villain" and "accomplice" of the older criminal. Mrs. Althorpe, a long-time acquaintance of the Mervyn family, presented the most devastating indictment of all. In contrast to Arthur's pretensions, she accused, he was notorious in Chester County for a "disposition to inactivity and laziness" and an "aversion to school . . . as great as his hatred of the plough." Moreover, she continued, the young man himself had a sexual relationship with the family servant, and only later accused her of being a "prostitute" when she married his father. Arthur then had been accused of stealing his father's horse and a considerable sum of money when he angrily left the family farm for Philadelphia. Dr. Stevens, reeling under this barrage of accusations, struggled to maintain confidence in his young friend. Arthur's conduct had been suspicious, but the doctor persisted in his belief that the youth's face was "the index of an honest mind." Stevens could reach but one weary conclusion: "If Mervyn has deceived me, there is an end to my confidence in human nature. All limits to dissimulation, and all distinctions between vice and virtue will be effaced."[6]

Arthur did not help his case with words or conduct. He admitted that things looked bad regarding his relationship with Welbeck and his dalliance with his stepmother, for instance, but he blamed false impressions and coincidences for creating misunderstandings. At other times, he proudly owned up to creating false appearances, noting at one point that "the stuff that I was made of was damnably tough and pliant." Even more distressingly, Arthur frequently betrayed a flexible, even expedient morality that justified any action. "My behavior," he conceded, "was ambiguous and hazardous, and perhaps wanting in discretion, but my motives were unquestionably pure." Mervyn elaborated upon this ends-justifies-the-means sensibility that directed his course. "Good intentions, unaided by knowledge, will, perhaps, produce more injury than benefit," he explained. "Meanwhile, we must not be inactive because we are ignorant. Our good purposes must hurry to performance, whether our knowledge be greater or less." Such a creed, while comforting to its holder, did not answer satisfactorily questions of mendacity raised by his detractors.[7]

Thus, the central problem of *Arthur Mervyn*—the integrity of the protagonist and the truth of his tale—admitted of no easy resolution. Brown, by virtue of Arthur's own explanations, linked much of the difficulty to the familiar Lockean dilemma of sensory delusion. The young man only *seemed* to lie, steal, embezzle, plagiarize, seduce, and murder. The vast weight of evidence in the narrative itself suggested another answer. The novel demonstrated that alienation, not mere misperception, fueled the suspicious ambiguity attached to young Mervyn's conduct. Adrift in a dangerous and unfamiliar world, he did not so much jettison morality as seek it. Arthur Mervyn, pathetically searching for values, moorings, and meanings, was more than a biological orphan. He was a moral and social one as well.[8]

Confusion and vacuity lay at the heart of Arthur's supposed "unshakeable centre," and they seeped out everywhere in the text. The sympathetic Dr. Stevens, analyzing his young friend, noted that "He stept forth upon the stage, unfurnished by anticipation or experience, with the means of security against fraud." Another acquaintance confirmed that innocence made Mervyn a "stranger to a deceitful and flagitious world." The protagonist himself confessed shock when, in his encounters in the city, "a scene of guilt and ignominy disclosed where my rash and inexperienced youth had suspected nothing but loftiness and magnanimity." Arthur blamed his naivete not only on his provincial upbringing but also on a bent toward withdrawn self-reflection that left him open to deceit: "My existence is a series of thoughts rather than motions. Ratiocination and deduction leave my senses unemployed. The fullness of my fancy renders my eye vacant and inactive. Sensations do not precede and suggest, but follow and are secondary to the acts of my mind."[9]

Not just innocence, but fluctuation and doubt also marked Mervyn's uncertain course through plague-ridden Philadelphia. As the plot took its various twists and turns, he veered wildly between virtue and self-interest, sacrifice and ambition. In trying to decide whether to marry Eliza Hadwin, for instance, he felt guilty when the fact of her modest circumstances came to mind, and he scolded himself that "the gratification of boundless ambition and inexhaustible wealth were contemptible and frivolous." In another case, that of the servant girl who seduced and married his father, he refused to utterly condemn her. In her position, he concluded, he "should have formed just such notions of my interest, and pursued it by the same means." Most of the time Arthur simply felt traumatized by the pressures and demands inflicted by the commercial city upon the individual. The dangers of "reasoning loosely on the subject of property" became painfully apparent to him. The young man frequently lapsed into self-pity: "Is every man, who leaves his cottage and the impressions of his infancy behind him, ushered into a world of revolutions and perils as have trammeled my steps?" Ultimately, however, young Mervyn defined his problem bluntly. In the uncertain and deceitful world of Philadelphia, the meaning of virtue and vice, right and wrong was simply unclear. "I am incapable of any purpose that is not beneficent; but in the means that I use and in the evidence on which I proceed, I am liable to a thousand mistakes," he confessed ruefully. "Point out to me the road by which I can do good, and I will cheerfully pursue it."[10]

The treachery of that road, and the alienating environment through which it passed, finally carried Mervyn to the precipice of personal disintegration. At several crisis points in the narrative, he threatened to crumble from within, to fragment his identity into splinters. As Arthur admitted early in the text when reflecting on his misadventures, "Nothing, indeed, more perplexes me than a review of my own conduct." Somewhat later, he again betrayed a sense of inner confusion when replying to the charges of Mrs. Althorpe and other neighbors. It was as if the young man had stepped outside his own skin. "It was not me whom they hated and despised," Mervyn averred. "It was the phantom that passed under my name, which existed only in their imagination, and which was worthy of all their scorn and all their enmity." Near the end of the text, as Arthur fell under the sway of Ascha Fielding and agonized over whether to marry her, he had a terrifying nightmare that brought him face to face with his own confusion. Wrestling with nocturnal images of self-destruction, he feared that "a latent error in my moral constitution" had boiled up to destroy him. Looking inward, the young man cringed before a horrifying vision: "a mind lost to itself; bewildered, unhinged; plunged into dreary insanity." This pathetic character was no dangerous and conniving manipulator. This Arthur Mervyn appeared as a bumbling, traumatized, rootless victim of a pestilential social milieu.[11]

Brown buttressed this complex image of his protagonist as imperiled survivor with a precise and powerful rendering of social setting. In something of a departure for the young novelist, he boldly sketched a social atmosphere for Arthur Mervyn's travails that pervaded and shaped every aspect of the narrative. It was a portrait shaped by withering social criticism, and the author painted it in a variety of dark tones. The post-Revolutionary Philadelphia of Brown's third novel was not an attractive place.[12]

The first hint of what was to come occurred as Arthur entered the city for the first time. Fresh from the rural regions, he fell victim to unscrupulous innkeepers who cheated him out of his small supply of money. Then tricked into entering a large house by a young man who falsely claimed to live there, the abandoned youth fled to a closet where he overheard an elaborate plan for fraud unfolded by the real inhabitant of the estate. Reeling from these incidents, Mervyn stumbled into the protectorship of Thomas Welbeck, who promptly made him an unwitting instrument in the swindling of a large amount of money from a wealthy woman. Such incidents quickly established the bustling commercial city as an impersonal arena characterized by fraud and selfish ambition. Overwhelmed by Philadelphia's "discords," "unwholesome labour," and "irksome companions," young Arthur came to feel that every day brought "some new artifice to baffle my conclusions and mislead my judgement." He grew so wary that meeting a perfect stranger prompted this appeal: "Be not a deceiver, I entreat you. I depend only on your looks and professions, and these may be dissembled." It is little wonder that Brown borrowed from Milton's

*Paradise Lost* to characterize the city as a hellish place "pendent with many a row of starry lamps and blazing crescents fed by naptha and asphaltos."[13]

In delineating this harsh atmosphere of lying and self-seeking, Brown focused on the pernicious effects of commercial pursuits. The volatile world of buying and selling was, to his mind, a haven for cheating and gouging as individuals vied for advantage. In the words of one prosperous merchant in the novel, it was an age of "mercantile anxieties and revolutions" where at all times one's fortune "an untoward blast may sweep away, or four strokes of a pen may demolish." Throughout the text commercial exchanges and money were tainted by destruction and death—Watson's defrauding, Clemenza Lodi's embezzled inheritance, Welbeck and Thetford's swindling scheme. Brown, speaking through the character of Dr. Stevens, laid the blame at the foot of greedy citizens

> who employed money, not as the medium of traffic, but as in itself a commodity. . . . He thought it a tedious process to exchange today, one hundred dollars for a cask or bale, and tomorrow exchange the bale or cask for an hundred and ten dollars. It was better to give the hundred for piece of paper, which, carried forthwith to the moneychangers, he could procure an hundred twenty-three and three-fourths. In short, this man's coffers were supplied by the despair of honest men and the stratagems of rogues.

In such a society of paper speculators and mercantile sharpers, honest men and virtuous labor seemed doomed.[14]

The greatest danger arising from this commercial calculus, however, went beyond mere fraud and was much more subtle and insidious. Throughout *Arthur Mervyn*, Brown suggested that deception and distrust, almost unnoticeably, had become the very stuff of everyday social relations. Arthur himself, of course, spent much of the book wandering about Philadelphia trying to decipher who was who and what was what in the inhospitable city. The novel also abounded—here Brown indulged in one of his favorite ploys—in a dizzying array of mistaken identities and alter egos. In Mervyn's commercialized Philadelphia, practically nothing and no one were what they seemed. Once again, Dr. Stevens cogently expressed the novel's disturbed sensibility on this point. "A smooth exterior, a show of virtue, and a specious tale, are, a thousand times exhibited in human intercourse by craft and subtlety," he explained. "Wickedness may sometimes be ambiguous, its mask may puzzle the observer; our judgement may be made to falter and fluctuate." Masked figures lurked everywhere and distrust lay heavy in the air as individuals in the mercantile city had to protect themselves and approach one another warily. Arthur concluded, "Never, in the depths of cavern or forest, was I equally conscious of loneliness" (pp. 229–30, 141).

This unsettling sense of social disease found its most brilliant reflection in the dominant symbol of *Arthur Mervyn*: the physical disease of yellow fever that ravaged Philadelphia in 1793. Brown's descriptions of the plague, particularly its horrible devastation of human life and social institutions, provided a consistently gloomy backdrop for the action. It also served as a vehicle for broader concerns. His sketches of the "confusion and panick" caused by the yellow fever uncannily replicated his social criticism of rampant individual greed and ruptured community ties. "Some had shut themselves in their houses, and debarred themselves from all communication with the rest of mankind. The consternation of others had destroyed their understanding," the author related. "Men were seized by this disease in the streets; passengers fled from them; entrance into their own dwellings was denied to them; they perished in the publick ways." Such scenes of isolation, distrust, and havoc produced a widespread mental state of "melancholy bordering on madness" (pp. 128–29, 130).

Brown's sketches of the Philadelphia pestilence gained particular power as they evoked several images. Significantly, one of the most haunting descriptions concerned the city's "marketplace," usually bustling but now an arena of darkness and death. It was occupied only by a small coterie of figures, "ghost-like, wrapt in cloaks, from behind which they cast upon me glances of wonder and suspicion," he wrote. "And, as I approached, [they] changed their course, to avoid touching me." In this desolate atmosphere, a diseased social intercourse had made even cash worthless. As young Arthur reported upon his return to Philadelphia with its hordes of frightened and dying citizens, "I had money, but an horse shelter, or a morsel of food, could not be purchased." Trapped and terrified, the protagonist fell victim to a kind of living death when he was knocked unconscious by a looter and nearly interred by exhausted undertakers who were roaming the streets. Arthur's "terrors were unspeakable" as he struggled to regain his senses. He did so just in time, and saw that "appearances had misled these men, and shuddered to reflect, by what hair-breadth means I had escaped being buried alive" (pp. 139, 141, 148–49).

This chilling portrayal of a world nearly devoid of social connection reached its greatest intensity in one particular character. Thomas Welbeck, one of Brown's most intriguing literary creations, stalked through the pages of *Arthur Mervyn* as the American individual turned sociopath.

From the time he rescued a desperate young Mervyn and made him his private secretary to his lonely death in debtor's prison, Welbeck operated according to his own utterly scurrilous logic. His apparent wealth and prestige, along with the mysterious origins of such grandeur, prompted Arthur's famous question: "Who and what was Welbeck?" As the young man discovered rather quickly, the "order and pomp" of his benefactor was actually "the mask of misery and the structure of vice." Welbeck worked as a professional confidence man who enriched himself by preying on his fellow citizens. He was a master of fraud and deception. With an accumulation of money from several small-time schemes, he arrived in Philadelphia in search of even bigger game. Renting a mansion and retinue of servants, Welbeck created the persona of a mysterious man of opulence and power. This served as a clever prelude to bilking the wealthy. In discussion with his new-found protégé, he betrayed a smirking pride in his talents:

> The facility with which mankind are misled in their estimates of characters, their proneness to multiply inferences and conjectures will not be readily conceived by one destitute of my experience. My sudden appearance on the stage, my stately reserve, my splendid habitation and my circumspect deportment were sufficient to entitle me to homage. The artifices that were used to unveil the truth, and the guesses that were current respecting me, were adapted to gratify my ruling passion. (pp. 70–71, 95)

Brown utilized a vocabulary of "masks," "veils," and "artifice" to describe this man and his remarkable facility for deception. Arthur was astonished, for example, when he accompanied Welbeck to a high-society party and discovered his mentor's ability to exchange his normal solemnity for an animated mask of eloquence and charm. In Mervyn's words, " I could hardly persuade myself it was the same person" as Welbeck covered his "secret torments and insidious purposes, beneath a veil of benevolence and cheerfulness." This capacity for "dissimulation" fueled an array of fraudulent schemes. A revealing, if somewhat botched, example of the con man's duplicity occurred when he tried to trick Mervyn into returning to him a large sum of money found in a book. Welbeck claimed that the bills were without value as products of a shameful "scheme of forgery," and insisted that they should be surrendered back to him. Arthur, however, swallowing Welbeck's tale with its "every token of sincerity," promptly burned the forged notes to avoid criminal prosecution. Welbeck exploded: "Maniac! Miscreant! To be fooled by so gross an artifice! The notes were genuine. The tale of their forgery was false, and meant only to wrest them from you." In this murky moral swamp of tainted money and false appearances, Welbeck personified a pressing social problem: Could any ambitious individual be trusted, and if so on what basis? (pp. 73, 335, 208–9).

Beneath the many masks of Welbeck there appeared a more complex character. The author, in part, clearly created this villain as a shadowy alter ego of Arthur Mervyn. The parallels and connections were too obvious and frequent to be mere circumstance. Mervyn and Welbeck, for instance, shared both a willingness to circumvent the law and a proclivity for playing fast and loose with others' property. From early in their lives they also shared an aversion to hard, honest work. In an admission strikingly similar to Arthur's, the older man told of his own youthful contempt for the "vile and ignominious drudgery" of manual labor, and confessed that "to perform any toilsome or prescribed task was incompatible with my nature." For his part, Mervyn admitted that he had learned much from Welbeck on "the principles of human nature; on the delusiveness of appearances; on the perviousness of fraud; and on the power with which nature has invested human beings over the thoughts and actions of each other." In turn, the wily confidence man believed that his protégé had learned his lessons all too well. On his deathbed, Welbeck bitterly denounced the young man as a villain more artful than himself. "Thy qualities are marvelous," he scornfully told Mervyn. "Every new art of thine outstrips the last, and belies the newest calculations. . . . Under that innocent guise there lurked a heart treacherous and cruel." In this perverse, twisted father-son relationship, Thomas Welbeck made manifest the latent evil within the novel's protagonist. Shaping deception and self-interest into a way of life, he represented a nightmare vision of what a society of ambitious individualism could produce (pp. 89–90. 137. 258–59).

To complete its bleak depiction of late eighteenth-century America, *Arthur Mervyn* returned again and again to a final theme. In a compulsive subtext, the novel forcefully alluded to an upheaval in family structure and gender relationships. By focusing intermittently on the unraveling ties that connected the solitary individual to overarching social institutions, Brown illuminated the destructive advance of ambition, deception, and isolation. In the liberalizing atmosphere of the post-Revolutionary republic, both traditional family structures and male/female attachments seemed to be crumbling. More powerfully than he ever knew, the young writer revealed the convergence of public and private disintegration.

Arthur's situation provided a beginning. As he related his life story to kindly Dr. Stevens, it became clear that family turmoil had prompted the young man's journey to the city. Mervyn's beloved mother had died, leaving him intensely lonely and dejected. His sister had been victimized by a seducer and had fallen into disgrace. His father's stupidity and licentiousness so disgusted Arthur that they inspired a desire for escape. Determined to be independent and successful, the son viewed with contempt "that feebleness of mind which degraded my father, in whatever scene he should be placed, to be the tool of others." Later in the novel the elder Mervyn would die an alcoholic. Brown's book, however, was also littered with the wreckage of other families: that of Thomas Welbeck and Ascha Fielding, among the major characters, and the Hadwins, Watsons, and Lodis among the minor actors. The disintegration of these families usually involved the death, often by self-destruction, of their paternal figures. Such scenes amplified the creaks and groans of the traditional patriarchal family as it was stretched to the breaking point by swelling liberal individualism. Once again, Brown utilized the metaphor of the plague to drive home this image. In the appalling atmosphere of the Philadelphia yellow fever, he wrote, "Terror had exterminated all the sentiments of nature. Wives were deserted by husbands, and children by parents."[15]

Scenes of familial failure provided a backdrop for the presentation of equally problematic relationships between men and women. The treachery of urban marketplace society was replicated in interactions between the sexes, and Brown punctuated *Arthur Mervyn* with incidents of destructive gender tensions: the rape of Arthur's sister by the cowardly schoolmaster Covill, Ascha Fielding's abandonment by her venal and bigamous husband, the elder Mervyn's unhappy coupling with the young milkmaid Betty Lawrence after his wife's death, Wallace's desertion of his fiancée Susan Hadwin. The novel's two primary characters, Arthur and Thomas Welbeck, took the lead once more. The older man's encounters with women produced a particularly vicious pattern of abuse, vice, and deceit. On the run from a failed marriage, Welbeck seduced a married woman and then left her ruined and penniless. He encountered the Lodi family and became the guardian of their daughter, whom he promptly made his mistress, impregnated, and then abandoned to a house of prostitution.

True to the larger pattern of the novel, Arthur echoed many of Welbeck's dastardly acts but in a pale and ambivalent form. Mervyn's sexual dalliance with Betty Lawrence brought him no honor, especially when he subsequently accused her of being a whore for marrying his father. His subsequent love affair with a Quaker farm girl, Eliza Hadwin, also smacked of opportunism. The young man's affection varied according to

his own whims and opportunities, and also, not coincidentally, to fluctuations in her family's fortune. At one point, after a particularly condescend-
ing dismissal of her intellect and inexperience, Eliza struck back at Arthur.
Echoing the sentiments of Brown's *Alcuin*, she angrily denounced Arthur's
apparent view

> that no scene is fit for me, but what you regard as slothful and inglorious. Have
> I not the same claim to be wise, and active, and courageous as you are? . . . but
> you desire it all for yourself. Me, you think poor, weak, and contemptible: fit for
> nothing but to spin and churn. Provided I exist, am screened from the weather,
> have enough to eat and drink, you are satisfied. As to strengthening my mind
> and enlarging my knowledge, these things are valuable to you, but on me they
> are thrown away. I deserve not the gift.[16]

Arthur's curious involvement with Ascha Fielding culminated the novel's troubled portrayal of gender relations. In the closing sections of the
text, the youth fell madly in love with this older widow (age twenty-six),
whom he came to view as the epitome of female virtue, grace, and intelligence. Several peculiar facts, however, muddled this apparently conventional sentimental ending. First, Ascha's evident ugliness violated literary
convention. Even the usually benevolent Dr. Stevens described her as "un-
sightly as a night-hag, tawny as a moor, [with] less luxuriance than a
sharred log, fewer elasticities than a sheet-pebble." Moreover, her un-
orthodox background as a Jew of English background did not deter her
young suitor but only prompted enthusiasm for marriage and residence in
Europe. Most striking, however, was the fact that Ascha clearly represented for Arthur an Oedipal resolution of his family and gender anxieties.
"Are you not my lost momma come back again?" he asked her bluntly.
"And yet not *exactly* her, I think. Something different, something better, I
believe, if that be possible. . . . methinks I would be wholly yours." This
twisted retreat to the bosom of his "mamma" provided young Mervyn with
an escape, both from his family problems and from the social pressures demanding assertive individualism. As he admitted with obvious relief near
the novel's end, "I was wax in her hand. Without design and without effort, I was always the form she wished me to assume. My own happiness
became a secondary passion. . . . I thought not of myself. I had scarcely a
separate or independent existence."[17]

*Arthur Mervyn* came to a close with its protagonist reconstituting family and renouncing self, then joyfully retiring to Europe. Brown's unsettling
portrayal of social disarray, institutional failure, and personal incoherence

in late eighteenth-century America ended on a note of cultural capitulation. Broadening his earlier novelistic endeavors, the author had half-consciously ventured into the frightening social territory of liberalizing change, and his expedition reached a point of no return. Faced with a moral spectacle of rampant fraud, venality, and confusion, young Arthur offered a complex vision of the new American individualism: alternately well-meaning and self-interested, a mass of insecurities covered by a thin veneer of excessive confidence, drifting wildly between greed and benevolence with no firm moral bearings. It seemed appropriate that at the novel's conclusion he fled almost frantically from this array of dangers, pressures, and quandaries into the "motherly" arms of European tradition. For Brown, Arthur's tranquility came only with a return—both personally and culturally—to the womb.

## II

In a variety of ways, *Arthur Mervyn* begat *Edgar Huntly*. The trajectory of flight that concluded Brown's Philadelphia novel continued in his last major work of fiction, only this time it led into the natural wildness of the frontier rather than the security of Europe. The author's need for an imaginative exploration of the transforming American republic also persisted. While *Arthur Mervyn* had ventured outward to chart the social parameters of liberalizing change, however, *Edgar Huntly* burrowed inward to gauge the psychological resonances of that momentous shift. And if the yellow fever metaphor had suggested a "diseased" society for young Mervyn, a powerful atmospheric image in the later narrative evoked the "wilderness" of the human mind. As the last in a flurry of novels flying from Brown's pen in the late 1790s, *Edgar Huntly* provided a kind of closure as it probed deep into the innermost recesses of liberal individualism. Its conclusion was a gloomy one.

In many ways, the plot of Brown's wilderness tale was the most exciting and gripping of all his novels. Published in the late summer of 1799 after a frenzied burst of composition over the previous few months, *Edgar Huntly; or, Memoirs of a Sleepwalker* was a dark, complex murder mystery set on the frontier edge of civilization. The narrative opened in a setting near the forks of the upper Delaware River as Edgar Huntly was mourning the violent death of his close friend Waldegrave, to whose sister, Mary, he was engaged. Later one evening, Edgar discovered a mysterious young man, Clithero Edny, digging and sobbing at the base of the elm tree where the murder had occurred. Even more oddly, as they conversed it became clear that the stranger was a sleepwalker who was acting in a nocturnal daze. When later confronted by Huntly, Clithero told the strange story of his life: his youth in Ireland under the care of his patroness, Mrs. Lorimer; his engagement to her niece, Clarice; his accidental murder of Mrs. Lorimer's brother; his panic-stricken flight to a remote section of the New World in Pennsylvania. Proclaiming his innocence of Waldegrave's death, Clithero won Edgar's friendship. Without warning, the Irishman then disappeared into the wilderness and eluded his new friend's efforts to track him down.

At this point, two subplots intervened. First, another stranger named Weymouth appeared, claiming that the estate of the late Waldegrave (some $8,000) was actually *his* money and had only been in his friend's hands for safekeeping. Thus, Edgar's fiancée was threatened with a loss of inheritance and impoverishment, as well as an indefinite postponement of her marriage. Second, a packet of Waldegrave's early letters mysteriously disappeared. These letters, espousing radical Godwinian ideas about materialism and atheism, had been in Edgar's possession and he had promised to destroy them. Unnerved by these developments, Huntly became convinced that Clithero held the key to these mysteries, and he determined to find him. Before Edgar could do so, however, he was forced to embark upon an enigmatic and terrifying journey of his own.

The protagonist awoke one night in complete darkness, bruised and disoriented, on the floor of a wilderness cave. He did not know how he got there. Dazed and confused, he gradually worked his way to the entrance and began a nightmarish trip back to civilization. He became involved in several murderous Indian battles, the killing of a ferocious grey panther, and the crossing of a wild river in a hail of gunfire from white settlers who believed him to be a marauding savage. Upon his return to familiar territory, Edgar was stunned by several discoveries. Friends informed him that Indians in the area, under the urging of an aged and revered woman, Queen Mab, had gone on a murderous rampage against white settlers over the last several days. Edgar also reunited with Sarsefield, an old instructor and paternal patron, who had just returned to the area as the husband of Mrs. Lorimer, Clithero's old patroness. He finally learned, to his dismay, that Clithero was in fact a dangerous homicidal maniac.

Perhaps the greatest shock, however, came with Edgar's discovery that he *himself*, like Clithero, was a sleepwalker who had unconsciously hidden Waldegrave's letters, and then stumbled into the cave on a nighttime ramble. The novel drew to a close as Clithero emerged from the wilderness, learned of recent events from Huntly, and headed to New York to murder

Mrs. Lorimer. The madman was intercepted, but he escaped his guards and committed suicide. Edgar was left alone and baffled at the end of the narrative, staggered by his consistent misreading of other people and external events, and even more disturbed by his own self-deception.[18]

*Edgar Huntly* offered many familiar Brownian features: the dark tones and mysterious textures of Gothic fiction, a preoccupation with human deceit and violent obsessions, a focus on abnormal psychology, in this case somnabulism, or sleepwalking. The author's own explanation of intent with this novel differed from his earlier efforts. In an introductory section entitled "To the Public," Brown claimed to be a "moral painter" using a fictional palette of colors to depict American sensibility. His comments also reflected a nascent cultural nationalism:

> That new springs of action and new motives to curiosity should operate; that the field of investigation, opened to us by our country, should differ essentially from those which exist in Europe, may be readily conceived. The sources of amusement to the fancy and instruction to the heart, that are peculiar to ourselves, are equally numerous and inexhaustible. It is the purpose of this work to profit by some of these sources; to exhibit a series of adventures, growing out of the condition of our country.[19]

As a moral painter trying to capture the various shadings of American motivation, Brown eschewed the biting social criticism of *Arthur Mervyn*. Instead, his treatment of a wilderness theme employed subtle gestures and tantalizing references to construct a skeletal critique of liberalizing society. Weymouth, for example, with his tales of incredible travail as a merchant speculator in the Atlantic world, prompted this commentary from Edgar about his fellow Americans:

> Is such the lot of those who wander from their rustic homes in search of fortune? Our countrymen are prone to enterprise, and are scattered over every sea and every land in pursuit of that wealth which will not screen them from disease and infirmity, which, when gained, by no means compensates them for the hardships and vicissitudes endured in the pursuit.

Ironically, given this rhetorical criticism, Edgar never disdained his *own* materialist ambition. When Mary Waldegrave lost her inheritance, he concluded rather quickly that their marriage must be postponed because it "could not take place while both of us were poor."[20]

An inchoate but stronger social theme in *Edgar Huntly* concerned the crumbling of patriarchal authority. Here, as in his earlier novels, Brown deployed the imagery and explored the consequences of paternal decline. Most of Edgar's family, including his father, had been massacred by marauding Indians in a frontier war. Along with his surviving sisters, the youth had been shuttled to the home of an uncle, whose natural son despised these family intruders. Edgar feared that his cousin, upon inheriting the uncle's estate, would make his first act of authority "to turn us forth from these doors." Thus, Huntly tried to build a father-son relationship with an older acquaintance, Sarsefield. The older man treated his young friend with "paternal tenderness" and "parental affection" and, in Edgar's words, was constantly "consulting for my interest as if he were my real father." By the novel's end, this relationship too fell apart as Edgar's thoughtless actions accidently resulted in Mrs. Sarsefield's miscarriage. Edgar's surrogate father denounced his son's "rashness" in bitter terms. "You acted in direct opposition to my council, and to the plainest dictates of propriety," he accused. "Farewell."[21]

These frayed lines of paternal social authority unraveled even further with Clithero. His mysterious appearance among these frontier farmers disturbed a social arrangement that was, "for the most part, a patriarchal one. Each farmer was surrounded by his sons and kinsmen." As an unknown and possibly dangerous individual, the Irishman represented a subversive social threat. The disclosure that Clithero had fled to the New World to escape from a murderous Oedipal conflict proved equally disturbing. Living under the benevolent care of Mrs. Lorimer, he had been violently accosted in the street by a stranger, who turned out to be his benefactress' malicious twin brother, Arthur Wiatte. Defending himself, Clithero shot the robber only to discover the man's true identity. Overcome with the horror of this symbolic patricide, the killer could only whisper, "I was impelled by an unconscious necessity. Had the assailant been my father the consequence would have been the same. . . . I have killed the brother of my patroness, the father of my love." Thus, Clithero, even more dramatically than Edgar, was a young man cut adrift from paternal authority, burdened with the weight of isolated individualism, and radiating an aura of emotional ill-will and self-hatred.[22]

Brown's most potent social criticism in *Edgar Huntly*, however, lay between the narrative lines. His last major fiction consistently, if often unwittingly, evoked the atmosphere and imagery of brutal competition. Eschewing *Arthur Mervyn*'s skewering of financial intrigue and social distrust, this novel provided an even stronger emotional jolt with its outlandish rendering of a vicious Hobbesian world "red of tooth and claw."

The milieu of Edgar Huntly was one of violent self-preservation, as became vividly clear in the middle section of the novel, where the protagonist emerged from the cave only to endure a series of murderous confrontations. In the exhausted words of the young man,

> No sooner was one calamity eluded, than I was beset by another. I had emerged from the abhorred darkness in the heart of the earth, only to endure the extrem- ities of famine and encounter the fangs of a wild beast. From these I was delivered only to be thrown into the midst of savages, to wage an endless and hopeless war with adepts in killing, with appetites that longed to feast upon my bowels and to quaff my heart's blood.

Struggling to survive in this ferocious context, Huntly concluded that destruction, mayhem, and greed were the natural stuff of human existence. "Such are the deeds," he exclaimed, "which perverse nature compels thousands of rational beings to perform and to witness . . . [as] zealous and delighted actors and beholders" (pp. 223–24, 202).

Two particular images, the brutal Indian and the wild animal, recurred throughout *Edgar Huntly* to give particular force to Brown's picture of life as a struggle for survival. Deploying a crude anthropology of juxtaposed "Civilization" and "Savagery"—it appeared, for instance, in the detailed descriptions of the steadily more sophisticated dwellings Edgar encountered as he made his way from the Indian wilderness to the Anglo settlements—the author chronicled a series of life-threatening situations. Blundering into several Indian raiding parties, the protagonist found himself in several fights to the death. This enemy, he grew convinced, was a barbaric murderer who lived to kill and "to drink the blood and exult in the laments of his unhappy foes, and of my own brethren." After one such battle in which Edgar killed an Indian attacker, he described a frenzied phallic triumph: he "made prize of his [opponent's] tomahawk . . . and stuck his musket in the ground and left it standing upright in the middle of the road." The young man also engaged in a death struggle, on two separate occasions, with a ferocious grey panther whose eerie cry, by "its resemblance to the human voice," sounded especially terrifying. In the end, Huntly survived by imitating his aggressors as he refused "to be outdone in perspicacity by the lynx, in his sure-footed instinct by the roe, or in patience under hardship . . . by the Mohawk." With this depiction of a savage atmosphere of every man for himself, Brown offered a hyperbolic vision of the individualist ethic with which he had contended for much of his early life. In the liberalizing American republic with its "new springs

of action," this novel suggested, violence lurked just beneath the social surface and within every man beat the heart of a beast (pp. 200, 203, 124,
212).

This threatening world of hunters and hunted offered little room for
women. In contrast to earlier Brown novels in which females had played
leading roles as narrators or protagonists (Clara in *Wieland* and Constantia
in *Ormond*) or functioned as important supporting players in the drama
(Eliza Hadwin and Ascha Fielding in *Arthur Mervyn*), *Edgar Huntly* betrayed virtually no sign of women. This distinction was even more striking, of course, in comparison to *Alcuin*, the author's early fictional dialogue
on the rights of women. Only three females made very brief and shadowy
appearances in this wilderness novel, and they were pictured either nega-
tively or in highly abstract terms. Edgar's fiancée, Mary Waldegrave, was a
cameo figure of virtue, refinement, and, as the author made clear, laziness.
Her "love of independence and ease, and impatience of drudgery," Huntly
reported, were "carried to an erroneous extreme" and detracted from her
character. Mrs. Lorimer, the benevolent Englishwoman, primarily functioned as a foil for the lunatic misapprehensions of Clithero. Finally,
Queen Mab, the eccentric Indian matriarch, flitted in and out of the narrative as a witch-like creature. While Edgar had maintained initially a certain affection and sympathy for this peculiar old woman, eventually he,
like his neighbors, recoiled upon discovering that she had engineered the
Indian uprising against white settlers. In Brown's description, Queen Mab
had "brooded a long time over nothing but schemes of revenge" against
Anglo intruders, and after the Indian uprising she had "readily confessed
and gloried in the mischief she had done." These fleeting, often distasteful
female images in his last major novel implied that for Brown, the acute social tensions of liberalizing change were creating gender tensions as well.
In a world of bloodthirsty male competitiveness, female refinement, not to
mention female equality, seemed somehow beside the point (pp. 155, 200–
9, 280, 281).

Various fragments of social characterization and criticism, however, ultimately comprised a preface to the real thematic thrust of *Edgar Huntly*.
Edgar's confrontation with the dangers of the wild, his encounters with
the volatile Clithero, and his struggle to grasp the meaning of his own actions and motivations all pointed in one direction: an exploration of the
innermost recesses of individual consciousness. As one critic has observed
presciently, this novel was "not so much written as dreamed." Indeed,
Brown's compulsive preoccupation with several themes—sleepwalking, al-

ter egos, dream states, unconscious actions—reinforces the suspicion that Brown used this narrative to plunge deep into the unknown regions of the human mind. Early in the text, Edgar provided the first of many hints that the coming adventure would be internal and psychological as much as external and geographical. Sitting at the edge of the forest, looking out upon a wild panorama of nature as he prepared to hear Clithero's life story, Huntly briefly opened a window into his inner state:

> My stormy passions had subsided into a calm, portentous and awful. My soul was big with expectation. I seemed as if I were on the eve of being ushered into the world, whose scenes were tremendous, but sublime. The suggestion of sorrow and malice had, for a time, taken their flight, and yielded place to a generous sympathy, which . . . had more in it of pleasure than pain.

As Brown clearly intimated here, the frontier setting of *Edgar Huntly* in many ways reflected the tangled undergrowth and terrifying grandeur of an even more intimidating wilderness: the volatile, unknown human unconscious. The bulk of the novel would be devoted to uncovering that hidden underside of rational individualism.[23]

Numerous images reinforced the sense of *Edgar Huntly* as a fictional foray into the unconscious. Throughout the text, for instance, Brown associated the mystery of the wilderness with dark, unknown dimensions of human motivation. Stalking Clithero through an uncharted region of forest, rivers, and mountains, Edgar described both geographical obstacles and the Irishman's enigmatic psyche in terms of wild, impenetrable terrain. Pursuing Clithero in a double sense, he related the "maze, oblique, circuitous, upward, downward" through which he was traveling. This path, Edgar reported, tended

> to pierce into the deepest thickets, to plunge into the darkest cavities, to ascend the most difficult heights, and approach the slippery and tremulous verge of the dizziest precipices. . . . I plunged into obscurities, and clambered over obstacles, from which, in a different state of mind, and with a different object of pursuit, I should have recoiled with invincible timidity.

This commingled wilderness/unconscious imagery recurred once again when Edgar awoke at the bottom of a cave, suffering "excruciating sensations" and "a species of delirium." Believing that somehow he had been buried alive, the protagonist concluded that he "existed as it were in a wakeful dream" in which "my state was full of tumult and confusion, and my attention was incessantly divided between my painful sensations and my feverish dreams." For Brown, the caves and wilderness mazes of the natural world reflected the turmoil seething beneath the surface of rational perception in the psychic world.[24]

The author also consistently employed the symbol of a secret box to evoke the concealed consciousness of both Clithero and Edgar. Both figures, it turned out, were skilled cabinetmakers who had constructed wooden containers that were nearly impossible to open. Edgar's was a cabinet with a secret drawer "opened by the motion of a spring, of whose existence none but the maker was conscious." Given Brown's commitment to discovering the "new springs of action" among ambitious Americans, it seemed no accident that this secret container became the receptacle for Waldergrave's scandalous letters. Significantly, Edgar opened the box and removed the letters only when he was in the unconscious state of sleepwalking. Clithero also had built a mysterious wooden receptacle that Edgar discovered in the course of investigating the immigrant's disappearance. In Clithero's box, too, "some spring . . . secretly existed which might forever elude the senses." Within this box, Edgar believed, were discoveries that would "throw light upon the conduct of this extraordinary man" and "his character might assume a new appearance." Once again, the secret compartments of human motivation that so preoccupied the author found symbolic expression in artifacts of the physical world (pp. 133–34, 115–16, 117).

At times Brown averred his fascination with the human psyche more directly. For instance, he liberally sprinkled *Edgar Huntly* with references to altered states of consciousness. Upon reuniting with Edgar, for instance, an astonished Sarsefield proclaimed, "Am I alive? am I awake? Speak again, I beseech you, and convince me that I am not dreaming or delirious." After Weymouth reappeared to rightfully reclaim his money, Edgar could only come to grips with this "unexpected and extraordinary interview, as if it had existed in a dream." Waldergrave, a ghostly figure constantly hovering at the margins of the narrative, directly entered it only once when he appeared in Huntly's sleep as a "half indignant apparition." The author constantly returned to the underside of consciousness, noting that things "nearly banished from my waking thoughts, occurred, in an incongruous and half-seen form, to my dreams" (pp. 242, 154, 130).

Brown's fixation on irrational dream-states found its most theatrical expression, of course, in the prevalent sleepwalking motif of *Edgar Huntly*. Clithero's somnabulism—unconscious motor activity without consent or guidance of the will—underlay many of his peculiar actions. Edgar's patronizing attempts to comprehend Clithero's motives also ran aground upon the discovery that he shared the Irishman's sleepwalking malady. Wandering about with his unconscious in command, Huntly stalked country roads frightening his neighbors, hid Waldergrave's letters, and stumbled into caves hidden in the forest. Edgar's initial analysis of somnabulism returned with a vengeance to haunt him. Upon observing Clithero physically moving while sound asleep, he had discerned a "fantastic drama" of the mind, a kind of "bewitchment" that bubbled up from "the recesses of his soul." In fact, Edgar defined sleepwalking as a species of insanity:

> The incapacity of sound sleep denotes a mind sorely wounded . . . [and in] the possession of some deadly secret. The thoughts, which considerations of safety enables them to suppress or disguise during wakefulness, operate without impediment, and exhibit their genuine effects, when the notices of sense are partly excluded, and they are shut out from a knowledge of their entire condition.

Somnabulism, by offering release from repression for wounded minds, promoted the dominion of the instincts and threatened to undermine the social order. The liberation of "deadly secrets" from the unconscious, Brown suggested, would be a gruesome sight (pp. 14, 13).

*Edgar Huntly*'s obsession with hidden, dangerous dimensions of rational individualism ultimately focused on a pair of closely drawn characterizations. First, Brown's extended analysis of Clithero Edny made this figure a barometer of unconscious instincts as they rose to the narrative surface throughout the novel. The reader first encountered this enigmatic character as a ghostly "apparition," a "robust and strange, and half-naked" figure digging and crying at the foot of a tree whose activity was both "mysterious and obscure." As Clithero recounted, he could not fully control his actions because of frequent episodes of sleepwalking. "My thoughts found their way to my lips without my being conscious of it," he noted about his condition, "and . . . my steps wandered forth unknowingly and without the guidance of my will." Moreover, his ungovernable instincts reflected "a violent internal struggle" that made him unknowable to others. His appearances and actions were misleading, he informed an acquaintance, and attempts to interpret them comprised "a tissue of destructive errors" (pp. 10, 89, 34, 35-36).

Accused of murder before plunging into the wilderness, the fleeing Clithero was a tormented man. Having killed before in his native land, he carried a heavy burden of guilt as he fled to America "not . . . to accuse others but myself." Fearing that "the worm that gnaws me will never perish," Clithero anguished over his domination by the darker impulses of his nature: "My fate is uniform. The demon that controuled me at first still in the fruition of power. I am entangled in his fold, and every effort that I make to escape only involves me deeper." It is important to note that Sarsefield—who demonstrated the superior power of paternal authority— quickly recognized Clithero's lunacy while Edgar never did. As the older man warned of this libidinous figure, "here, all remedies are vain. Consciousness itself is the malady." Equally significant, Sarsefield perceived the sleepwalker's threat of social subversion. In words resonant with the imagery of declining paternalism, he denounced Clithero as a "madman" and "atrocious criminal" whose conduct illustrated a clear principle: "liberty is dangerous" for the unfettered individual (pp. 36, 277, 291).

Brown's fascination with the murky underside of human rationality ultimately settled on Edgar Huntly. As both the narrator of the novel and its key figure, this protagonist slowly revealed himself as a creature of confused perceptions and profound unconscious impulses. Indeed, much of the novel's drama stemmed from Edgar's dawning awareness of his intense internal divisions. As the story opened, the young protagonist appeared dramatically alone. While still a boy, both of his parents and one sibling had been murdered by an Indian raiding party. Unable to contemplate "the image of a savage without shuddering," he grew up under an uncle's roof with a distinct sense of lonely self-reliance. This sensibility flowered into a kind of Lockean individualism, as Huntly grew convinced that his own sensory experiences would lead to knowledge as a light that would "burst upon my ignorance of myself and of mankind!" This confident individualism at times slipped into an arrogant solipsism. As Edgar once described himself,

> Few, perhaps, among mankind have undergone vicissitudes of peril and wonder equal to mine. The miracles of poetry, the transitions of enchantment, are beggarly and mean compared with those which I had experienced. Passage into new forms, overleaping the bars of time and space, reversal of the laws of inanimate and intelligent existence had been mine to perform and to witness. (pp. 173, 6, 239)

Huntly's self-assurance flowered in a Godwinian creed of materialism and reason. Edgar maintained an enlightened commitment "to deify necessity and universalize matter, to destroy the popular distinctions between soul and body." This protagonist, for instance, declared his faith in human rationality in his initial encounters with Clithero. The Irishman's problems, Edgar mused, "argued phrenzy rather than prejudice; but phrenzy, like prejudice, was curable. Reason was no less an antidote to the illusions of insanity like his, than to the illusions of error." He confidently asserted that his powers of intellect and sympathy, brought to bear through "the perserverance of benevolence," would replace Clithero's desperate impulses with "better thoughts" (pp. 132, 133, 95, 111).

This buoyant belief in rationalism and individual efficacy, however, rapidly began to capsize in *Edgar Huntly* as its protagonist embarked upon a nightmarish journey of self-discovery. With his terrifying awakening at the bottom of a cave, Edgar found himself plunged deep into both the wilderness and his own psyche. Subsequent discoveries shocked him. Lying on a rocky floor in the darkness, Edgar concluded that he was either experiencing a horrible dream or suffering from some "tormenting vision . . . in my own distempered imagination." Facing his libido for the first time, Huntly became aware of a powerful, murderous impulse. Hungry and desperate, he anticipated "the delight I should experience in rending some living animal to pieces, and drinking its blood and grinding its quivering fibres between my teeth." After killing an attacking panther and eating part of the raw carcass, Huntly then murdered an Indian blocking the escape route by plunging a hatchet into his chest. Pausing from this orgy of killing, he was shocked by a primitive surge of revitalization: "Never was any delight worthy of comparison with the raptures which I then experienced. Life, that was rapidly ebbing, appeared to return upon me with redoubled violence. My languors, my excruciating heat, vanished in a moment, and I felt prepared to undergo the labours of Hercules" (pp. 164, 180).

Edgar's regeneration through violence continued through a libidinous bonding with his Indian adversaries. On the one hand, a series of brutal encounters fostered within him "a spirit vengeful, unrelenting, and ferocious" and he admitted to developing "the misguided fury of a maniac" regarding these aborigines. On the other hand, Huntly claimed a passing knowledge of the Delaware language and expressed admiration for the "patience under hardship, and contention with fatigue" displayed by Indian warriors. This latent, half-conscious attraction to the dark, forbidden values associated with Indian life crystallized in Brown's sensational rendering of one of Edgar's battles. Having vanquished his foe and passed out from the incredible physical exertion, the young man later awoke to this scene:

My head rested upon something, which, on turning to examine, I found to be one of the slain Indians. . . . My head had reposed upon the breast of him

whom I had shot in this part of his body. The blood had ceased to ooze from
the wound, but my dishevelled locks were matted and steeped in that gore
which had overflowed and choked up the orifice.

Having become an unwitting blood-brother to his dead, savage opponent,
an exhausted Huntly finally reached a stage of genuine insight into his
own potential for brutality. He "aspired to transcend the rest of animals in
all that is common to the rational and the brute," he admitted, "as well as
in all by which they are distinguished from each other."[25]

Thus, Huntly's terrifying wilderness adventures transformed his perception of both the world and himself. His earlier love of nature and its
delights—"my devotion to the spirit that breathes its inspiration in the
gloom of forests and on the verge of streams"—now gave way to a profound distrust of the "mysterious power" lurking in the woods and rivers
and caves. Moreover, the dark and irrational instincts that had first welled
up with Waldegrave's murder—Edgar once described them as his "impulses of vengeance," "hasty rage," and "fiery sentiment"—grew so large as to
overwhelm his normal mildness of manner. Somehow the journey through
the wild had plumbed the depths of his nature and uncovered a heart of
darkness, and Edgar was stunned to discover that he was not the rational
creature he had assumed: "All my education and the habits of my life tended to unfit me for a contest and a scene like this. But I was not governed
by the soul which usually regulates my conduct. I had imbibed from the
unparalleled events which had lately happened a spirit vengeful, unrelenting, and ferocious."[26]

An unsettling feature of this growing self-awareness, however, was
Huntly's discovery of an obsessive identification with Clithero. In fact,
Brown depicted the maniacal Irishman as almost an alter ego for the protagonist. Striking parallels and similarities appeared. Both young men grew
up with adoptive parents. Both shared a common father-figure, Sarsefield,
an older man who had taught Edgar and then married Clithero's patroness. Both disappeared into the wilderness for an isolated testing of
their will to survive. More important, these linkages began to preoccupy
Huntly. Early in the narrative, Edgar wondered about why he chose to
chase down Clithero, "to tread, as closely as possible, in his footsteps, and
not to lose sight of him till the termination of his career." Conversing with
the stranger at another point, he extended sympathy and offered the possibility of becoming "my best friend." "I am no stranger to your gnawing
cares," Edgar reassured Clithero; "to the deep and incurable despair that

haunts you, to which your waking thoughts are a prey, and from which sleep cannot secure you." These strong sentiments of bonding finally prompted Huntly to ask a blunt, self-examining question: "why should my whole attention and activity be devoted to this man?" (pp 18, 31, 32, 131).

Edgar's discovery of his own sleepwalking clinched the tie between the two characters. Sarsefield, the novel's emblem of paternal authority, had first deduced Edgar's somnabulism and offered it as the solution to a number of mysterious occurrences. Instantly accepting this proposition, Edgar confessed that he must be subject to "a freak of noctambulation." Moreover, he immediately connected this sleepwalking habit to his alter ego. "What explanation was more obvious?" he admitted. "What but this solution ought to have been suggested by the conduct I had witnessed in Clithero?" This common proclivity, Huntly concluded, bound the two together in a tangle of irrationality and distress. As a shocked Edgar noted when he became aware of his own sleepwalking,

> Clithero had buried his treasure with his own hands as mine had been secreted by myself, but both acts had been performed during sleep. The deed was neither prompted by the will, nor noticed by the senses of him, by whom it was done. . . . By his own hands, is constructed the mass of misery and error in which his steps are forever involved.

For Huntly, this empathy grew so strong that he came to see the lunatic Irishman as almost a secret partner in his own unconscious, a dark reflection of his own personality (pp. 247–49, 260, 261, 278, 263).

Brown's "doubling" of character in this novel did not restrict itself to Edgar and Clithero. Many intertwined or duplicated figures darted in and out of the narrative with striking effect. For instance, in Edgar's mind the Waldegrave siblings seemed inseparable since, in his words, "connected with the image of my dead friend was that of his sister." With Weymouth's sudden appearance, another doubling appeared. "I loved Waldegrave," claimed this stranger. "With his life, my own existence and property were, I have reason to think, inseparably united." Clithero's life history revealed still more mirrored images. Mrs. Lorimer and her niece Claire so powerfully resembled each other that "nature seemed to have preeluded every difference between them but that of age." Even more important for Clithero's plight, his patroness had an actual biological twin, Arthur Wiatte, and "the resemblance between them was exact to a degree almost incredible." While Mrs. Lorimer was benevolence incarnate, her twin reveled in depravity, wickedness, and "pure unadulterated evil." When Clithero accidentally killed the vicious Wiatte, of course, it triggered his descent into madness. Thus, *Edgar Huntly* presented a pantheon of characters that, far from existing in splendid isolation, were stalked by doubled personalities and shadowy alter egos (pp. 130, 141, 49, 45–46).

Such themes ultimately converged in the broadest and most unsettling motif of Brown's final major novel: the fragmentation of individual identity. For characters whose social roots were torn from the earth, whose actions often seemed inexplicable even to themselves, and whose personalities faced grotesque mirrored images at nearly every turn, self-deception became the horrible stuff of daily existence. Several spokesmen in the novel confirmed this conclusion. The madman Clithero, in a momentary flash of lucidity, flatly told Edgar that "You, like others, are blind to the most momentous consequences of your own actions." Huntly eventually confessed that he had erred "not through sinister or malignant intentions, but from the impulse of misguided, indeed, but powerful benevolence." He brooded that perhaps everyone was a subject of destiny wherein each was caught in a trap of his own making. Entangled in error and misperception, a person's "efforts to relieve himself are fruitless as those with which he attempted the relief of others." Finally, at the novel's end, when the validity of his actions and judgments had collapsed like a house of cards, Edgar let loose his anguish and frustration: "Disastrous and humiliating is the state of man! By his own hands, is constructed the mass of misery and error in which his steps are forever involved. . . . How little cognizance have men over the actions and motives of each other! How total is our blindness with regard to our own performances!" These literary strokes painted a disturbing portrait. The vaunted individualism of the expanding liberal republic, Brown suggested in *Edgar Huntly*, was in fact a hollow conceit. Coming apart from within under the pressures of social performance, the isolated individual disintegrated into a "personae"—a fragmented, splintered creature for whom self-deceit was unavoidable and the deception of others natural. An American society of Edgars and Clitheros indeed portrayed "new springs of action," as Brown had predicted, but the results were more unsettling than inspiring. Individual liberation, it seemed, had only led into a new wilderness of social, cultural, and psychological confusion.[27]

III

An exhausted Charles Brockden Brown paused wearily at the dawn of the nineteenth century. Investing an incredible amount of intellectual and psychological energy into the writing of four novels in just two years, the twenty-nine-year-old author had achieved a great deal almost in spite of himself. The appearance of *Wieland, Ormond, Arthur Mervyn,* and *Edgar Huntly* offered a fitting climax to the conflicts and traumas—many of them self-imposed—of his early career. These texts composed a kind of literary diary that recorded the internal struggles, fluctuations, and displacements that had marked Brown's confrontation with the liberalizing tendencies of post-Revolutionary America. Relentlessly probing both self and society, these novels had depicted erratically but brilliantly the changing social forms and fluid states of mind characteristic of this volatile age. They focused on the internal and external travails of individuals swept up in the powerful currents of early capitalist culture. They featured young male and female protagonists perched on the threshold of maturity, making life-shaping decisions while under unfamiliar pressures for social performance. Ultimately, Brown's major novels helped mediate transforming social practice and cultural perception in the early republic. They did so in several ways.

In the manner of Richardson and Rousseau, Brown tried to use the novel as a powerful instrument of moral instruction. Combining striking Gothic atmospheres, outlandishly emotional literary style, and heavy-handed moralizing, he created a didactic fiction aimed at a popular audience of literate, educated readers. His goal was the promotion of virtuous self-control among an ambitious and restless population. In an essay, the writer explained the moral thrust of his fiction:

> Those who prate about the influence of novels to unfit us for solid and useful reading, are guilty of a double error: for in the first place, a just and powerful picture of human life in which the connection between vice and misery, and between facility and virtue is vividly portrayed, is the most solid and useful reading that a moral and social being . . . can read; and in the second place, the most trivial and trite of these performances are, to readers of certain ages and intellects, the only books they will read.[28]

Less deliberately, Brown also shaped in his fiction a forceful social critique that rested on a rather dark reading of individual human agency. Perceiving a cloudy cast to the liberationist atmosphere of the post-Revolutionary republic, Brown explored a crumbling of paternal authority and hierarchical tradition, and its replacement by a lonely and morally uncertain individualism. His characters continuously betrayed strong instincts for deception and fraud, masks and manipulation, social ambition and ethical fluidity. Stretching from *Wieland*'s religious mania to *Ormond*'s moral

confrontations, from *Arthur Mervyn*'s diseased city to *Edgar Huntly*'s violent wilderness, Brown's books illuminated a dark and bloody social ground
in late eighteenth-century America.

Brown's frenzied novel writing ultimately penetrated the veneer of social practice and cultural perception to reach the psychological interior of
liberalizing values. His late 1790s fiction doggedly searched for genuine,
coherent selves behind the inflated rhetoric of individual aspiration. Such
figures never appeared. Instead, Brown's novels paraded a collection of
fragmented characters as they stumbled forth from their hiding places in
basements and secret studies, closets and caves. Desperately sounding the
hidden depths of their own personalities while gauging the artifice of others, these anguished individuals struggled with mirrored images of themselves and frantically tried to hold together their faltering perceptions and
splintering identities. In many ways Carwin and Ormond, Clara and Constantia, Arthur and Clithero, Welbeck and Edgar were at odds with themselves as well as their society.

This uneasy juxtaposition of self and society, this precarious balancing
of warring elements within the personality, had made for a creative tension
in this young Philadelphia author. It had provoked and inspired four novels in an astonishingly brief period of time as Brown became a skilled in-
terrogator of the fragmented "personae" of emerging market society. His
private struggles had produced a striking analysis of the public pathology
of the liberalizing republic. Such a pressurized sensibility, however, had
taken a heavy toll. By 1800 an emotionally spent and frustrated Brown was
looking for a way out.

SIX

# 鐵‖ The Writer as Bourgeois Moralist

On or about April 1800 Charles Brockden Brown changed. In a despondent letter to his brother James, the young author confessed that "gloominess and out-of-nature incidents" had tainted his early novels. The time had come, he wearily admitted, "for dropping the doleful tone and assuming a cheerful one, or at least substituting moral causes and daily incidents in place of the prodigious or the singular. I shall not fall hereafter into that strain. Book-making, as you observe, is the dullest of all trades, and the utmost that any American can look for in his native country is to be reimbursed his unavoidable expenses." This rather sullen, forlorn admission seemed to belie the upward trajectory of Brown's literary endeavors. The burst of novel writing over the previous few years had fulfilled his literary agenda, focused his radical social criticism, and relieved his intense adolescent build-up of psychological pressure. The result had been a quartet of brilliant, wild, complex fictions that would elicit much critical commentary over the next few decades. The Philadelphian seemed poised at the threshold of a distinguished literary career, prepared to become, perhaps, America's first entry into the pantheon of great writers in the early modern Atlantic world.[1]

Brown's efforts as a professional writer, however, began to collapse almost as quickly as they had accelerated. His novels sold poorly, and this failure sapped both emotional and financial reserves. The inexorable forces of marketplace individualism in the expanding republic—the very forces Brown had confronted and struggled with in his fiction—seem to have cornered him by the end of the century. Economic success as a writer depended on sales, which in turn demanded popularity. Both of these eluded Brown. Moreover, by 1800 the struggling author's growing desire for a wife, children, and family stability lent even greater urgency to his plight. Genteel poverty, if an acceptable condition for an unmarried and aspiring author, offered no attraction to any respectable young woman.

Thus, by the early nineteenth century, Brown began a significant retrenchment in his life. While earlier pressures of career choice, parental expectations, and emotional upheaval had produced the decision to become a professional writer, a gradual erosion of those hopes now led to a second transformation. Brown began a withdrawal from the literary scene. He took one more half-hearted stab at fiction writing with two domestic novels that seemed deliberately aimed at a popular audience. As this literary endeavor fell flat, he bitterly rejected fiction altogether—at least for the public—and moved in different directions. Brown became involved with his family's mercantile business, married the daughter of a Philadelphia minister, and became a father. In addition, he entered the world of journalism as editor of, successively, three journals of letters and opinion in his native city. In the process, this intense intellectual began to formulate an important new public role: cultural critic and defender of bourgeois values.

Pulling back from radical social criticism, moving away from the breathtaking possibilities of the new novel genre, settling into the routine of family and business life, by 1805 Brown had remade himself once again. He negotiated an uneasy peace with America's expanding market society, and with himself as well, and engaged in a process of cultural and political redefinition. With his customary emotional cycle of fits and starts, deep doubts and utopian enthusiasm, Brown began to reposition himself as a bourgeois moralist in an ascending culture of capitalism. Hints of this dynamic change came in a final, futile attempt at novel writing. Connecting the personal upheaval and creativity of the 1790s with the moral consolidations of the new century, Brown's last two books of fiction built a cultural bridge to the future.

I

Charles Brockden Brown's final pair of published novels offered an obvious contrast to his earlier efforts. Their titles (*Clara Howard* and *Jane Talbot*) indicated a decided shift of gender sensibility away from the male-titled and dominated books of the 1790s. Their content, however, revealed this to be but one part of a broader literary and cultural change. As stories of domestic maneuver in which virtuous, morally willful female characters tamed restless, morally adrift males, these texts fulfilled their author's new determination to abandon "prodigious," "gloomy," and "singular" themes.

Yet these works were much more than sentimental, didactic tales cynically aimed at a popular audience, as many critics have long believed. Instead, these domestic novels explored, in fairly complex fashion, the cultural and ideological dimension of Brown's early nineteenth-century adjustment. The author may have utilized the sentimental form in an attempt to sell books, but that form became the vehicle for a more profound reconsideration of American values. These books answered many of the why's and wherefore's of Brown's retreat from radicalism and embrace of bourgeois moralism.[2]

While a certain amount of overlap probably occurred, *Clara Howard* seems to have been written before its counterpart. Likely begun in the late summer of 1800 and finished in the spring of the following year, the novel was published in June 1801.[3] The highly sentimental plot revolved around the romantic and moral entanglements of three primary characters: Edward Hartley, Mary Wilmot, and Clara Howard. Initially, the focus of this epistolary novel fell on Edward, a poor rural boy who had been befriended and tutored by an English gentleman named Mr. Howard. When Howard departed rather suddenly for Europe, his young protégé headed for the city to become a watchmaker's apprentice and begin the climb to social respectability. At this point romance entered the picture. Shortly after his arrival, Edward met Mary Wilmot, a plain young woman almost ten years his elder whose once-wealthy family had fallen into decline. Mary now supported herself and her brother by working as a seamstress, and she fell in love with her new acquaintance. Edward did not reciprocate Mary's love, but considered marriage because of her virtue. He grew more attracted to matrimony, however, when the young woman unexpectedly inherited $5,000. Edward and Mary agreed to wed after a six-month waiting period. In the meantime, Howard surprised everyone by returning to America with a wife and lovely stepdaughter, Clara. At the same time, a man named Morton suddenly appeared and claimed Mary's inheritance.

Here the novel's narrative became mired in a swamp of complexity. Edward entered Howard's household, was treated as a son, and rapidly became infatuated with the beautiful Clara. Mary, believing that her inheritance was lost and that Edward should not enter a loveless marriage with her, fled the city in the company of friends. When an explanatory letter to her fiancé was misplaced, her disappearance seemed final. At this point, Clara Howard moved to center stage. Although she had fallen in love with Edward, her sense of self-sacrifice proved more powerful. She demanded that her suitor find Mary and wed her, even offering half her fortune to support the match. Edward, forced to marry a woman he did not love by the one he did, dutifully set off in search of Mary. Before finding her, however, he fell ill with a near-fatal fever and the saintly Clara rescinded his banishment. The overjoyed young man revived and departed to make his peace with his former fiancée. The narrative now offered its central, if rather stilted, moral dilemma. After accidentally meeting Mary, Clara insisted once again that Edward marry the older woman. Mary, in the meantime, had fallen in love with a Mr. Sedley, and thus rejected her previous suitor's proposal. Caught in the middle of a tortuous situation in which neither woman seemed to want him, a despairing Edward left the city for life in the wilderness. Again he fell ill, and letters reached him which finally resolved the situation. Mary informed him of her intent to marry Sedley, a move that allowed Clara to drop her opposition and declare her love for Edward. The novel ended with plans in motion for both weddings.

Without doubt, *Clara Howard* was the weakest of all Brown's novels. As critics have observed, the tale liberally borrowed many incidents and situations from the author's earlier works. Its moral situations were contrived, its characters stereotyped and artificial, and its language heavy with overwrought sentimentalism. In terms of literary merit, the book represented a long step backward for Brown. Even with these defects, however, *Clara Howard* contained much of interest for students of early American national culture. Buried beneath the vapid prose and inane plot lay certain ideological and cultural treasures that revealed a great deal about Brown himself and the transforming era in which he wrote. With its self-conscious rendering of gender and morality, and its ongoing juxtaposition of romantic love and utilitarian profit, the novel illuminated certain aspects of the consolidating capitalist culture that its author was coming to embrace. This appeared especially in Brown's central trio of characters.

Edward Hartley, the driving force early in the novel, presented an intriguing portrait of aspiring individualism. His self-description in the book's opening epistle introduced the whole story as a variant on the Franklinian success tale:

> You once knew me as a simple lad, plying the file and tweezers at the bench of a watchmaker, with no prospect before me. . . . I was sprung from obscurity, destitute of property, of parents, of paternal friends; was full of that rustic diffidence, that inveterate humility, which are alone sufficient to divert from us the stream of fortune's favor.

Such was I three years ago! Now am I rich, happy, crowned with every terrestrial felicity.

Underlining this theme throughout the text, Edward frequently denounced his own rural origins and their quietistic traditions. When his early benefactor, Mr. Howard, urged him to appreciate the dignified integrity of the farmer's life, the young man scoffed. "The rustic life was wholly unsuitable to my temper and taste," he recalled, as the prospect of status and money lured him to the city. Edward admitted that wealth and social position awed him with their "mysterious elevation." Even the friendship of the Howards fired his ambition, as the personal attention "from beings invested with such dazzling superiority, almost intoxicated my senses." In fact, midway through the novel Edward affirmed a dictum—"to retain humility and probity in spite of riches, and to effect the highest good of ourselves and others, by the use of them"—which epitomized his ambitious social creed.[4]

Mary Wilmot provided a study in contrast. In Brown's hands, she became a moral counterweight to the impetuous, aspiring Edward. Nine years older than the young man from the country and full of benevolence, she attracted his intense admiration. Mary fell in love with Edward, but slowly realized that his affection contained no passion. Thus, she refused to accept Edward's dutiful offer of marriage, and sacrificed her contentment to his. As she explained to him, "I sought your happiness. To be the author of it was an object of inexpressible longings. To be happy without you was impossible, but the misery of loneliness, however great, was less than that of being the spectator of your misery, or . . . defrauding you of the felicity attending marriage with a woman whom you could truly love." True to sentimental forms, Mary's nobility took a severe toll on her physical well-being. Emaciated and drained from her moral endeavors, she felt the steady "progress of death" and believed that "every hour accelerates my decay" (p. 16).

Even the virtues of Mary Wilmot, however, paled before those of the novel's namesake, Clara Howard. Combining the older woman's selflessness with a strength of will entirely her own, she was an apostle of self-denial. Denouncing "selfish regards" and "selfish gratification," she insisted that one should derive "more satisfaction from disinterested than selfish conduct." As part of her firm moral code, Clara also rejected mere "sensuality" and placed the material pleasures of wealth and status far back in the rank of values. "Have I not known, from infancy the pleasures of affluence and homage? Cannot I conceive the mortifications to one thus bred up, of poverty and labour?" she exclaimed to Edward. Nonetheless, she made clear her intent to sacrifice such comforts if necessary. Clara's willingness to give up the man she loved seemed to transcend a utilitarian calculus of pleasure and pain, gain and loss. She tried to explain to a puzzled Edward that his despondency reflected

> an heart incapable of perceiving the possibility of sacrificing my own personal gratification to that of another, and of deriving, from that very sacrifice, a purer and more lasting felicity. It shews you unable to comprehend that the welfare of another may demand self-denial from us, and that in bestowing benefits on others, there is a purer delight than in gratifications merely selfish and exclusive. (pp. 71–72, 77–78, 20, 24)

Brown's three primary characters in *Clara Howard* created a fascinating configuration of gender and ideology. Edward suggested that men threatened to become victims of the very social instincts that drove them to success. Lashing out against moral restraints that curbed his passions—"It is the system of nature that deserves my hatred and my curses; that system which makes our very virtues instrumental to our misery"—he acknowledged their validity and his own depravity. Ashamed of his "peasant" background and filled with "self-contempt and humiliation which pertain to that condition," he sought the "confidence and self-respect" that accrued to wealth and social advancement. Such striving produced great ambivalence, however, and Edward frequently chastised himself as a "mere earthworm" and an "obscure clown." In his bitter words, "all my desires are the instigators of guilt, and all my pleasures those of iniquity." Near the end of the novel, he had become so frustrated that he threatened to flee into the wilderness and "make myself akin to savages and tigers, and forget that I was once a man" (pp. 18, 53, 55, 112, 134).

Edward's personal incoherence eventually produced a clear result. He became a moral cripple desperately searching for healing and guidance. Clara Howard happily obliged. Even though in love with the young man, she upbraided Edward for his "cowardly and ignoble designs" in abandoning Mary and warned of the folly attending his greed: "Thou art fiery and impetuous, my friend. Thy spirit is not curbed by reason. There is no outrage or discretion—no crime against thyself—into which thy headlong spirit may not hurry thee." For his part, Edward humbly, even gratefully, submitted to Clara's moral dictations. Calling her "an angel" and his "heavenly monitor," he surrendered with the declaration, "Clara, thou hast conquered me." Even more important, he credited the young woman with healing his inner confusion and putting him on the path to virtue. "I am now master of my actions and thoughts," Edward told her, "and will steadily direct them to a single purpose" (pp. 21, 26, 90, 144, 22).

The force of Clara Howard's benevolence took on another important dimension in Brown's novel. Her task as moral lion-tamer broadened to include women as a group and emerged as a gendered cultural prerogative. By the end of *Clara Howard*, a sisterhood of moral teachers had arisen to dominate the text. For instance, Mary and Clara explicitly joined forces to guide Edward down the correct course of virtue. Only after consulting Mary was Clara prepared to wed Edward and heed "the sweet voice of an approving conscience." For her part, Mary reciprocated by telling her new female friend, "I exult that my feelings are akin to yours, and that it is in my power to vie with you in generosity." As if to underline their sisterhood, Brown disclosed that the two female protagonists were distantly related to one another as second cousins. Most important, perhaps, both women made clear to Edward the goal of this female crusade: moral authority. Near the end of the novel, Mary warned Edward: "Your Clara, the noblest of women, joins me in recalling you . . . to virtue and felicity." Clara put the matter more bluntly. As she told the young man, his "worldly knowledge and acumen may be greater, but in moral discernment much art thou still deficient; here I claim to be more than equal." In the face of this formidable female phalanx, Edward could only retreat while meekly acknowledging that Mary and Clara had rescued him from "disease," "anxiety," and "melancholy," a condition that had made him "half-crazy, shivering and glowing by turns" (pp. 141, 131–32, 96–97, 143, 147, 145).

Thus, *Clara Howard's* stilted form belied the intriguing cultural content within. Adopting sentimental literary conventions, Brown depicted a male-dominated public ambition harmonizing with female-dominated private self-restraint. Success, wealth, and happiness resulted for everyone: Clara and Edward wed riches and benevolence, while Mary did likewise in agreeing to marry the affluent businessman, Mr. Sedley. So Brown's first fictional foray after his passionate efforts of the 1790s, while doing little for his pocketbook and even less for his literary reputation, represented a critical stage in his ideological development. Distancing himself from the political and cultural radicalism of earlier books like *Alcuin* and *Arthur Mervyn*, the author moved decisively toward the moral consolidations of bourgeois society in early nineteenth-century America.

*Jane Talbot, a Novel* took an even longer step in the same direction. Although conceived by Brown as a more dramatic moral battleground—here a knot of seduction, religion, and money replaced *Clara Howard*'s rather insipid moral benevolence as the main theme—the story resonated with similar cultural overtones. The Philadelphian's second domestic novel had been started probably in early 1801, set aside while *Clara Howard* was rushed to completion and publication, and then resumed in the late summer of that same year. Finished sometime in the fall, the book finally appeared from a Philadelphia press in December 1801. Even though the novel would see an 1804 publication in England, it received scant critical notice and its sales remained quite low. Once again, however, *Jane Talbot*'s sentimental strategies and domestic devices disguised its important cultural content.[5]

The plot of *Jane Talbot* concerned the frustrated love affair of the novel's heroine, a young widow, and Henry Colden, a Godwinian radical. While deeply in love and determined to marry, these two characters found their plans thwarted by Mrs. Fielder, Jane's strong-willed, adoptive mother, and by Henry's father. The resistance flowed from a combination of political, religious, and moral issues. Mrs. Fielder, Jane's mentor and guardian, grew outraged when informed of Henry's religious skepticism, moral rationalism, and political nonconformity. To make matters even worse, she grew convinced that this profligate had plunged the two into adultery while Jane's husband was still alive. Digging in her heels, Mrs. Fielder used every power at her command to stop the match. The alleged seduction, of course, had never occurred and most of the novel consisted of long epistolary explanations and romantic maneuvers. Jane, caught between love for Henry and respect for her mother, anguished over the correct course of action. Mrs. Fielder refused to budge. Henry, pulled in different directions by his head and his heart, struggled to resolve the situation but ultimately began to crack under the pressure.

Throughout this travail—this is what elevated *Jane Talbot* several notches above the normal run of early sentimental fiction—Brown sustained an ongoing discussion of serious moral, religious, social, and epistemological questions. Arguments over the respective merits of religious faith, worldly wealth, reason and emotion, and male and female sensibility added a strong intellectual element to the book's rather maudlin love story. Such tendencies in the novel were reinforced by its subplots and minor characters. Jane's brother Frank, for instance, occasionally appeared in the text as a spendthrift, embezzler, and insatiable seeker of wealth. Playing on his sister's affection, he successfully overcame her scruples to borrow and waste large sums of money. Jane's late husband, Lewis, also made several ghostly appearances as a paragon of hard-working, self-satisfied bourgeois habits. And Miss Jessup, a flighty young woman carried away by her secret passion for Lewis Talbot, turned out to be a key in the plot: she forged the letter falsely implicating Jane and Henry in adultery. So by the time the story reached its rather predictable conclusion—the two young lovers surmounted all obstacles to finally marry—the novel had ventured beyond mere sentiment to engage some interesting cultural issues.

As in several of his earlier novels, Brown created in *Jane Talbot* a mutable atmosphere of fluctuating financial and moral values. Here, however, the contrast between the stilted, mawkish love story and its fluid social backdrop became striking. In a world increasingly driven by market forces and individualist ambition, the novel's characters slipped and staggered on the shifting cultural ground beneath them. Jane's brother, for instance, with his maneuvering and scheming, prompted from her this reflection: "I know that those who embark on pecuniary schemes are often reduced to temporary straits and difficulties; that ruin and prosperity frequently hang on the decision of the moment; that a gap may be filled up by a small effort seasonally made, which, if neglected, rapidly widens and irrevocably swallows up the ill-fated adventurer." In such a world of contingency and peril, moral fraud seemed even more threatening than financial fraud. As Jane pointed out, forgery and embezzlement were public crimes that could be punished. A loss of moral character—for example, an accusation that "robs a helpless woman of her reputation"—cut much deeper by producing enmity between the individual and "those whose affection is necessary to render life tolerable." In such a context, it was little wonder that the novel's characters frequently fell into agonizing reappraisals of religion and its correct moral principles. All agreed that "true religion" must consist of more than piety and doctrine, and must somehow include "*rational* activity for others' good." The precise benevolent principles remained elusive, however, and caused Brown's characters to fear a moral "void." Each struggled, in the words of one, "to comprehend myself."[6]

Full of moral flux and social uncertainty, Brown's second domestic novel evinced an additional theme: the nature of correct gender roles. This question centered on the issue of love and morality. Early in the novel, for instance, Jane felt compelled to compare males and females in matters of the heart. Men, she argued, were "sanguine and confident" while inclined to let "their words outstrip their feelings." Those of "ardent temper" could easily, and probably sincerely, love several women in one year. Women, by contrast, were naturally creatures of self-restraint. They "feel deeply but boast not," Jane insisted, and "their words generally fall short of their sentiments." Yet their passion, when aroused, was "hard to be escaped from." As if to illustrate the impulsive nature of men, *Jane Talbot*'s male figures ran the gamut of unacceptable emotional extremes. Lewis Talbot, Jane's first husband, exemplified the sturdy dullness of the bourgeois businessman in the early Republic. His religion was "steadfast and rational" and had produced a highly rationalized conduct that was "regular, sober, and consistent." "He was addicted to industry, was regular and frugal in his manner and economy. He had nothing of that specious and glossy texture which captivates inexperience and youth, and serves a substitute for every other virtue. While others talked about their duty, he was contented with performing it." Lewis's temperament made him an impassive, tedious companion, however, and his marriage to Jane had been a dreary one. At the other extreme, of course, stood Frank. Even as a boy Jane's brother had been "boisterous, ungrateful, imperious," and as an adult appeared "selfish and irascible beyond most other men." He displayed an attraction to "active amusements and sensual pleasures," and had deserted school for the illicit pleasures of gambling and whoring. Frank's embrace of "idleness and dissipation" gradually led him into various speculative schemes that proved financially disastrous. His lack of restraint brought ruin to himself, and near-ruin to his family before he fled the country for France (pp. 170, 223–24, 156–59, 172–200).

Regarding women, *Jane Talbot* offered a contrasting picture of social roles and moral principles. In a liberalizing society in which public activity remained regulated by gender, Brown's female characters sought to solidify their moral dominion in private life and domestic affairs. Their struggles illustrated the complexity of women's cultural plight. As Jane noted early in the narrative, even as a young girl she had become convinced that while males were ambitious, self-seeking, and aggressive, females were "soft, pliant, affectionate." These female qualities could lead to self-destruction, as the example of Miss Jessup showed. With an insatiable hunger for love and emotional connection, the desperate young woman had displayed a "volatile, giddy, thoughtless character." Nearly sick with passion for Lewis Talbot, she was driven to acts of forgery, lying, and character assassination before recanting in a deathbed confession. Mrs. Fielder, however, compensated for the sentimental indulgences of Miss Jessup. As Jane's mother, she emerged in the narrative as a massive, unmovable moral force. When informed of Henry Colden's radical views on social and religious matters, and after learning of Henry and Jane's supposed adultery, she denounced Henry as a sensual "visionary and romantic" who loved "to intoxicate the women with melodious flattery." Bitterly opposed to this dangerous rationalist with his agenda for revolutionary social change, she pictured him as "the grand deceiver." "How nicely does he select, how adroitly manage his tools!" she accused. Both Jane and Henry eventually submitted to this "stern and inflexible spirit" and acknowledged her moral dominion. Significantly, marriage between the two took place after Mrs. Fielder learned the truth about the false adultery charge shortly before her own death, and after Henry had reformed his character to meet her standards. As a counterweight to women like Miss Jessup, this formidable matron became a symbol of female moral influence in the domestic realm (pp. 156, 333–35, 225–29, 303, 376, 326, 394, 431).

This entire mélange of social stresses, religious turmoil, gender definition, and moral struggle settled on the shoulders of the novel's two primary characters, Jane Talbot and Henry Colden. Brown's male protagonist, for instance, stepped forward as a seething mass of emotional insecurities, half-held convictions, and self-loathing. Describing himself as "sensual and volatile," Henry confessed that the "image of myself in my own mind is a sorry compound of hateful or despicable qualities." An alienated Godwinian intellectual struggling in a utilitarian society, his elevated views of science and letters brought spasms of self-doubt: "I cannot labour for bread; I cannot work to live. . . . My very nature unfits me for any profitable business. My dependence must ever be on others or on fortune. . . . I am not indolent, but my activity is vague, profitless, capricious. No lucrative or noble purpose impels me. I aim at nothing but selfish gratification." Henry's inability to find a purposeful career led to fears that a species of "insanity" had destroyed his capacity to act. Desperately seeking to "unfold myself *to* myself," the young man began to believe destiny was slipping ever more out of his control. "Let things take their course," he lamented. "I can do nothing." Following its own emotional logic, this internal fragmentation threatened a dark conclusion. Overwhelmed by "this excruciating, this direful melancholy" and feeling "comfortless and friendless," Henry contemplated suicide as a source of relief: "Nothing is sweet but the prospect of oblivion" (pp. 204, 266, 267, 382, 383, 378).

Henry's death wish never came true. Instead of disintegration completing its fatal course, the faltering young man found his cultural bearings and righted himself emotionally. The way in which he did so—relying upon female morality to restore his shattered persona—proved highly revealing. Despairing over the direction of his life, Henry frantically sought to steady his fluctuating character through "some kind of principle by which to regulate my conduct." When his Godwinian principles—enlightened self-interest, scientific rationalism, utilitarian morality—failed to support him on this count, Jane Talbot stepped into the void. As an advocate of benevolence, self-control, and Christianity she became a source of "steadfastness and virtue" for Henry. His deep respect for "this feminine excellence, this secondary and more valuable self" led him to describe the young woman as "my sweet physician." Her influence was slow-working, however, for only after a long, meditative overseas voyage could Henry truly embrace pious morality as a means to reconnect his fragmented character. Jane's principles of Christian benevolence, he concluded, had shored up his moral framework and "made *my mind whole*" (pp. 390, 228, 309, 382, 311).

As for Jane herself, moral solidity and virtue had not come easily. This heroine had struggled to conquer her own baser instincts as a prerequisite for helping Henry overcome his. "I am very far from being a wise girl," she admitted at the novel's outset, and acknowledged that "there are bounds beyond which passion cannot go without counteracting its own purposes." Fearing that her passions threatened to overwhelm moral barriers, she vowed to "enjoy the rewards of self-denial and forbearance." Through a strong measure of self-control, Jane thus felt able to treat her suitor benevolently. " I want to act with a view to your interests and wishes," she informed Henry in the spirit of self-sacrifice. Jane was so sincere that when Henry's father threatened to disinherit him if he became engaged, she pledged to give him up for his own material well-being. Her explanation summarized the spirit of virtuous self-denial: "What I did was in oblivion of self; [it] was from a duteous regard to his genuine and lasting happiness." Henry became the ultimate object of Jane's moral crusade, as she sought not only to gain his love but to shape his character. The determined young woman envisioned herself as Henry's wife, happily playing the role of domestic manager, patroness of the cultivated arts, mother, and not least important, moral instructor. His lack of religious belief—"the most deplorable calamity that can befall a human creature"—became the particular target for her endeavors. What Jane called her "unconquerable zeal to rescue him from this calamity" aptly summarized her self-imposed task of moral stewardship (pp. 141–52, 255, 317–20, 399, 284–86, 302–3).

Thus, the conclusion of *Jane Talbot*, with a newly pious Henry set to wed the morally triumphant Jane, reached the same destination as *Clara*

*Howard*. In both cases, sentimental forms and language masked an important cultural realignment at the heart of the stories. Intertwined with their author's own personal struggles, Brown's last two published novels suggested the emergence of a profound new pattern in early nineteenth-century America: the old republican tradition of self-sacrificing "virtue" was becoming feminized and privatized, while an emerging liberal imperative of "self-interest" appeared increasingly masculinized and publicized.[7] Most important, these instincts could be, indeed should be, harmonized through the mediation of sentimental love and marriage, with liberty and profit for all. For Charles Brockden Brown, this process rescued him from the ideological and moral upheaval of early manhood in the 1790s, and pulled him into a calming new world of bourgeois stability. It demanded wrenching accommodations on his part, but it was a world that would win both his emotional loyalties and literary talents.

II

*Clara Howard* and *Jane Talbot*, in terms of sales, failed miserably. Their sentiment and romance did not attract a popular audience, as their despairing author had hoped. Ironically, this collapse of literary hope reinforced the larger cultural accommodations represented in the novels themselves. Brown's psychological state around the dawn of the nineteenth century, for instance, in its evolution from rage to resignation, embodied a process of *embourgeoisement*. So too did his personal life as it became submerged in courtship, marriage, and children. In a marked development from anguished artist to family man, Brown's own life seemed to mirror the social and cultural forces transforming the American republic by the early 1800s.

With the opening of a new century, the Philadelphia author revamped his writing activity, slowly abandoning fiction for other genres. Brown had been involved in several journalistic enterprises throughout the 1790s. In 1798, for example, he had been a primary contributor to the Philadelphia *Weekly Magazine*, a journal of opinion and belles letters. Now Brown's journalistic endeavors quickened as his novelistic ones faded. From April 1799 to the autumn of 1800 he served as editor of the *Monthly Magazine and American Review*, a publication backed by his circle of intellectual friends in New York City. Then, in 1803, the enterprising writer founded another monthly journal in Philadelphia, the *Literary Magazine and American Register*, and edited it until its demise in late 1807. Finally, he was editor of the *American Register, or General Repository of History, Politics, and*

*Science* from 1806 to 1810. Brown also contributed generously throughout the early 1800s to his friend Joseph Dennie's *Port-Folio*.[8]

The abandonment of the novel for journalistic enterprises came at a heavy personal cost. Brown evinced extreme bitterness about his failed literary career and attempted to dismiss it altogether. In a public confession in 1803, he denigrated his earlier writings. "I should enjoy a larger share of my own respect at the present moment," he stated bluntly in the first number of the *Literary Magazine*, "if nothing had ever flowed from my pen, the production of which could be traced to me." This self-hatred also flared outward into a stinging critique of American cultural values. The republic's citizens had become so enamored of the "love of gain" and "the main chance," he angrily wrote, that a genuine appreciation of literature and science was all but impossible. He continued:

> Perhaps there never was such a theatre for *speculation* as the United States have presented for the last twelve or fifteen years. On this theatre thousands have played a part, equally astonishing to the sober calculator and humiliating to the moralist. The influence of this system has extended to the remotest corners of the union; so that perhaps a more mercenary and speculating nation than our own hardly at this day exists.
>
> The natural and necessary influence of such a state of public taste and public sentiment, must be in various ways highly mischievous. . . . When an idea becomes prevalent, that wealth is everything, and that nothing can atone for the want of property, we may expect to see most men bending their whole attention to this object, and neglecting the cultivation of their minds as an affair of secondary moment.[9]

Brown's reassessment of his writing and its relation to American society also came from deep in his own psyche. Once again, an intense self-absorption boiled to the surface as it had earlier in the 1790s. Now the psychological effects remained more muted, and the lashing out was more controlled. Brown wrestled with a strong sense of social isolation, observing at one point in 1801 that "we know nobody, and can therefore seek employment and amusement only in ourselves." At other times this solitude appeared a mere "wretched possession" far beneath the invigorating "images flowing from society." Such ambiguous reactions eventually settled into a pattern of impassive, morose alienation. Describing "the surface of his life" as "tolerably smooth," he admitted to getting by in terms of mere "food, raiment, and repose." Intellectual vigor seemed to have evaporated. "All the inanimate objects in this city are uniform, monotonous, and dull,"

Brown wrote a correspondent from Philadelphia in 1800. "I have been surprised at the little power they have over my imagination, at the sameness that everywhere reigns." Literary fame, he decided, was a despicable thing while "obscurity" offered "numberless delights." By 1801 the disgruntled ex-novelist presented a persona that was part self-pity, part sullen resignation.[10]

In this context Brown gradually came to terms with journalism as a career that would allow a modicum of both writing and profit. The task proved difficult, as economic and ideological pressures pulled in several directions. On the one hand, he upheld the journalist's pursuit of gain, albeit a bit defensively. In the 1803 inaugural issue of the *Literary Magazine*, his "Editor's Address" offered self-assurances on this point. "The project is not a mercenary one," he wrote. "At the same time, he [the editor] cannot but be desirous of an ample subscription, not merely because pecuniary profit is acceptable, but because this is the best proof which he can receive that his endeavors to amuse and instruct have not been unsuccessful." On the other hand, however, Brown frequently complained about "the apathy and disregard apparently shown by Americans to literature and science," an attitude that made serious journalistic writing a risky financial proposition. The typical citizen's concern with material interests, the writer noted sourly, did not create a public atmosphere for "estimating the productions of genius, taste, and learning." Overall, Brown was forced to admit that journalistic success depended on the American proclivity for newspapers. This habit was unavoidable in a commercial republic, he granted, where political information and market information were necessary for survival. The journalistic combination of "literature, lucre, and politics," Brown admitted, must be granted its usefulness. In less sanguine moments, however, the editor described popularity as a shallow achievement fleetingly bestowed by "the veneration of the multitude." It usually attended a writing enterprise "with no moral or beneficial purpose whatever."[11]

Such ruminations led Brown to confront head-on a cultural predicament in the expanding liberal republic. The entrepreneurial ambition of the middling orders provided the vitality in American society, he admitted, yet this fact created tremendous difficulties for aspiring writers and artists. The people of the United States, he wrote in 1801, were "more distinguished than those of Europe as a people of business, and by an universal attention to the active and lucrative pursuits of life." This may have been politically desirable, but the artistic consequences were troubling. Aristocratic wealth, Brown pointed out, traditionally produced a "superfluity" of funds that flowed into the coffers of painters and writers. When wealth was more evenly divided in society, however, people concentrated on "a provision of absolute necessaries, before they think of conveniences; and . . . before they can indulge in the agreeable arts." For the Philadelphian this brought an obvious dilemma. Aristocracy, of course, was ideological anathema to this self-proclaimed radical. He also rejected the romantic opinion that genteel poverty stimulated literary genius, since a struggle for material survival only drained artistic energy. The writer's only alternative was to accept the republic's liberalizing society and work within its confines, attempting to harness its energy. Brown exposed the foundation for his new position in 1805: "Poverty is far from being a spur to genius; wealth is far less unfriendly, though its influence is certainly not propitious to it. It is the middle class that produces every kind of worth in the greatest abundance. We must not look for fertility on the hill top, nor at the bottom of the glen. It is only found in the plains and intermediate slopes."[12]

Brown's reconciliation to America's growing market society in the early nineteenth century appeared clearly in another aspect of his life. After nearly ten years of resistance, he finally caved in to family pressure and became a partner in his brothers' commercial enterprises. In 1801 he began office work in their trans-Atlantic trading company, and particularly focused on problems involved with mercantile and maritime law. In March of that year he ruefully told a correspondent, "I write to you in company, & with all the sounds, tools, & symbols of the gain-pursuing merchant about me." Brown assured friends that his new labors took only part of his time, so that many hours could still be devoted to reading and writing. Equally important, the business provided more financial security than fiction ever had. While mercantile activity certainly had its share of fluctuations and disappointments—particularly when intensification of the Napoleonic Wars brought maritime harassments and blockades—the profits still far outdistanced sales of his books. "This period is eminently prosperous for all with whom I am bound by the dear ties of relationship or friendship," he reported in 1803. "The more so by contrast with ancient difficulties and humiliations."[13]

A brief piece of fiction provided a tantalizing glimpse of the emotional currents that were sweeping Brown from the world of literature to that of business and journalism. Published in the *Monthly Magazine* of July 1800, "The Trials of Arden" was a short story about the tribulations of an intellectual wronged by public opinion. The plot involved a young immigrant teacher named Arden who became entangled in a murder mystery. When the eldest daughter in the family whom he tutored, Harriet Finch, was found murdered, suspicion fell immediately upon Arden. Having arrived in this New York town only three months before, the young man had been spotted in the area where the killing took place. His nervous behavior and abrupt resignation from the Finches' service sealed his fate. Smoldering community suspicion flamed into outrage, and Arden was pursued, arrested, and imprisoned. Circumstantial evidence and popular outcry made a guilty verdict at his trial all but inevitable. One juror, however, held out for Arden's innocence. An angry mob then attempted to capture and lynch the prisoner. When he escaped, their wrath turned upon the isolated juror who had insisted on his innocence, and this gentleman also fled the community. Almost a year later, a counterfeiter was arrested in Albany and, under interrogation, confessed to the Finch murder. Arden's vindication prompted embarrassment and apologies from his former accusers, and events reached a happy conclusion. The teacher married a young woman from the community whose support had helped rescue him, and their future prosperity was assured when it was revealed that Harriet Finch had bequeathed to Arden her entire estate.[14]

In the context of Brown's early century retrenchment, "The Trials of Arden" had fascinating implications. The protagonist was, as the author considered himself to be, an outsider in American society. The story's plot also involved another issue identified with Brown's own life: the young intellectual struggling to maintain his virtue against unpopularity and mindless persecution. Examining an evil perpetuated upon "the fame, peace, and life of one who merited a better fate," this tale pitted a deluded mob against a dignified, self-contained, even Christ-like individual:

> Nothing confounded observers more, than the sedateness of the man. . . . When called upon to defend himself, he complied with apparent reluctance; but, when he opened his mouth at the bar, averred his purity with astonishing collectiveness and fervency; while, at the same time, he declared his hopelessness of acquittal, his acquiescence in his fate, and his forgiveness of his persecutors.

Brown's sublimation of his own literary fate became even more obvious in his depiction of Mayo, the actual murderer. This criminal not only murdered, but embodied two other "demons" that Brown saw arrayed against him in turn-of-the-century America: the "counterfeiter," who feverishly sought wealth immorally, and the manipulator of false appearances who, "being specious and addressful, insinuated himself into Finch's confidence." In such a society of moral caprice and social distrust, the weary writer could wear his alienation as a badge of honor.[15]

The conclusion of "The Trials of Arden" provided a final indicator of Brown's cultural realignment in the early 1800s. Arden's courtship, marriage, and prosperity again paralleled the author's own life. In this period the Philadelphian not only embraced business and journalism, but desperately grasped for the security of marriage and family. As the financial failure of fiction writing had driven him away from the arena of letters, the slow evaporation of his old circle of intellectuals in New York City helped drive him back to the bosom of his family in Philadelphia. The death of Elihu Smith in 1798 had a particularly powerful impact. In January 1799 Brown wrote to his brother: "I have neither wife nor children to look up to me for food; and, in spite of all refinements, conjugal and paternal cares can never be fully transferred to one who has neither offspring nor spouse." Around the same time, he confessed to another correspondent that "my conception of the delights and benefits connected with love and marriage are exquisite." This lonely young man thus began to search for stability in emotional as well as material terms.[16]

In 1801 he began to find it. In that year Brown initiated a serious courtship of Elizabeth Linn, the daughter of a prominent Presbyterian minister from New York City. He had first met the young woman in November 1800 when she visited her brother—the Rev. John Blair Linn, also a minister—at his home in Philadelphia. Taken with her good looks, pleasant manners, and shy demeanor, Brown started to call regularly on Miss Linn and to correspond with her both at her brother's home and at her regular residence back in New York. The courtship would be an extended one—they would not be married until November 1804—and during that time the young writer would become close to the whole Linn clan. He grew quite fond of Elizabeth's three sisters, Susan, Rebecca, and Mary, while a strong friendship evolved with her brother John. The Philadelphia minister was a poet and essayist whose literary interests coincided with Brown's. The two developed a rich personal and professional relationship, with Linn even publishing pieces in Brown's *Literary Magazine*. When the minister died prematurely in August 1804, his brother-in-law wrote a public memorium.[17]

Brown's relationship with Elizabeth Linn proved crucial to his new life. The lonely writer had come to yearn for the security of marriage, as he revealed in 1803. Gaining a wife, he wrote, "may not be the only species

of felicity, and of all kinds of terrestrial bliss, it may be . . . [most] precarious in possession, but to *me*, THIS is the highest bliss." With great enthusiasm, and his usual lack of emotional subtlety, Brown plunged headlong
into romance and began a barrage of attention and letters. Miss Linn remained cautious. Perhaps bothered by religious reservations—Brown's
family had nixed several earlier love affairs because of the young women's
non-Quaker status—she also possessed a reserved temperament and was
intellectually insecure to the point of self-deprecation. Hence began a long
process of maneuver between the impetuous, impassioned Brown and the
chary, discreet Miss Linn.[18]

A fascinating record of this romantic minuet has survived in the form
of a fat cache of letters from Brown to his future wife. Written from December 1800 up through the spring of 1804—most were posted in 1801—
these missives provide much intriguing information about their author's
state of mind during this period. They also opened another angle of vision
on Brown's social and cultural readjustments in the early nineteenth century. More than just declarations of love for Elizabeth Linn, these didactic
letters formulated gender roles and cultural values in the aftermath of the
tumultuous, challenging 1790s. Subtly seeking to shape the character of
this young woman, and simultaneously realigning his own persona in light
of these gendered prerogatives, Brown clarified some of the outlines of an
emerging bourgeois culture.

He compulsively stressed the necessity of self-control. Brown's admonitions on this point permeated his letters to "my sweet friend," "my Elisa"—
two favorite terms for his correspondent—and most of them focused on
his own physical passions and moral character. Not unexpectedly, sexuality
emerged as the primary object of repression. The young man wrote frequently of his desire for "that sacred privacy so dear to lovers" and confessed that his "imagination was sometimes in danger of becoming too
strong for me." As he told Elisa, the "passion of the sexes is the source of
existence and happiness" and it could not be ignored either intellectually
or emotionally. "I should not be human," Brown argued, "if I did not muse
with rapture on the dear privileges of the wedded life." As soon as sex
raised its head, however, he leaped to restrain it on moral grounds. Reflection, he observed in many letters, was the most powerful "antidote to passion" and "the mind of genuine force will need no other expedient to restore its self-possession." Bringing reason to bear on instinct was difficult,
he admitted, and "I sometimes have need to struggle with the rising gust
of my impatience. But I shall always effectually struggle with it." While

reflection and passion tugged in different directions, they were not completely incompatible. As the Philadelphian vowed to his beloved, "My reason, as well as my heart, is thy worshipper."[19]

Brown's search for self-control also transcended the realm of physical lust. His flood of letters to Elizabeth Linn suggested a broader impulse toward character formation defined by sincerity, forthrightness, and moral solidity. This shaping of self involved the regulation of a host of libidinous drives and weaknesses – greed, pride, manipulation, anger. Cumulatively, such restraints would create a coherent, decisive, self-propelled individual. Brown's developing relationship with Elisa, for instance, brought forth an emotional defense of his sincerity. Lengthy assertions of "the purity, the fervency" of his feelings for her tumbled over one another in his letters. An intense struggle to "obtain the victory over my selfishness and vanity" prompted this explanation of his moral character: "My inmost soul is not to be heard or seen. Into that you cannot enter. You must rely for your knowledge on my sentiments, on my words and looks. You have no interest in misapprehending these. If *they* mislead you, who but I am to be blamed . . . for my happiness requires that you know me for what I am." For Brown, this harnessing of emotion and selfishness created a simple imperative: "Self-denial is a wholesome thing." Pronounced with varying degrees of enthusiasm or resignation, this emerged as the motto for many Americans with the cultural *embourgeoisment* of the early nineteenth-century republic.[20]

Brown's "Elisa Letters" also demonstrated, however, that self-control became primarily a gendered directive for males. A stern code of emotional regulation placed somewhat different demands on women. Brown, like other bourgeois moralists in the early nineteenth century, believed that female sexuality was "naturally" less intense and less problematic. Female character formation therefore presented other tasks. Women, as Brown suggested constantly in his missives to Elisa, should strive to become models of genteel sensibility. Less vigorous and willful than men—this was "a sexual distinction, a feminine property: to be addicted to misgivings, reluctances, forebodings"—they were also deficient in the "branches of knowledge." Because of these weaknesses, Brown wrote frankly, "from the multitude of women we may turn away with indifference or contempt." Yet compensation could be found in the female capacity for aesthetic, moral, and cultural refinement. Ensconced in the private realm with "freedom from all brutalizing toils, all ignoble wants, all heart-depressing cares," women could and should read, paint, write, and converse. Wisdom would come to the cultivated female while "truth, by being coupled with delight, shall more easily seduce thee to her side."²¹

An ideologically progressive impulse inspired this idealized vision of feminine culture. In contrast to earlier moralists who downplayed female capabilities, Brown insisted that women did have an important role beyond childbirth and domestic chores. Influenced by revolutionary republicanism and his own earlier concern with women's rights, he roundly condemned John Gregory's *A Father's Legacy to His Daughters* (1774). Having mentioned her reading of this popular American moral primer for young women—a highly conservative work that insisted that vitality and learning were unfeminine and that passive meekness and strict decorum were most appealing in women—Elisa was unprepared for her suitor's outburst.

> Jn. Gregory is an egregious fool, Elisa. Never consign thy conversation and behavior to his government. If I remember rightly, his errors are properly exposed in the "Rights of Women." How remote, indeed, from simplicity and rectitude, are the systems of theorists on the laws of sex. . . . Yet in my narrow and indirect experience, I have met with scarcely anything among women but exceptions to the systems of punctilio.

For Brown, the theorist of gender, Wollstonecraft had distinct advantages over Gregory—but this preference had important limitations.²²

The writer's litany of instructions to Elisa unveiled a model of active female behavior that was carefully restricted to the realm of genteel culture. Brown urged the young woman to gain confidence, to overcome her tendency to view herself as "homely and unlovely" or "stupid and insipid." He probably contributed to Elisa's self-denigration, as suggested by the comment that "I wish I could cure thee, my love, of thinking thyself a simpleton & me a fastidious hypercritic." Nevertheless, Brown relentlessly urged her to read and write in order to cultivate "reason, reflection, memory" and thus improve herself. He urged her to express emotions frankly, but gracefully, so that "your pen thus faithfully [will] depict your character, your sentiments." Praising Elisa's talents profusely, he pleaded with her to express her inner moral beauty: "your purity, your good sense, your taste, your sensibility, your liberal curiosity, your knowledge, your dignity . . . the unaffected delicacy of your feelings." In a letter of April 1, 1801, the Philadelphian summarized his vision of Elizabeth Linn as idealized woman of genteel learning and discretion: "She will be one whom your reason will as zealously revere, as your heart adore. All that your fondest imagination can conceive of pure, modest, and engaging: with all the benefits of education and society; rectitude of taste; freedom from prejudice & all frivolous propensities."[23]

As part of the cultural bargain, however, the educated and sensitive female of Brown's imagination was expected to perform important emotional tasks. Terming Elisa "my good angel" and "mistress of my destiny," Brown elevated her to a position of moral eminence. She served as a source of religious direction, as an exemplar of "rational piety," and she calmed his libidinous outbursts as a model of "Truth, goodness, virtue, harmony, & love." As Brown confessed rather emotionally to her, she had rescued him from the "ancient difficulties and humiliations" that had plagued him in the 1790s and made his past life a "dreary" one. In the eyes of her suitor, this young woman was such an icon of emotional calm, moral inspiration, and intellectual stability that he must strive to be "not only worthy of you, but in your eyes, worthy."[24]

These gender ideals, however, were but part of a larger project of cultural construction. In Brown's blueprint, willful, self-controlled males and genteel, morally scrupulous females would serve as pillars for a massive edifice of bourgeois respectability. With men striving for success in the competitive marketplace while women served as moral managers in the domestic sphere, the bourgeois vision offered a picture of gender congruity and social harmony. Love, of course, served as the great binder. As Brown explained to Elisa, his love for her was part altruism, part self-interest. "I shall be soothing my own disquiets, beguiling my own pain, in alleviating yours," he observed. Brown elaborated in another letter: "We surely value the happiness of those we love, but then we wish them to owe that happiness to us. We rejoice that they seek their good in our store . . . ; but that they can do without us is our woe." This tug between independence and interdependence suggested how love mediated tensions over individualism in a rapidly growing market society. In the family such fears could be calmed and anxieties overcome. Brown, for instance, wrote of the "vehement longing" and "inebriating rapture" attached to his image of "our home, our fireside." Typically, the writer revealed his longing for domestic happiness by employing a dream motif. Asking Elisa for permission to remain "in quiet possession of my dream," he announced that "my dream will be far exceeded by reality." Thus, home and family, love and marriage promised to provide a great bulwark against the external dangers and internal stresses of a competitive society.[25]

The domestic bliss of Brown's imagination, however, concealed hidden fissures and unrecognized dilemmas. His myriad letters to Elizabeth Linn revealed these clearly. Brown's correspondence, for instance, frequently gave glimpses of the emotional turmoil and power relationships behind the assurances of gender compatibility and social cooperation. His long-standing insecurities often leaped to the fore as he constantly pleaded with Elisa for love and attention. "I will not say you sport with my feelings; but you wound them sorely," he admonished her at one point. "I have *no* security, I tell you, against *you*." Brown accused her of being "full of doubts, mistrusts, misgivings" and of communicating with him only when she had "some request to refuse, some mortification to inflict." Browbeating Elisa into making greater effusions of her love—"do you think I can have patience with your silence? No, I shall insist upon your writing as the only proof admissible that you have not forgotten me"—the young man frequently fell into bouts of whining. His "health of body & peace of mind" depended on the young woman's devotion, one letter insisted, and mortification grew from the fear that he held her "affections by no other tenure than incessant supplication." Falling prostrate at the feet of Elizabeth Linn, Brown appeared as an emotional cripple in desperate need of female succor.[26]

The irony of this situation became clear only in light of Brown's persistent claims of intellectual strength and superiority. While bowing to Elisa's moral and religious eminence, he saw their relationship as a heuristic opportunity. Proclaiming himself her "task setter," "monitor," and "instructor," Brown claimed intellectual authority.

> I would fain now be very wise, be very monitory, very lessonful, I would play the tutor with you; the elder brother with his head a mere storehouse for the harvest of experience; retailing his wisdom with the authoritative air of eldership. . . . Have I any influence over you? Yes, I have. . . . What a sacred duty to employ that influence in cherishing in you the seeds of excellence.

He took this sacred duty to rather extreme lengths. Promising to open new intellectual horizons for Elisa, Brown announced: "I wish to be a sort of visible divinity to my girl, to have all her thoughts, wishes, fears entrusted to my keeping." Such overweening paternalism involved considerable projection on Brown's part, of course, as became evident in a long letter of March 18, 1801. Contrasting Elisa's pessimism and insecurity with his own supposed emotional confidence, he observed, "Strange, my friend, that thou art not as sanguine as I." To one familiar with Brown's own history of hysteria, self-pity, and outlandish behavior, this claim must appear rather amusing. Clearly concerned with overcoming his own agitated past, the writer seized an opportunity to project those fears onto a "weaker" female and thereby establish a newfound emotional dominion.[27]

These patterns within the developing private relationship of Brown and Miss Linn (at least from his perspective; her letters have not survived) replicated larger archetypes in an emerging culture of capitalism. Maneuvering, accommodating, and defining anew around the onset of the nineteenth century, the young writer's attitudes toward love and life linked a pair of gendered cultural principles. Men, as his many letters to Elisa illustrated, would likely suffer an emotional buffeting from their competitive, assertive roles in the public arena of an acquisitive society. Thus, in the domestic sphere, these weary figures required the security of genteel family life and the serene guidance of females. Women, on the other hand, were to shape themselves as attractive, civilizing public ornaments through modest education in the humanities and fine arts. Yet in the home they were to function as pillars of emotional strength and morality, busily promoting a genteel, religious code of benevolence and self-control. This idealized model of complementary gender behavior unfolded by Brown in the early 1800s was, of course, gradually developed by many other moralists as well. It became the basis of a bourgeois Victorian culture that would slowly become dominant by the 1830s and 1840s, a culture in which the private cult of domesticity reinforced the public world of marketplace endeavor. As the "Elisa Letters" demonstrated with great clarity, Brown's private life at the turn of the century had begun to move in the same cultural channels as his final pair of domestic novels.[28]

III

Brown's wooing of Elizabeth Linn came to a happy, if rather delayed, conclusion. Elisa's caution, in concert with some serious financial setbacks suffered by the Brown family's mercantile business, postponed their marriage until 1804. On November 19 of that year the two were finally married by the Rev. William Linn, the bride's father, in New York City. Predictably, Brown suffered censure and expulsion from the Philadelphia Society of Friends for marrying a non-Quaker. Happier events soon followed. In an interesting twist of fate, given Brown's long-standing fascination with doubled identities, the new couple saw the arrival of twin sons in 1805, Charles Jr. and William. In 1807 there followed another boy, Eugene, and two years later a daughter, Mary.[29]

From all accounts Brown's private life entered a stage of contentment and security, in marked contrast to his personal unhappiness as a young man. Shortly before his marriage, he complained of poor health and the fact that "the world of business has been darkened by unusual vexations, disappointments, and embarrassments." By the end of 1805 the situation had brightened greatly. Reporting to his old companion, William Dunlap, Brown painted a glowing picture of domestic felicity with his "adored wife" and "two healthy and lovely babes." "As to myself, my friend, you judge rightly when you think me situated happily," he wrote. "As to my own personal situation, I have nothing to wish but that it may last." Elizabeth Brown seemed to share her husband's sense of joy at their domestic life. Upon his death several years later, she composed an obituary that stressed her husband's delight in family affairs. "It was in the endearing recesses of domestic life," she wrote, "that the character of the deceased shone with its loveliest lustre."[30]

Brown's series of early nineteenth-century realignments—his immersion in business and journalism, his wholehearted embrace of marriage and family—set the stage for an important new public role: bourgeois cultural critic. During the 1790s this restless young intellectual had challenged cultural, religious, and social traditions as part of his struggles with marketplace individualism. Now he moved to occupy a defensive position in protection of bourgeois society. In journals like *The Literary Magazine and American Register* and *The Monthly Magazine*, Brown appeared increasingly in a dual role: articulator of genteel behavior and advocate of cultural stability. A code of self-controlled individualism became his moral map for both private and public endeavor. A young man's intense frustration with a competitive market society, it seemed, developed into a middle-aged man's determination to stabilize that society, clarify its principles, and identify its transgressors.

In 1803 Brown made a dramatic appearance in his new role. The opening issue of the new *Literary Magazine* contained an "Editor's Address to the Public" that was part public confession, part statement of principle. This statement noted somewhat bitterly that the editor took no pride in his earlier writings. Then he announced at some length the cultural maxims that would henceforth guide his work:

> In ages like this, when the foundations of religion and morality have been so boldly attacked, it seems necessary . . . to be particularly explicit as to the path which the editor means to pursue. He therefore avows himself to be, without equivocation or reserve, the ardent friend and willing champion of the Christian religion. . . .

> As, in the conduct of this work, a supreme regard will be paid to the interests
> of religion and morality, he will scrupulously guard against all that dishonours
> or impairs that principle. Everything that savours of indelicacy or licentiousness
> will be rigorously proscribed. His poetical pieces may be dull, but they shall, at
> least, be free from voluptuousness or sensuality, and his prose . . . shall scrupu-
> lously aim at the promotion of public and private virtue.

In the years that followed, the editor attempted to uphold these principles.[31]

Brown vigorously promoted a moral creed of self-control throughout
his journalistic essays of the early 1800s. In a startling turnabout from his
passionate emotional displays of the 1790s, he now denounced those who
acted "according to their impulses without heeding the restraint of rationality." Rampant emotion, he maintained, created a wealth of private and
public dangers. It led to widespread mischief and destruction flowing from
the consumption of "inebriating liquors." It promoted the perverse blending of honor and violence in the practice of "dueling." It encouraged the
pernicious activities of gambling, lotteries, and political partisanship. Finally, it prompted that lust "excited by mere sex, . . . a gross appetite distinguished by no humanity, no delicacy, from that which stimulates the
goat and the bull." These activities, Brown insisted, were particularly dangerous in a republic because they enticed "the mechanic and husbandman
away from their usual wholesome and virtuous employment, to chimerical
and ruinous visions."[32]

The Philadelphia editor leveled some of his sharpest criticism at money
making, perhaps the greatest passion in a liberating society of individualism. For too many ambitious Americans, profit had become "the *one thing
needful* " in life, and its pursuit had overwhelmed many virtues with "depravity and selfishness." In a *Monthly Magazine* piece entitled "A Miser's
Prayer," Brown presented a satirical sketch of the greedy citizen offering
his hopes to the Almighty:

> Give humility to the poor and beggarly, and make them contented . . . so they
> may not pester thy faithful and thrifty servants with their outcries for charity. . . .
> Save us, we pray thee, from perishing by fire . . . and let a particularly large
> share of thy regard be bestowed upon the buildings on Third Street, between
> Vine and Sassafras. . . . Have compassion on all those who are sick and in
> prison. . . . Have an eye of special regard to Richard Harris, and give him
> wherewithal to pay thy servant what he oweth him, to wit the sum of three

hundred dollars and sixteen cents due, with interests thereon, since the fourth instant.[33]

Such dangerous passions lurking in the shadows of the early nineteenth-century republic led Brown to search for instruments of restraint. He found one in the civilizing influence of women. While tempted by certain cravings—particularly fashion, with its frippery and temptations to physical immodesty—females nonetheless had a unique capacity for self-control. Adopting the model of Lockean psychology, he argued that women were more susceptible to sensory impressions than men because of their worldly inexperience, lack of education, and emotional sensitivity. Yet this was also their greatest source of moral strength. Women, Brown contended, were attuned to the noble sentiments of music and painting and thus were able to promote their "laudable and generous emotions." These activities, however, threatened to degenerate into sensuality or idle amusement, so females needed to engage in serious reading and religious study. Moreover, the editor contended, women should maintain a strict "chastity" in order to control the animal desires of men. While males should seek an "inward conviction of rectitude," women best monitored their conduct through a code of sexual virtue, something that would be "a more effectual preservative against licentiousness, than any penal statute." So while Brown concluded that social equality between the sexes was "quite impossible," he proposed an important public role for women in a bourgeois republic: paragons of self-restraint in a society constantly seduced by self-interest.[34]

In Brown's new cultural ideology, literature emerged as another important means for inspiring sensual repression and social stability. The genre of the novel appeared especially rich with possibilities. While Brown granted that a large number of immoral, insipid, and frivolous stories had come forth under this heading, he insisted that many fictions of "merit and genius" stood out from "the promiscuous crowd." Novels had the capacity to gain an emotional grip over their readers, and then drive home a moral of "virtuous and noble sentiments." Through "the principles they have inculcated, and the sensibilities they have exercised," Brown wrote in 1804, fictional narratives had reached a pinnacle of cultural influence. While the "profligate novel" was a fact of life, Brown focused on the many "novels that may be read with benefit and pleasure by persons of good morals and good taste."[35]

Brown's old hero, Samuel Richardson, stood foremost in the ranks of virtuous novelists. Other fiction writers like Rousseau and Defoe had merit, of course, but in the early 1800s the Philadelphian sang the moral praises of Richardson loudest and longest. Defining the English author as "the father of the modern novel of the serious or pathetic kind," Brown lauded his ability to combine emotional, gripping stories with "salutary maxims" and "dignity of the sentiments." Like no other author, Richardson demonstrated "the beauty and the usefulness of virtue." This figure of "moral grandeur," in Brown's adoring eyes, was like a skillful preacher "in introducing useful maxims and sentiments of virtue . . . and he has besides the power of pressing them upon the heart through the best sensibilities of our nature."[36]

For Brown the bourgeois critic, literature provided only a prelude to his larger movement for cultural stability. From the editor's chair in Philadelphia, he used the *Literary Magazine* in particular to advocate an array of morally uplifting projects. Brown promoted, for instance, a national plan to develop "the fine arts of painting, sculpture, and architecture" in the United States. Urging both a private subscription drive and a congressional grant of public money, he maintained that the construction of art galleries and public monuments would help cohere a "civilized, peaceful, free, industrious, and opulent nation." In addition, by the early 1800s Brown had become a firm advocate of religious instruction. Abandoning his own youthful skepticism, he now insisted that religion must be instilled early in children to "balance the counter-impulse of the passions." If their impressionable minds encountered religion "at a time when the passions are most violent," impulsive behavior could be restrained. Religion, if it was to have social utility, must avoid the extremes of "enthusiasm," on the one side, and "dull conformity" on the other. It "must be taught rationally," drawing upon the individual's reason for comprehension. This cultural critic now saw religion as "the best safeguard against the impulses of the passions."[37]

Given the restless ambition of early nineteenth-century America, education loomed equally large in the Brownian blueprint for stability. He began to address the subject in numerous essays which argued that schooling was critical to the shaping of a virtuous, hard-working citizenry. Education, Brown maintained, worked to "form the mind of youth, . . . to mold the disposition of a new generation." It served as an agent of cultural transmission by handing down "the acquisitions of our forefathers." It helped "produce a virtuous and enlightened race," a necessity in an American society given to licentious temptation. Yet Brown was no simple reactionary on this matter. Granted, he did oppose reformers like Noah Webster who sought to create an American language with its own grammar, spelling, and vocabulary. Instead, he favored an Anglo-American cultural imperialism with a "diffusion of the English lineage and language" throughout the entire New World. Brown also denounced advocates of a "classical education" for American children, arguing that the study of modern languages and science was more appropriate to a utilitarian, market society. As he wrote in the 1805 essay "On Classical Learning," in a voice filled with bittersweet experience,

> If a boy be intended for trade or business, a classical education will be injurious to him. . . . [M]en, who have been educated at the university, seldom make it as active, expert, and successful merchants or tradesmen. . . . Habits of indolence, or of studious industry, are formed at college, which are inimical to the mechanical processes of trade, and to the activity and bustle of a man of business. . . . The dull uniformity and confinement of a shop or accounting room, are irksome to men of genius and studious mind.

Overall, Brown envisioned an educational process that would socially channel and morally restrain the activities of liberated individuals.[38]

As this process of cultural logic unfolded, "taste" emerged as its most intriguing dimension. As a bourgeois critic seeking anchors of stability in a gathering storm of social competition, Brown increasingly formulated principles for correct aesthetic judgment and cultural practice. Such standards, he hoped, would encourage mental stability and moral restraint. In an 1806 essay entitled "On Standards of Taste," Brown made the argument clearly. The laws of taste were partly "natural," in that writing, painting, and music inevitably raised emotional associations and affections in an audience. Yet they were also "partly arbitrary" because of the necessity for "observance of those rules with which critics are conversant." Here Brown minced no words: "As there are rules of taste, which are absolute and universal, and founded only on the common nature of human beings; so the rules of ethics are universal, and obligatory on all intelligent creatures who have received the same constitution as ourselves."[39]

Brown suggested several axioms in elaborating this unbreakable connection between "rules of taste" and morality. First, he demanded a soberminded sensibility. The habit of witticism was entertaining, but it was also a foolish and "childish practice." Moreover, "the wit" usually proved to be a trite and superficial figure unable "to discuss any subject soberly, to reason or to speculate, or to moralize." Second, the Philadelphian demanded not only seriousness, but realism. The American writer or painter should strive to accurately present "a picture of his age and country, by minutely and faithfully portraying himself." Nature's abundance in the New World provided particular opportunity here. By realistically presenting the "picturesque beauty" of natural landscapes, Brown suggested, the artist could evoke "a gratification the nearest akin and most friendly to the ennobling and domestic virtues."

Turning to his own province of writing, the essayist issued several directives after the turn of the century. In "The Difference Between History and Romance," published in the April 1800 *Monthly Magazine,* Brown set out his mature critical position. The writer should strive to be both a realistic "historian" (one "who carefully watches, and faithfully enumerates the appearances which occur" in life) and an imaginative "romancer" (one "who adorns these appearances with cause and effect, and traces resemblances between the past, and future, with the present"). The narrow scope of history, with its attempts to affirm "what is known by the testimony of our senses," required enrichment from the vast scope of romance, which maintained an "empire absolute and undivided over the motives and tendencies of human action." The result of tasteful artistic endeavor would be an audience of individuals whose "observations are as diligent as their theories are adventurous." The ideal person of "taste"—this included not only producers but consumers of culture, men and women—advanced sober reason against the barriers of mindless custom and tradition. He or she did so calmly and rationally, avoiding wild speculation and unfounded theorizing. Brown envisioned a cultured individual who could fight off "the caprice and instability of human nature" with a wide-ranging curiosity and synthesizing intelligence. Such citizens, he hoped, would bring a forbearing, rational realism to the cause of moral stability in America, and thereby save a volatile market society from its own worst instincts.[40]

One episode, more than any other, illustrated what might happen if human passions were left unrestrained: the French Revolution. Like many American intellectuals and politicians, Brown anguished over the meaning of this upheaval in the life of the Western world. Although he found the course of events in France to be deeply disturbing, he was no reactionary. In fact, by the early nineteenth century Brown developed a reading of the Revolution that was carefully in line with his broader cultural principles. The revolt in France had been initiated by philosophers and moderate republicans, he argued, whose activities were driven by "a love of liberty and a desire of reform." Moreover, the turbulence of the Revolution was no cause for automatic denunciation. Human nature demanded "the exercise of freedom, and the indulgence of a liberal and beneficent temper" rather than "mere tranquility," Brown insisted. The political disputes, angry meetings, attacks on the monarchy, and general public contention in revolutionary France were to be expected as "the collisions of free society."[41]

However, the Revolution had plunged into disaster, Brown believed, and for specific reasons. Passions had gradually gained the upper hand over reason and sent the French into an abyss of "massacre, confiscation, and exile." Restless popular anger had produced "a reliance on force" and the machinations of demagogues. "Virtuous and enlightened" judgment had been crushed by "acclamations of the mob" and monarchy had given way to "military despotism." Society, Brown believed, was organic in nature with a "natural aristocracy" of leaders who were "the natural organs of a great living body." Such figures, because of their education, status, and wealth, embodied the restrained and rational judgment of the whole. By ignoring this leadership class and indulging themselves in wild political and social experimentation, French revolutionaries had abandoned all hope for reforming the profound "properties and powers" of civil society. For Brown, the triumph of "misguiding passions" in France since 1789 had seriously injured "the cause of rational freedom." This nightmarish scene was one that ambitious Americans ignored only at their peril.[42]

So by the early years of the nineteenth century, Charles Brockden Brown had traveled far on his intellectual and emotional journey. In part, his path reflected a growing conservatism that often typifies the human life cycle. Challenges to the social order had marked his adolescence and early manhood as issues of personal ambition, gender definition, economic pursuit, and cultural performance tormented the young individual. In the same way that American revolutionaries had defied the sovereignty of Great Britain, Brown had worked to undermine traditional paternalism and its restraints. Even in 1800 Brown still emphasized that filial duty was in fact a contractual relationship: "our treatment of parents must be regulated by their characters. When vicious, our duties lie in rejecting their demands." Such freedom, however, could be frightening as well as exciting. The implications of unfettered individualism—its demands and possibilities, pitfalls and liberations—had provided the raw material for his frenzied fiction writing up through the 1790s. After a long struggle, Brown arrived at middle age a different and sobered man. No longer the brash intellectual maverick, he had become a persistent, articulate spokesman for social stability, cultural authority, and self-discipline.[43]

The meaning of this writer's evolution went far beyond personal development. It replicated a broader process of historical change in post-Revolutionary America. First, like many other citizens of the republic, Brown had gradually come to terms with a growing individualism. Fully recognizing the danger of this powerful social and economic force rampaging through the early modern Atlantic world, he grudgingly came to view it as an instrument of progress. This reluctant admission, however, was made possible only by a second crucial proposition. If individual agency was allowed free play in the social arena, the potent forces of "culture" must be mustered out to prevent anarchy and brutality. The passions, in Brown's words, arose from "the deplorable imperfections of human nature, absurd and pernicious." The incredible diversity of the United States—its vast "motliness, the endless variety of habits, ranks, and conditions"—presented additional perils of incoherence and instability. Given these assumptions, Brown the moralist concluded that a culture of self-control provided the strongest barrier to chaos. Genteel standards of conduct, stern moral codes that repressed sexual and violent impulses, and civilizing habits closely tied to the arts stood the best chance of throttling individual licentiousness and its horrors.[44]

Ultimately, the thrust of Brown's social and cultural maneuvers veered in the direction of irony. By elevating "culture" to a level above the tawdry impulses of competitive social and economic life and granting it civilizing powers, Brown in fact helped legitimize a society of marketplace individualism. His promotion of an abstract cultural aesthetic advanced the notion that creativity and imagination had been rationalized out of everyday life and into a specialized realm of human activity. Implicitly, but powerfully, this implied that the social world must be accepted as driven by competition, profit, and productivity. By 1803, for example, Brown had concluded that the typical "poor author" was someone who abandoned steady work for "habits of improvidence and heedlessness, as to all economic matters" and sunk into "the refuge of idleness and poverty." A more admirable kind of writer was one "who devotes to composition the leisure secured to him by hereditary affluence, or by a lucrative profession or office." This artistic role, which clearly disassociated work from creativity, he deemed "the pinnacle of human elevation." Brown's crusade for cultural coherence thus furthered, in unintended fashion, the very social fragmentation that had unsettled him for so many years.[45]

Brown's willingness to don the mantle of cultural "critic" completed this significant historical odyssey. In a public sphere that idealized marketplace social relations—free and equal exchange, debate, and decision making among autonomous individuals—the critic acted as referee. His task of establishing genteel guidelines of rationality and taste was a complex one. The critic sought, in part, to uplift an energetic but provincial mercantile and entrepreneurial class; in part, to defend the social and property interests of that class; in part, to soothe the pressures and heal the wounds inflicted by expanding market competition. Within this culture, Brown believed, the critic would shape a true "paradigm of reason" inspired yet restrained. As he instructed his countrymen in his 1806 essay "Standards of Taste,"

> Criticism is a science, and taste can only be rendered accurate by much study and attention. . . . Nothing is more truly cant, either in morals or in criticism, than the language of those who profess to decide from the impulse of their immediate feelings, without listening to so cold an arbitress as reason. . . . The imagination is the source of all error; and it is hard for taste to keep a rein over so festive a faculty.[46]

In its blending of enlightened reason and genteel repression, this writer's gradual evolution into an arbiter of cultural taste was part of a vast realignment in early modern America. By the early nineteenth century, he was helping validate the hegemony of liberal capitalism by clothing it in the sober, respectable garb of bourgeois civilization. In his final years, Brown would explore his new role, uncovering its capacity both for achievement and self-destruction.

# SEVEN

# ※‖ The Writer and the Liberal Ego

By 1805 Charles Brockden Brown seemed to withdraw into a cocoon of personal and professional quiescence. This Gothic novelist turned bourgeois cultural critic had abandoned almost completely his innovative, emotional fiction of the 1790s, while journalism, his second career, also fell increasingly by the wayside. More and more he devoted himself to less provocative work as a geographer, compiler of statistical and literary information, and serializing historical novelist. Turning his back on the cultural and ideological dissent of his earlier career, Brown fell back upon the genteel standards of social order and personal self-control that he had articulated in the early 1800s. With a certain sense of weary bemusement, he now presented himself to the public as a mere "scribbler." The fledgling writer, he confessed with chagrin in 1809, imagined that "every reader will find as many charms in his performance as he has found. . . . This error will, however, have had a very short reign." Experience had taught a hard lesson to this man of letters: in the long run "public approbation" was far less important than the affirmation of one's "own feelings."[1]

This stance suggested complacency on the part of this middle-aged Philadelphian. In fact, Brown's attitude evinced a more complex sense of disengagement, one with emotional as well as intellectual dimensions. As the first decade of the nineteenth century wore on, his imagination stood ever more remote from the social, cultural, and ideological questions that had preoccupied him over the previous two decades. He retreated, in large part, into an involvement with technical, abstract subjects. After 1805, for instance, Brown apparently spent much time composing a massive geographical work. Entitled *A System of General Geography: Containing a Topographical, Statistical, and Descriptive Survey of the Earth*, this 1,200-page text prompted the issuing of a prospectus in 1809, but it remained unfinished at Brown's death and the manuscript subsequently was lost. In 1806 he also moved to downgrade the *Literary Magazine* , which had enjoyed only modest success, into a semi-annual compendium of historical, literary, scientific, and political information called *The American Register, or General Repository of History, Politics, and Science.* Brown's imagination contracted even further. Withdrawing to the "seclusions of the closet," he became enamored of architectural drawing, according to close friend William Dunlap. Spending long hours measuring and drawing "plans of Grecian temples, of Gothic cathedrals, monasteries or castles," the writer became "addicted to every kind of abstraction and . . . reverie."[2]

The writing that Brown did attempt in this period, both fiction and nonfiction, only reinforced a sense of emotional distancing. He spent much of the period from 1803 to 1807 engaged in the composition of what one observer has termed "a massive historical novel." Typically left incomplete and published only in fragments, this fictional work dug deep into the ancient and medieval Western past to present a mythical picture of historical development. For the first time, Brown also made several forays into partisan politics as a pamphleteer. Jettisoning any Jeffersonian sentiments that he harbored from the 1790s, he now mixed skepticism of democratic tendencies with an imperialist vision of America's expansionist future. The market and its profit-seeking ethic, this critic recognized grudgingly, had become the driving force of the young republic. His old instinct for social reform and cultural radicalism, it became ever clearer, had receded before a new respect for wealth and power, stability and responsibility.[3]

Brown's personal life undoubtedly fed this process of shrinking imagination and intellectual retraction. In the years following his marriage, the writer celebrated the birth of four children and the development of a secure domestic life. At the same time, however, he suffered a steady emotional buffeting from a series of family deaths and financial setbacks. The years from 1804 to 1808 saw the deaths of his sister Elizabeth, his brother Joseph, his father-in-law, and his brother-in-law and close friend, John Blair Linn. Then in 1806 the Brown brothers' mercantile firm went under. Charles was forced to establish a small retail business selling pots and pans, the income from which he supplemented with small earnings from subscriptions to the *American Register.* Failing health completed this cloudy picture. Always rather frail, by 1806 he began to exhibit a steady cough, physical weakness, and other signs of "consumption," or tuberculosis. Increasingly unable to work for extended periods, he sought relief in brief vacations to New Jersey and New York. By the summer of 1809, a worsening condition prompted increasing despair. As he wearily asked a friend, "When have I known that lightness and vivacity of mind which the divine flow of health, even in calamity, produces in some men? . . . never; scarcely ever; not longer than half an hour at a time, since I have called myself man." Brown's withering powers of imagination seemed mirrored in his steady physical degeneration.[4]

Yet an emphasis upon this writer's evident resignation by 1805 paints a somewhat misleading picture. A shrinking of moral fervor, a pronounced ideological retrenchment, and a lingering bitterness about his authorial fate certainly tainted his attitudes and pronouncements. Beneath the surface, however, an even stronger impulse shaped his endeavors. Permeating his historical fiction, geographical commentary, belles-lettristic essays, and political pamphlets in the early nineteenth century was a quietly desperate search for sociocultural unity and personal grounding. Having finally reconciled himself to the dynamic energy of a liberalizing society, Brown persisted in one final, protracted struggle: to escape the confines of lonely individualism and find a secure sense of place.

I

After the radical challenge of fiction writing in the 1790s, followed by an outpouring of stern bourgeois moralizing in the early 1800s, Charles Brockden Brown half-consciously began a period of synthesis. During what turned out to be the last half-decade of his life, he labored to fuse a mature, coherent vision of culture and society that somehow brought together divergent tendencies in his earlier career. While not fully articulated, deliberate, or systematic, this attempt was more successful than Brown ever knew. Coming from several directions and filtering through different genres, a central impulse moved his intellectual work forward by 1805. Brown haphazardly, often awkwardly, attempted to merge the expansionist ethos of the liberalizing American republic with a creed that elevated and glorified genteel culture and the individual artist. This *mentalité*, with its taut internal bracing of assertion and restraint, ambition and repression, would become the ideological framework for liberal culture in nineteenth-century Victorian America.[5]

Brown's moves in this direction became evident in an 1804 project. Urged on by intellectual companions like playwright William Dunlap, the Rev. Samuel Miller, and geologist Samuel Latham Mitchill, the Philadelphia writer completed a translation of C. F. Volney's *A View of the Soil and Climate of the United States of America*. In addition to translating the original French into English, he also appended numerous footnotes to the text that comprised in themselves brief essays. This running commentary proved highly revealing. For Brown, the American republic offered a wealth of praiseworthy features in the early nineteenth century. Its energy and vigor elicited admiration, especially in terms of geographic expansion. Brown strongly endorsed American growth, and the recent purchase of the Louisiana Territory caused him to anticipate "the extension of this empire . . . east and west from sea to sea, and from the north pole to the Isthmus of Panama." The prospect of annexing territory in South America provided even greater "cause of pride and exultation." The author also saw much to commend in the American proclivity for "working diligently," widely educating its citizens, and pursuing trade and commerce.[6]

Brown's footnote essays in the Volney volume mixed ample chastisement with such praise. American drunkenness, violence, bad hygiene, and tradition-bound thinking came in for severe censure. The translator suggested that overindulgence in food and liquor was the "great curse of the country." Such crude habits fed an appetite for physical assaults and licentiousness, and served as a "most effectual method of shortening and destroying life." Brown's attack on the "ferocious passion" of his countrymen prefaced a general critique of tradition and its pernicious effects. The typical American, in his view, appeared practically immune to reason and scientific principle; "no reasonings could have changed his inclinations, already moulded and fixed irrecoverably by the force of habit." Tradition, Brown ruefully concluded, "reconciles us to everything." As he was fond of pointing out—reflecting, perhaps, a latent fear of the barbarizing impact of the wilderness—the American Indian illustrated the dangers inherent in this amalgam of tradition and unrestrained passions. Endorsing the dominant anthropology of this period, the author argued that American aborigines were given to savage outbursts of sex and violence, or what he described as "excessive indulgence of the appetites." They approached the world as creatures bound by superstition and custom while remaining nearly oblivious to reason and science. Given the fact that Indians were "hastening to extinction with a much quicker pace than to civilization," the lesson for licentious, irrational Americans was obvious.[7]

This ambivalent view of American society—equal parts approval of energetic expansion and disapproval of crude profligacy—ultimately led Brown to a larger issue in his shaping of Volney's *Soil and Climate of the*

*United States.* He used the volume to proselytize for a coherent, genteel civilization in the restless republic. In many ways, he perceived this as a crusade transcending national boundaries. Brown disapproved of Americans' fervent cultural nationalism, terming it a "positive, dogmatic spirit which is so generally inculcated by the popular modes of education." The infant United States, he pointed out, often reproduced the social and intellectual forms of Europe, "especially of England and Germany." For Brown the Volney tome offered an opportunity to postulate that religion, self-control, and gentility were parts of a unifying impulse in civilization. Spiritual ideas about moral "rewards and punishment" and "the notion of a future state," he argued, were natural to the human mind. In turn, the "regulation of the passions and discipline of the manners" sprang from such religious instincts and only required nurture to flower. This critic drew his conclusion near the end of the text: "The only just theory of the physical, moral, and religious condition of mankind is founded upon this solid truth, that all nations are derived from a common stock, and that the dispersion of nations did not take place until after the seeds of those religious truths and prejudices, which are everywhere to be met with, had been implanted in their minds."[8]

Other essays on literature and morality further developed Brown's advocacy of cultural cohesion. Toward the end of the nineteenth century's first decade, he published several short pieces in his own *American Register* and in the *Port-Folio, A Monthly Magazine*, a Philadelphia journal edited by his friend Joseph Dennie, which buttressed the structure of a dynamic, yet genteel liberal society. By 1805 Brown repeatedly insisted that the pursuit of wealth must be accepted as the mainspring of American life. He implored intellectuals to grasp this salient fact. His 1807 "Sketch of American Literature," for instance, argued that the state of literature could not be traced abstractly to the "constitutional genius" of the people. Instead, he insisted that it lay "in the common and obvious circumstances on which the fruits of literary genius and industry, *like all other commodities* [my italics], depend for their abundance and scarcity. Authors will, in fact, be always found, and books be written, where there is a pecuniary recompense for authors, and a ready sale for books." This market view of literary production contained a considerable ideological element. An 1809 essay in the *Port-Folio* maintained that while many moralists denounced the pursuit of "wealth and power," most citizens sought them feverishly. As Brown noted rather sharply, intellectuals had contempt for wealth because they "are generally unqualified to get rich . . . [and] are naturally prompted to depreciate what is unattainable." Additionally, they failed to realize that wealth "may be employed to the lasting benefit of others," that its power may be made "subservient to the public happiness," that it could be put to "beneficial purposes." The prosperous should be taught, Brown argued, that their riches might be wisely employed to elevate American society through promoting "pictures and books, music and conversation."⁹

Here Brown took a crucial step in his cultural theorizing. If the market was an unavoidable fact of life, the man of letters must use culture as a tool to civilize its excesses and channel its energies. This required a strong, even bitter, dose of reality for the typical early nineteenth-century American intellectual. The United States, Brown insisted, was still little more than "a province of the British empire" in terms of its culture and literature. Very few "original books" could be found since most writing appeared in daily newspapers and gazettes. While these tabloids were unquestionably valuable in practical terms—their mercantile information about "what is to be bought and sold, is useful to everyone who buys and sells; and that is the case of every member of society"—their cultural content paled in comparison. Newspapers, Brown noted sourly, cultivated copious, shallow, glib writers whose fame may "be of short date, yet . . . it is very wide and very noisy while it lasts." Moreover, to the extent that literary culture existed, the professional classes—lawyers, doctors, and ministers—absolutely dominated it. In short, America's cultural context of provincialism and gain seeking demanded that the purveyor of literature prepare stoically for a career of lonely, frustrating struggle. Facing a society of "frivolous readers" pandered to by "trivial or worthless" writers, serious men of letters could only seek from the typical American the "acknowledgement that our pursuits are as meritorious as his own." Meritorious writers might attempt to ameliorate the miseries of mankind through genteel moral appeals, rather than by exciting ridicule through satirical wit and "the sting of derision." Most of all, the artist should muster his transcendent abilities to uplift, inspire, and civilize his rough-hewn countrymen. Brown described the artist's burden in 1809:

Common objects he [the artist] frequently groups in an uncommon manner. Though he pictures an ordinary scene, he selects and holds forth these lineaments and features which the eye or the ear is apt to overlook. It is like viewing the morning star through a telescope, by which we are enabled to see, what we never saw before, as often and as intensely as we have gazed at it. The world that we look at through the poet's optics is so much our world that we recognize it easily again, but it is still in many respects a world different from ours.[10]

A distinct cultural politics gradually emerged from such scattered ruminations in the early 1800s. Brown's attempts to fuse a dynamic, energetic market society with a genteel culture of self-restraint colored his diverse literary efforts throughout this period. In particular, his vision of a civilization of striving, noble individualism began to permeate two major projects. It prompted Brown's entry into the contentious partisan world of political pamphleteering. It appeared even more clearly, however, in a huge historical novel that purported to chart the development of Western civilization.

## II

It has been described as "one of the most ambitious and one of the most eccentric works" in American literary history. It is unclear whether the author abandoned the project, continued to work on it sporadically throughout the early 1800s, or simply decided to break up the whole and publish the fragments separately. In any event, Charles Brockden Brown's massive *Historical Sketches* marked a fascinating departure in his career as a writer of fiction. Rather than abandoning the novel altogether after 1801, the author apparently reoriented his efforts into a modified genre more in tune with his developing ideological sensibilities: historical fiction. The historical novel provided more fertile ground for the nurture of a unified cultural vision of stability and self-restraint.[11]

Coming to grips with this mysterious work is no easy task. No outline or general description of the unfinished novel has been found, and it can only be reconstructed through combining some ten printed, but scattered, fragments. Brown's intentions nonetheless seem fairly clear. The *Historical Sketches* was to have chronicled the fictional history of a prominent English family from the conversion of its ancient patriarch by St. Paul up to the nineteenth century. The fragments that came to light—some appeared in the *Literary Magazine*, others in William Dunlap's 1815 biography of Brown—focused on two ancestral branches of the family, one in Sardinia and the other in England, throughout the medieval and early modern ages. Dunlap described these loosely connected tales as "works of imagination in which historical facts are mingled and the air of history imitated." Moreover, he believed that Brown intended "an Utopian system of manners and government . . . to complete the whole." A utopian impulse may have been at work, but the texts suggest that it was of a particular sort. With its nostalgia for certain organic, medieval social forms, this grandiose work ventilated Brown's lingering dissatisfactions with the flux and ambitious individualism of post-Revolutionary America. By opening a wide avenue for grand historical interpretation, the project allowed its author to define and promote a particular vision of civilized progress. Brown seized the opportunity.[12]

As a whole, this saga presented a complex reconstruction of the medieval past. The author consistently denounced the corruption and superstition, the cupidity and oppression of traditional European society. His treatment of events in Sardinia, or "Carsol," as he terms it, focused on recurring episodes of religious strife. Sympathy for the Reformation triggered the terror of the Counter-Reformation, as Catholic fanatics moved to stamp out the influence of Protestants, Jews, and Moslems. For Brown, the Church of Rome was a study in corruption:

> The injurious effects of this [Roman Catholic] system, the venality, tyranny, and negligence of the prelates and their delegates, may be easily imagined. The continual draining away of money was of ruinous tendency. The administration of justice, among the vassals of the clergy, was totally neglected or perverted; poverty, depopulation, and depravity were the consequences of this system.

Brown's account of feudal conditions in England continued the theme of degradation, but substituted a social critique for a religious one. The setting for this story, an estate of some 25,000 acres in the northern region, featured an absentee aristocratic landlord who lived in London and his avaricious manager who collected rents from the impoverished inhabitants. While those in authority operated only by "pecuniary calculations," those who lived on small farms and in tiny hamlets harbored no ambitions and struggled along in a system of "negligent and slovenly cultivation." The entire scene was one of "vexations and oppressions."[13]

At the same time, however, Brown's attacks on the religious superstitions and social perversions of feudal society often yielded to a more positive assessment. As the Carril story frequently revealed, he found the security of tradition to be very appealing. The stable government and social order of Carsol, he argued, protected its people from internal commotion and external threats and rendered the island "the best possible for persons or property." The Philadelphian also approved the "love of literature and the arts" displayed by Sardinian feudal aristocrats and their avoidance of "that restless, turbulent, ambitious spirit so common among contemporary princes." More pointedly, Brown described with thinly disguised enthusiasm the cultural cohesiveness of life in Carsol. He insisted that "religious uniformity was a national blessing" and even offered the dictum that "uniformity, even in error . . . is better than dissension." Brown went so far as to approve the establishment of a theocratic tribunal. In his words, within this unified Carsolian culture

> all diversities of language and religion had entirely vanished, the distinction between freedom and servitude, between foreigner and native among residents, with all the jarrings and diversities of jurisdiction flowing from this motley assemblage, were no more. The new generation were as flourishing and numerous as the former, but they formed one body infinitely more compact and simple, and their harmony and energy . . . [were] much greater.

Thus, Brown presented an ambiguous fictional depiction of the medieval past. His denunciation of its narrow-mindedness, confinement, and privilege betrayed an equally passionate longing for its security and coherence. This nostalgic willingness to crush diversity and dissent, to create "one body," suggested more than mere fantasy. It revealed the author's lingering alienation from the separations and competition of a liberalizing market society, a society that he ostensibly accepted.[14]

Brown's complex recreation of premodern society in the *Historical Sketches* ultimately served a prefatory purpose. It set the stage for the farsighted efforts of the narrative's heroic reformer, Sir Arthur Carril. This idealized English aristocrat, who dominated the two fragments of the novel published in the 1805 *Literary Magazine*, was the most compelling of Brown's characters in this unwieldy tale. Sir Arthur, the product of a long line of British feudal nobility, united the novel's far-flung fictional families in the late seventeenth century by marrying the female head of the Carsolian clan, a woman who also maintained large landholdings in northern England. He then embarked on his life's work: the overhaul of the massive estate over which he had gained control by marriage. His wide-ranging efforts comprised something of a blueprint for Brown's mature vision of modernizing progress.

Pursuing his task over a thirty-odd year period from roughly 1680 to 1710, Sir Arthur Carril set in motion a comprehensive reform program defined by reason and efficiency. After surveying the vast acreage and numerous inhabitants of his new estate, he banished all feudal retainers—"official vermin who had hitherto preyed upon the vitals of the people"—and replaced them with his own intelligent and honest "agents." Carril then determined to provide each tenant farmer or laborer a means to "secure refuge from poverty," "enlarge his comforts, promote his health, and increase his independence." No mere altruist, he hoped reform would enlarge his own revenue in the bargain. After careful thought and planning, Sir Arthur moved in several directions.[15]

Agricultural reform spearheaded the effort. According to Brown's description, the new estate owner and his men began to drain swamps, fence pastures, import livestock for regulated breeding farms, plant trees on land that could not be cultivated, establish crop rotation and fertilization programs, and arrange for the marketing of surplus production. In the villages and towns on the estate, Sir Arthur moved decisively to revamp existing arrangements. Discarding the haphazard design of the typical "old crazy town," he worked from a plan that was "elegant, homogeneous . . . simple and uniform." In a kind of urban renewal project, this aristocratic reformer tore down many old and dilapidated structures and replaced them with neat rows of "contiguous buildings." He built broad avenues with trees and footpaths between the rowhouses. He tapped new water sources to create a steady supply for townspeople. He strengthened fortifications for defense. Finally, Sir Arthur created a "college" in the estate's old abbey where students could study the productive arts, the fine arts, and scientific subjects in an atmosphere tightly controlled by "sobriety and temperance." To knit together this complex system of reform, he established a well-ordered bureaucracy of "head stewards" and "substewards," all of whom were well-paid representatives of the estate owner's authority. Brown's appreciation of Carril's project was indicated by the titles of two stories that described it in the 1805 *Literary Magazine*: "Specimen of Agricultural Improvement," and "Specimen of Political Improvement."[16]

Beneath the flurry of practical activity on this English estate, however, several motivating principles were at work. Fueling this social reorganization, they represented Brown's new ideological position in the early 1800s. A creed of work-discipline and personal self-control appeared most powerfully. Sir Arthur sought to "introduce sober and industrious habits among a race of tipplers and idlers." He cracked down on gin shops and whiskey manufacturers, and demanded of farmers and craftsmen a rigid standard of hard work. The brunt of his effort, however, went into re-educating children. "Old habits he deemed incurable," Brown wrote, "and [he] believed that there was no safety for the common weal but in new modelling the rising generation."[17]

This culture of self-discipline, in turn, rested upon a clear conceptualization of wealth seeking. For Brown, speaking through his characters, it had become axiomatic that "the grand object of human activity is fortune or wealth. How to employ talents and industry so as to convert a little money into a great deal is the subject which employs the faculties of the greater part of mankind." At the same time, however, the author insisted that profit often went for "vulgar" uses: a mindless consumption of goods where people sought to increase "the splendour and variety of their dress, furniture, and equipage"; or a "passion for money for its own sake" where funds were accumulated simply to make more money. The appropriate approach to profit, Brown argued, was demonstrated by Sir Arthur Carril. While reform unquestionably augmented his personal property and wealth, he deemed them of "no value but as they were subservient to the public good." Carril's motives may have been selfish in part, but his endeavors "essentially produce the good of the whole society." As Brown explained, the crucial link between profit seeking and communal virtue was "productivity." One's own wealth could not be "built upon the poverty of others," but must be of a generative, compounding kind aimed at "exalting their condition; improving their morals; enlightening their understanding; and enlarging their comforts." In the case of his fictional aristocratic reformer, the key to creating the public good out of the sum of private ambitions "was to make the ground more productive."[18]

A theory of social relations provided a complement to productive self-discipline in the *Historical Sketches*. Once again, Sir Arthur Carril represented the author's reforming calculus. While respecting the instinct for advancement, this powerful magnate was determined to tame the spirit of ambition among his tenants by "keeping them stationary." Allowing some to raise themselves above the others, he believed, would undermine the harmony and productivity of his scheme. Sir Arthur's control over all property on the estate, Brown explained, did not discourage industry and independence among the inhabitants. Instead, it exchanged a measure of mobility for a larger measure of security. While there were limitations placed on individualism in Carril's plan,

> these disadvantages were amply counterbalanced by the cheapness, convenience, and luxury of personal provision and accommodation, by the invariable equity with which the great power of the landlord was exercised, and the facility, among the middling and lower class of adventurers, of acquiring competence, of accumulating stock in goods and money.

Stability and modest prosperity for all, Brown suggested, more than compensated for the restrictions of opportunity and advancement for the few.[19]

This vision of modernizing progress based upon efficiency, self-discipline, productivity, and stability came at a steep price. Simply put, Brown's system depended upon a benevolent dictator. Sir Arthur Carril—an idealized projection of the author's ideological fantasy life—was as a man above all restraints. Those who challenged his will on the estate were subject to complete banishment: "In judging his people he was bound by no laws, either written or prescriptive." In fact, the extent of his improvements required "an unlimited authority" and this imposing figure did not hesitate to exercise it. His absolute power was justified, Brown contended, because "to restrain the uses of spirituous liquors, to convert the ignorant, idle, and profligate into diligent, sober, and enlightened" citizens was an enormous task. Thus, the reformer of this tale took shape as a heroic individual, a superman who burst the chains of tradition and irrationality to realize his fantasy of the public good. Confident that he could create happiness for others, he mustered such great energy and sagacity that it enabled this "single man to perform what will vulgarly be deemed impossible." Brown admired Sir Arthur Carril's final product: a "new race . . . as different in their minds and morals as in their external condition from those who preceded them."[20]

The *Historical Sketches*, even in their unfinished and fragmentary state, offered a fascinating prognosis of Charles Brockden Brown's ideological condition in the early nineteenth century. This historical morality tale was highly ambivalent in its overt reformist simplicity and covert bitterness. The author's long struggle with liberalizing individualism gave rise to a fictional hero whose unrestrained power imposed order upon chaos. The irony in this vision—which combined extreme market individualism with premodern authoritarianism—influenced Brown's entire reconstruction of the past. The organic connections of medieval society, the author suggested, could be reconstituted to control, *not* reject, the flux and growth of the present. This ambiguous, nostalgic reformism—one scholar has described it as "antimodern modernism" in its later nineteenth-century form—reflected not so much utopianism as a profound frustration with the public separations and private dislocations of developing market society. It suggests that Brown's reconciliation with a transforming America by 1805 was more superficial than real. Desperately seeking to overcome the isolation and strife that often colored the social relationships of emerging liberal capitalism, he envisioned the creation of an efficient, rationalized social order melding productivity with security. In its enlightened totalitarianism, this somewhat chilling historical novel sought to locate personal rootedness in a structure of enforced social uniformity.[21]

Brown's other great writing project of this period—a series of political commentaries—transported this deeply ambivalent sensibility into the real world of the early nineteenth century. From 1803 to 1809 he composed a trio of long, polemical pamphlets, along with several briefer magazine essays, which plunged headlong into political controversy. Brown's *An Address to the Government of the United States on the Cession of Louisiana* (1803) appeared amidst the American uproar over the Spanish transfer of the Louisiana Territory to France. His *Monroe's Embassy; or, The Conduct of the Government in Relation to Our Claims to the Navigation of the Mississippi* (1803), published a few months later, urged a vigorous policy of American expansion into the trans-Mississippi west. Over the next few years, the fledgling political writer pursued his new interest with several pieces in the *American Register*. Then in 1809 Brown responded to President Thomas Jefferson's embargo policy with *An Address to the Congress of the United States, on the Utility and Justice of Restrictions upon Foreign Commerce*, a pamphlet that criticized commercial restrictions and stoutly defended principles of free trade. In part, the turbulent Atlantic world of the Napoleonic Wars triggered this explosion of political rhetoric. Issues of political rights, territorial integrity, and national survival preoccupied most American men of affairs by the early 1800s. Once again, however, an ideological logic crept beneath the surface of Brown's practical politics. He staked out a position that was vigorously expansionist yet sharply critical of American values, and then defended it with a message of disciplined unity and productivity.[22]

Throughout these pamphlets, Brown's advocacy of American commercial activity and geographic growth was striking. His countrymen, the Philadelphian asserted, were "remarkably addicted to trade, and ingenious in all its stratagems and artifices." An exchange of goods had woven extensive ties between the nations of Europe and their New World colonies. In fact, the American republic's commercial connection with nations all over the globe brought "the wonderful power of annihilating, in its usual and natural effects, even space itself." As Brown perceptively noted, these commercial proclivities also had pushed market networks deep into the American interior. The exchange of goods between east and west within the United States now involved "the whole mercantile class, throughout America." This web of commodity exchange entangled not only farmers—

still a great majority in American society—but "the whole chain of artisans, dealers and carriers, near or remote, who subsist by supplying his wants."[23]

This enormous swelling of commercial activity, in concert with a steadily increasing population, made expansion of the American republic almost inevitable. As early as 1798 Brown had calculated that vast expanses of cheap land, along with an explosive increase in population, would create a polity of great strength and magnitude. By 1807 he had grown convinced that "changes in the last twenty years" would increase "for at least another century." The scope of American development was breathtaking, he wrote, because since the Revolution "the American nation has increased in number and opulence, in a degree far beyond any known example . . . [and] it is not easy to set the due limits on it. We can discover no material obstacle to the continued extension of our settlements to the Pacific Ocean, nor can the increase be less than double in every twenty years."[24]

As a result, Brown became an ardent expansionist in the early 1800s, promoting American growth into "the property which God and Nature have made ours." Addressing the issue of the Louisiana Territory in 1803, he insisted that the United States had "a right to the possession" of it by virtue of the "reign of peace and concord" that American dominion would inaugurate. He even advocated war if necessary. Serious financial, moral, and human costs would accompany armed conflict, but the writer insisted that the benefits were worth it: access to the Mississippi River and western territories, protection of profit from free trade, extension of Republican sentiments. "Seasonable war," he assured readers, "is . . . the surest way to peace."[25]

Brown's deep-dyed expansionism, however, concealed a complicated ideological logic. His boisterous rhetoric of manifest destiny barely covered a stinging critique of American factionalism, unrestrained passions, and money grubbing. In these political writings of the early nineteenth century, expansion and war were as much an antidote for American weakness as a triumphant expression of strength.

The author provided a fascinating clue to his reasoning in the 1803 *Cession of Louisiana* pamphlet. In a clever literary ploy, Brown adopted the persona of a French counselor of state as a way to criticize American values without risking personal attribution. This fictitious French diplomat, advising the government in Paris as an expert on the Louisiana Territory, offered a clear critique of the United States and its proclivities in this situation. His remarks, written in a dispatch, supposedly fell into American

hands and Brown presented them to his countrymen. The report was far
from flattering. The Frenchman told his superiors that while the United
States had grown immensely over the past two decades, internal weaknesses hindered its capacity for further development. The North American republic, he argued, presented a "motley character" and its citizens were
moved by "forward passions." Only a "precarious authority" bound together the various hostile interests of this restless society. The American population was widely dispersed, the French counselor continued, while fully a
fifth of it was composed of disgruntled black slaves. The most damaging
weakness, he believed, was the American obsession with money.

> This is a nation of peddlars and shopkeepers. Money engrosses all their pas-
> sions and pursuits. . . . Their ruling passion being money, no sense of personal
> or national dignity must stand in the way of its gratification. These are an easy
> sacrifice to the lust of gain, and the insults and oppressions of foreigners are
> cheerfully borne, provided there is a recompense of a pecuniary nature. Insults
> and injuries that affect not the purse, affect no sense of what they possess.

Expressed through this fictional mouthpiece, Brown's conclusion sounded
clearly: America's greed would lead them to sacrifice long-term stability
and strength to short-term profit.[26]

This scathing criticism of American profit-mongering prefaced an even
broader attack on American civic values. In a number of published essays
from 1803 to 1809 Brown bitterly denounced certain political and social
trends. American public life, he asserted, had produced many contentious
groups who marched "under the banners of faction." In fact, the young republic had become a "hot bed for faction and sedition" as Jeffersonians and
Federalists, pro-English and pro-French groups, New Englanders and
Southerners accused one another of wickedness and folly. This spirit of
faction was not especially ferocious, but rather moved by "subtlety and
stratagem, . . . duplicity and artifice." The effects were poisonous. Demagogues and character assassins fanned the flames of public passion and
gained acclaim. Public discourse was degraded through flamboyant
rhetoric, "personal altercation and abuse," and partisan finger pointing.
Factionalism even threatened to undermine the Constitution, the Phila
delphian believed, since warring factions would likely assault the fabric of
government and "portions will be cut out, and replaced by patch after
patch, till no remnant of the original cloth shall remain." Perhaps the
greatest danger lay in the likelihood of foreign intrigue. With American

factions comprising "obvious and convenient tools," European powers could maneuver them into confrontation and easily "set this heterogeneous mass into commotion."[27]

Brown's lamentations about the demise of American virtue and the ascendancy of greed and factionalism did not dampen his enthusiasm for American expansion. In fact, those fears fueled his enthusiasm. The prospect of American movement into the Mississippi Valley, the author argued, would create a powerful unifying impulse within the American republic. Westward growth would bring together "the merchant, the artisan, [and] the planter" in common interest to work toward "ensuring the harmony and union of these states . . . [by] removing all obstacles to the future progress of our settlements." A "unity of manners, laws, and government" would emerge under pressure from opposing forces and obstacles. Brown's hopes for forging unity through geographic and economic conquest was reinforced by a barely concealed enthusiasm for war. If expansion brought armed conflict, so much the better. In war "we gain advantages, not to be bought by mere money," he wrote, and foremost among them was a strengthening of American character. The trials of war encouraged fortitude, moral focus, resilience, and a concern for the commonwealth. For proof, Brown returned to the American Revolution as a heroic example of martial virtue: "It was then evident that the ploughman and the mechanic at either end of the continent, would recognize a common interest with each other; could sacrifice their ease, their fortunes, their lives, to secure a remote and general benefit; that the passion for gain could not deter us from repelling encroachments on our liberty, at the cost of every personal advantage."[28]

Brown's position, significantly, did not demand a wholesale rejection of market values and commercial activity. Instead, it sought to tame the materialistic, self-interested impulses of a market society by administering temporary doses of purifying virtue and intermittent injections of noble purpose. Moreover, it promoted "productivity" as the healing balm for all stresses and strains in the body politic. The protection of American commerce and its future expansion, by force if necessary, would insure the republic's prosperity. As Brown took great pains to point out in his 1809 *Address to the Congress*, such protection would hasten the day when "we shall become the manufacturers of other nations." This economic development, in turn, would bring even greater social stability and economic security to the growing republic. The possibilities for unity were nearly endless. A protected American commerce would be free "to enlarge that circle which each man calls his country; to take away the grounds of dissension and rivalship; to create one nation out of many."[29]

Brown's political writing of the early 1800s ultimately envisioned an American imperial republic. His bellicose defense of the United States' commercial rights and territorial claims from 1803 to 1809 flowed in part from a simple sense of national self-interest. The real power and emotion of his sentiments came from a broader, deeper conviction of his country's "progress to greatness." This prediction of an "extended empire" linked together his hopes and fears in an ideology of geographic growth, commercial freedom, social coherence, and resolute, self-controlled character. Brown's future American republic would be "occupied by one language, one people; one mode of general government; one system of salutary laws." This productive, unified market empire promised to be the most magnificent in history. For Brown, it was the logical political expression of the bourgeois ideology he had forged early in the new century.[30]

### III

By 1809 Charles Brockden Brown's life entered its final, unhappy stage. His literary endeavors faded in the face of a dominating new factor: rapidly failing health. Growing weaker by the summer of that year, he took to his bed for growing stretches of time. Physically drained, he quit writing almost entirely. Then in November 1809 he suffered a violent pain in his side, according to close friend William Dunlap, and was bled before retiring to his chamber. Brown stayed there for the next three months, often suffering great pain from what was probably an advanced case of tuberculosis. Finally, on February 22, 1810, the author died, at age thirty-nine. It seemed almost a final scene from one of Brown's own Gothic tragedies: the sensitive, misunderstood artist whose heroic literary efforts produced only popular apathy and a truncation of talent, dies from consumption at a relatively young age.[31]

Overall, Brown's career in the early nineteenth century was not so much a story of tragic decline—the standard story from most literary historians—as a tale of escape and reformulation. It seems clear that the author's post-1800 reconciliation with bourgeois individualism had relieved the painful psychological and ideological tension of the 1790s. The cost had been high, however. This became partially evident, of course, in Brown's atrophied creativity as he pulled away from the innovative, forceful writing of his early career and struck a public stance as cultural schoolmarm. It also appeared, however, in a deeper, even more wrenching process within the psyche. Brown's struggle with a half-conscious but powerfully enervating impulse—a fragmentation of self, a splintering of psychological coherence—pervaded his life as he contended with the pressures of a consolidating market culture. A strong sense of fragmentation had colored his writing and intruded into his personal experience as a young man. It may have come to light most clearly in two extended pieces of fiction with a somewhat curious history.[32]

In an 1827 review essay of the first edition of Charles Brockden Brown's collected novels, writer and critic Richard Henry Dana found much to support in the project. Yet he lamented the omission of two little-known works: *Memoirs of Carwin, the Biloquist* and *Memoirs of Stephen Calvert*. These novelistic fragments were incomplete, the reviewer admitted, but they deserved inclusion as the most autobiographical, and hence most revealing, of all Brown's tales.[33] Much evidence supports Dana's insight. Both protonovels were begun in the heart of Brown's most productive period, the year 1798, only to be abandoned and later picked up early in the nineteenth century. Neither was published as a whole, but appeared only in serialized and fragmentary form. Moreover, some kind of creative link between the two works seemed to exist in the author's own mind, since he set aside *Carwin* in September 1798 to begin work on *Stephen Calvert*. Most strikingly, these two fictions shared an introspective, psychological theme that indeed seemed drawn from Brown's own life. Each story featured a desperate, floundering individual set loose in a society of confusing possibilities and terrifying choices. Each character seemed to splinter apart under the pressure. Frank Carwin and Stephen Calvert, two literary figures cast in the mold of their creator's experience, presented a ghostly spectre of the fragmented liberal ego of early capitalist culture. It is little wonder that Brown half-consciously tried to evade or repress their realization.

Apparently the Philadelphian began writing *Memoirs of Carwin, the Biloquist* in the summer of 1798 and worked on it for several weeks. The manuscript then sat untouched for several years before appearing in ten installments in Brown's *Literary Magazine* from November 1803 to March 1805. During publication their author seems to have composed additional sections for the narrative until it reached some sixty pages in its entirety. The story itself grew out of the novel *Wieland*, where Carwin, the mysterious ventriloquist, had been the catalyst for much of the action and psychological dynamics of that Gothic mystery. Believing that this fascinating

character could stand as the centerpiece of a separate novel, Brown began
composing an intriguing tale based on Carwin's life but deserted the manuscript just as it reached an emotional crisis that hit a little too close to
home.[34]

Frank Carwin's memoirs comprised a twisted tale of success seeking.
The youth, reared in the western wilds of frontier Pennsylvania, grew up a
study in provincial frustration. His boyhood saw an intense chafing against
patriarchal power and traditional expectations. The Carwin family farmed
a small plot of ground in the western district of the state. Frank's older
brother was content to be a farmer, while his father exercised a stern paternal authority. In contrast to the restricted vision and willful ignorance of
these two men—they were unwilling to consider "the possibility that to-
morrow could differ from today"—the younger son described himself as an
individual with "a restless and unconquerable curiosity," a deep "thirst of
knowledge," and a focus on "visions of the future." Frank's love of books
and hatred of manual labor clashed with his family's belief in a "thousand
superstitious tales" and their dogged work ethic. His father determined to
break his will. As a result, for several years the boy suffered the heavy hand
of paternal punishment: physical beatings, destruction of his books, forced
labor, oppressive sibling supervision. By mid-adolescence, a revolt was in
full flower as the young man desperately sought an opportunity to escape.[35]

Frank found his first chance when a prosperous aunt living in Philadelphia—who had always been fond of her bookish nephew—invited him to
live with her and receive an education. His reluctant father eventually re-
lented from a desire to get a hand on the old woman's inheritance. After
three delightful years, however, Frank suffered a great shock. Upon his
aunt's death, he discovered that she had bequeathed him absolutely nothing. The penniless youth found himself perched on the threshold of manhood with no means of support, and only a vague ambition to get ahead
and a contempt for mere money making. This career crisis, much like
Brown's own, featured an intense young intellectual with a passion for
books and geography seeking an arena for displaying his talents. Carwin
cogently expressed the commingled anxiety and hope, determination and
loneliness of the aspiring individual: "Without profession or habits of industry or sources of permanent revenue, the world appeared to me as an
ocean on which my bark was set afloat, without compass or sail. The world
into which I was about to enter, was untried and unknown, and though I
could consent to profit by the guidance, I was unwilling to rely on the support of others." This drama of self-made success took a sharp narrative

turn when the youthful protagonist encountered by chance an intelligent and sophisticated, but enigmatic European (pp. 258–62, 297, 298, 268–69).

Even in this novelistic fragment, the character of Ludloe made an arresting impact. Taking young Frank under his wing, this ambitious and visionary Irishman convinced the boy to return with him to his homeland as a step toward fame and fortune. First, Ludloe converted his new protégé to his philosophy of utilitarian radicalism. This doctrine, according to the young parvenu, aimed "to lay the foundations of virtue in utility." Since people "in their natural state are infirm and deceitful," Ludloe taught, "a just estimate of consequences may sometimes make dissimulation my duty." The Irishman frequently denounced "the artificial impediments of government" and proselytized his belief that a reordering of circumstance would improve human nature. He constantly discussed a "scheme of Utopian felicity, where the empire of reason should supplant that of force," where justice would be understood and practiced, where labor and wealth would be equally distributed, and where "the interest of the whole and of the individual should be seen by all to be the same." It slowly became clear to Carwin that his mentor belonged to an elite secret society—Brown's fascination with the fabled Bavarian Illuminati surfaced once again— whose members stood above "minds ordinarily constituted." Seeking to implement "a new model of society," this group demanded absolute fidelity and secrecy among its members. It also instructed each member to disclose to his fellows "every fact in his history, and every secret in his heart." Ludloe invited Carwin to join, and the young American leaped at the chance (pp. 263, 273–74, 276–77, 280–85).

This radical creed fed a reformist hunger in both the Irishman and his young friend. More immediately, however, Ludloe's radical utilitarianism found a less elevated target. With his hatred of manual labor looming in the background, and his new teacher's message of unscrupulous self-interest ringing in his ears, Carwin became a confidence man. Under Ludloe's tutelage, he sought "the straightest and surest avenues to wealth and power." A disregard for truthfulness and sincerity became his guiding principle: "Ludloe had taught me to model myself in this respect entirely with a view to immediate consequences. If my genuine interest, on the whole, was promoted by veracity, it was proper to adhere to it; but, if the result of my investigation were opposite, truth was to be sacrificed without scruple." Mrs. Bennington, a wealthy widow in Ireland, became the first object of the con game. Ludloe formulated plans for Carwin to seduce and wed her, thereby gaining access to her fortune (pp. 262–63, 285–86, 288).

In many ways the confidence schemes, the career crisis, and the revolt against paternalism in *Memoirs of Carwin* only set the stage for the real emotional drama of the story: Frank's remarkable talent for ventriloquism and its critical connection to his identity. This "biloquism," as late eighteenth-century usage termed it, was offered neither as a freak of nature nor as a flamboyant literary device. For Brown, it emerged instead as a kind of ideological motif that encapsulated the deceptions and fluidities of bourgeois individualism. Frank had discovered a talent for throwing his voice as a young boy, and had cultivated it innocently as a source of adolescent amusements. He flabbergasted acquaintances by having his spaniel, "Damon," conduct conversations in English. At an outdoor party in Philadelphia, guests were amazed to hear a ghostly "invisible figure" singing sweet songs from somewhere above the garden wall. Frank's thwarted ambition, however, gradually turned this skill toward a new object: the achievement of prosperity and status. This tendency first appeared when the young boy, furious at his widowed father's initial refusal to send him to Philadelphia, snuck into the older man's bedroom in the middle of the night to impersonate his dead mother's voice and urge permission for the trip. When Frank was left out of his wealthy aunt's will, he determined to terrorize the lucky heir—a working-class servant woman—by having his dead aunt's voice demand that the money be given to her nephew. The young man acquired a vague sense that somehow his "biloquial faculty" could be an instrument of ambition and "superior power" (pp. 252, 259–60, 261, 254–66, 259).

Ludloe, however, unintentionally convinced Carwin that his talent could be systematically utilized for deception and gain. The Irishman had observed the incident of the singing spectre at the garden party, and he told Frank his conviction that someone had performed the trick by verbal manipulation. Unaware of his young friend's agency in the matter, he mused on the possibilities of this skill. This "powerful engine" could mold "the ignorant and the credulous" to one's own purposes, Ludloe speculated, and thereby open new pathways to wealth and power:

> A voice coming from a quarter where no attendant form could be seen would, in most cases, be ascribed to supernal agency, and a command imposed on them, in this manner, would be obeyed with religious scrupulousness. Thus, men might be imperiously directed in the dispersal of their industry, their property, and even of their lives. . . . If it were his desire to accumulate wealth, or institute a new sect, he should need no other instrument.

To the ambitious but down-on-his-luck American, this was music to his ears (pp. 268, 264).

By the end of this story, however, Frank Carwin's verbal dexterity had evolved into something else entirely: the crux of a ferocious struggle for identity. The entire last section of the tale focused on Ludloe probing Carwin for every detail of his past, his beliefs, and his character as a prerequisite for joining the radical secret society. Frank confessed everything to his mentor except his precious powers of ventriloquism. As he explained,

> Some fatal obstinacy . . . got possession of me, and I persisted in the resolution of concealing *one thing*. We become fondly attached to objects and pursuits, frequently for no conceivable reason but the pain and trouble they cost us. In proportion to the danger in which they involve us do we cherish them. Our darling potion is the poison that scorches our vitals.

Demanding an absolute subjugation of will, a godlike Ludloe insisted that his protégé could find no peace "till *you* are what I am." For his part in this psychodrama, Frank resisted and literally held on to his biloquism for dear life. This power to deceive and manipulate others, no matter how self-destructive, had become the essence of his individual being. It was the only thing he had, and on this unresolved note the tale ended suddenly (p. 304).

In some ways, this picture of the psychologically torn and socially desperate ventriloquist captured the plight of Brown himself, for whom speaking through other voices comprised the act of writing fiction. In a larger sense, this dramatic portrait of multi-voiced incoherence reflected the inner turmoil of the fragmented self of early capitalist culture. The abrupt conclusion of *Memoirs of Carwin* only heightened the intense psychological and cultural tension it had created. The author could find no way out. The emotional theme of fragmented selfhood and its discontents, however, would bleed into another story to which the writer now hastily turned.

In September 1798 Brown began working on *Memoirs of Stephen Calvert* after abandoning the Carwin tale. As usual, he seems to have written at a frenzied pace but then was interrupted by an outbreak of yellow fever in Philadelphia. It is not clear when he picked up the story again, but eventually it appeared in serialized form in Brown's *Monthly Magazine*. Running in eight installments from June 1799 to June 1800, the "novel" eventually totaled some two hundred printed pages. The plot of *Stephen Calvert*, like many others from this author, combined romance, Gothic mystery, and a fascination with abnormal behavior to make an uneven psychological thriller. Moreover, the story's protagonist was another study in autobiography, complete with Brownian inner doubt, social angst, and paralysis of practical action.

Stephen Calvert was the offspring of family turmoil. His grandparents and parents had been deeply involved in religious and political disputes in England between Protestants and Catholics. When his Protestant parents fled to Pennsylvania, more trouble followed. Stephen's father died prematurely, forcing his mother to open a boarding school to support the family. The rest of the tale revolved around Stephen's clumsy, frustrated attempts to find his way in the world. First, he became the unwitting heir of a significant estate from a distant branch of the Calvert family. Then he became romantically involved with his cousin Louisa Calvert, daughter of Stephen's family benefactor, and Clelia Neville, a beautiful young woman whom he met by accident. All the while, the youthful protagonist grew increasingly erratic and impulsive in his behavior. As Stephen's passions entangled him in a knot of accusations and compromised principles, the story finally came to a surprising and rather dramatic conclusion.[36]

At the outset, *Stephen Calvert* established a narrative point of view with clear social and historical dimensions. It opened with a solitary, lonely individual living a reclusive life on the far western shores of Lake Michigan. Having fled to the edges of the frontier, Stephen Calvert harbored a disgust with society as a place of "temptation and calamity." He had developed "habits of corruption and idleness" in this bustling, competitive world and lost his integrity. The only alternative to an ignominious fate, Calvert had concluded, was withdrawal from "the haunts of mankind." An emotional cripple full of "guilt and remorse," this antisocial individual told his story and as it unfolded, it became evident that his isolation had been forged in a world of social and psychological disintegration. For Stephen Calvert, shifting values and constant deception had created an atmosphere where nothing was what it seemed.[37]

The demise of a paternal social order had played a key role in the making of this volatile world. Brown persistently used the early sections of *Stephen Calvert* to metaphorically portray a crumbling of patriarchal authority. A long chain of betrayal began when his grandfather, also named Stephen, engaged in plots to overthrow the Protestant king of England. When the protagonist's father, yet another Stephen, rejected his sire's reactionary Catholicism for Protestantism and emigrated to America, the grandfather promised revenge. Accusing his son of patricide, the older man bitterly vowed vengeance. According to the narrator, his father's mind became "distinguished by some degree of imbecility," a situation only exacerbated by his mother"s "masculine and daring spirit." The narrator's father eventually died from sheer fright, possibly as a suicide. Thus, this novel, written and set in the revolutionary upheavals of the late eighteenth-century Atlantic world, painted a backdrop of collapsing patriarchal tradition. The protagonist, the last in a line of angry and frightened Stephens, wandered alone into a world of uncertain expectations and dangerous possibilities (pp. 91, 92).

From such moral and social materials Brown reproduced an environment of flux, false appearances, and normlessness. At the very beginning of the novel, Stephen Calvert noted "the evils of society" in America and announced that he had grown "disgusted with its iniquities." The narrative subsequently illuminated a dark mosaic of selfishness, trickery, and expediency. Little escaped the author's denunciation. With males, according to young Calvert, claims to virtue were but "impostures which men practice on themselves. Such are the folds under which selfishness and passion hide themselves, and so easily are their boastful and arrogant pretensions to disinterestedness and magnanimity admitted by their fond slave." Women appeared little better, with the typical female practicing "a thousand stratagems and frauds, and cloaking her hypocrisy under the specious names of dignity, self-respect, modest reserve." In public life, eloquent and principled debate had sunk into the babble of "a market-place, and advocates and statesmen were supplanted by butchers and herb-women." Calvert's republic was an exercise in collective deception, where a malleable character could proclaim, "How invisibly faint are the boundaries of truth and falsehood!" (pp. 73, 165, 129, 162, 196).

Trapped in this fluid and frightening social milieu, Stephen Calvert unaccountably stumbled upon the means to success. As the young man was awkwardly plotting the course of his life, he learned that Ambrose Calvert, a distant uncle of fierce temperament, had willed him, as the nearest male relative, a mansion and estate of over three hundred acres. Brown, significantly, placed this good fortune in a highly problematic light. First, Stephen's success was as undeserved as it was unexpected. Second, Ambrose's position as a slaveowner who passed along fifteen black chattel morally tainted this inherited wealth and status. Finally, Stephen's fondness for Louisa, the disinherited daughter of Ambrose, made him hesitate to take the property out of her hands. The protagonist's agonized attempts to untangle this knot of issues produced only more confusion. Eventually they led him straight into a larger difficulty: a confrontation with himself.

This bewildered young man gradually became lost in the maze of his own psychological impulses.

As the *Memoirs of Stephen Calvert* told its tale, the narrator's intense, uncontrolled passion gradually became the driving force of the story. He slowly exposed himself as a mass of raw nerves and instinctual desires. Stephen's fantasies of wealth and status led him to concoct a half-baked plan: he would marry his cousin Louisa, a young woman he knew only by reputation, and thus hold on to his inheritance with a clear conscience. Louisa's homely appearance and pox-scarred face caused him to waiver, however, and he became attracted to Clelia Neville, a beautiful young woman of refinement and taste. Stephen first proposed marriage to one, then to the other. Louisa at first agreed to wed and then pulled back, while Clelia was forced to tell her impetuous suitor that she was already married to an Englishman. Careening between one young woman and the other, the frantic young man found that self-gratification had created a puzzle of conflicting desires. Wanting everything, he gained nothing.

Stephen's surging passion became especially evident in sexual terms. Fantasizing about the as-yet-unseen Louisa, the youth excited his physical ardor through "golden dreams and delicious palpitations." "I did not believe her exempt from sexual impulses," Calvert declared. "I believed her capable of being dazzled and seduced by a demeanor, characterized by all the impetuosity and tenderness of passion." Clelia, his other love interest, was described by another as a sensual woman eager for the "gratification of her passion" and prone to "forgetfullness of virtuous restraints." Offered as a warning, this only drove the hot-blooded young man in her direction. He became sexually aggressive. "Thou art mine," Stephen told Clelia flatly at one point. "It will be vain to refuse or hesitate. . . . I hearken not to scruples. Denials I will not hear." This forceful undercurrent of hungry, dangerous sexuality in *Memoirs of Stephen Calvert* was underscored by Clelia's tale of her estranged husband, Belgrave. He had married the young heiress only to get her money. Belgrave then rejected Clelia's affection and contemptuously allowed her to witness his sexual union with other men. The horrified young woman fled from these "savage pollutions" and "horrid images of voluptuousness and insensibility" (pp. 108–9, 110, 224–25, 188, 204–5).

Significantly, Brown traced Stephen's libidinous outbursts to a clear source. Books, he asserted, had made the young man "a slave of phantasies and contradictions" and corrupted his view of the world with passionate "imbecility and folly." A particular kind of book, the novel, especially stained Stephen's character. A romance by the seventeenth-century French-woman Madeleine de Scudery, he admitted, had been "the most powerful of all the agents who made me what I am." "If I am fickle and fantastic, not a moral or rational, or political being, but a thing of mere sex, *this* it was that fashioned me. I almost predict that I should owe an ignominious life, and a shameful end, to this book." For Brown the novelist, such an admission constituted a kind of self-denunciation in which vocation and corruption had become tightly joined (pp. 124–25, 192).

Stephen Calvert's uncontrolled passion eventually got the best of him. His avaricious libido began to devour his character from within, while his desperate attempts to restrain it became increasingly ineffective. Subsequent tensions and internal contradictions began to tear Calvert's psychological fabric. An escalating conflict between "the dictates of desire and the injunctions of reason" drained his energy and confused his aspirations. Driven by passion yet obliged by genteel restraint, his moods became "perpetually varying, . . . tranquil or stormy, torn by regrets or soaring into tranquility." Within Calvert's psyche "illusions of poetry" collided with "practical notions of happiness and dignity" to warp his very perceptions of reality. Much like his literary creator, the embattled protagonist even sought refuge in altered states of consciousness. His libidinous reveries with Clelia Neville, for instance, appeared as "the tissue of some golden dream" and a comforting source of "bewitching influence." Struggling unsuccessfully to gain mastery over himself, Stephen Calvert gradually succumbed to a fragmentation of self (pp. 110, 190, 124–25, 176).

This portrait of psychological disarray gained particular clarity through a central drama of the narrative: the clash between Calvert and Sydney Carleton, a stern male figure who demanded self-control. Carleton, a close friend of Louisa Calvert, befriended her impulsive suitor and vowed to save the young man from his own lust for "temporary gratification." He counseled Louisa to refuse marriage until Stephen had reformed his impetuous ways. Carlton then detailed a list of character weaknesses to Stephen's face. In the older man's blunt words, the youth was

raw, inexperienced, with principles untried and unsettled, impetuous, versatile, liable each day to new impressions, and enslaved by a thousand romantic and degrading prejudices. . . . You have hitherto dreamed away your life in solitude. . . . You have nothing but distorted and crude conceptions, and passions

lawless and undisciplined. You are governed by the present impulse, rebel
against all restraints, shrink from all privations, and refer nothing to futurity.

This withering indictment demanded a clear program of reform. Carlton
insisted that his young friend resolutely assert self-control, and struggle "to
discover and exterminate the suggestions of self-interest."[38]

Stephen's reaction mirrored his internal fragmentation. Sometimes he
perceived Sydney Carlton as a kind of alter ego. This demanding voice of
restraint—he had the same initials, SC, as the protagonist—appeared as a
"secret conscience" whispering truths that Calvert could not ignore. Sydney was right, he admitted, as his actions indeed appeared "more allied to
the impulses of sense and to the instigations of vanity, than to any better
principle." At the same time, however, Stephen resisted reform. Carlton's
injunctions triggered resistance as Calvert's emotional impulses "acquired
new strength from this unexpected opposition. These desires dictated my
opinions and my language." The central character in this novel became, in
his own words, a thoroughly "ambiguous being" whose external struggle
with the creed of Sydney Carlton replicated an inner struggle with his
conscience. The story of Stephen Calvert came to center on a dynamic
clash of instinctual drives and civilized restraints within himself. (p. 139).

Brown's study of character disintegration in *Memoirs of Stephen Calvert*
finally reached its crisis point when a submerged theme in the story finally
burst to the surface. Stephen, of course, had become aware of his own internal divisions. He grew troubled, perhaps even frightened, by "the rapid
transitions which my feelings had undergone from indignation and horror,
to complacency, and even rapture. Is there an human heart, said I, fashioned like mine; susceptible to such extremes; shifting guises and forms
with such celerity, and delivering itself up to such opposite emotions within the same short period?" This psychological volatility finally threatened
to erupt, however, when the author reintroduced at story's end a crucial
fact: Stephen was, in fact, an identical twin (p. 212).

As an infant, with religious and political turmoil assaulting the Calvert
family, Stephen's twin brother, Felix, had been left with friends and then
presumed lost and dead through a series of misfortunes. When distraught
parents began to call their surviving son Felix, the germ of identity confusion first appeared. The lonely, bookish Stephen began to fantasize about
this "sacred and tender" bond with another person "coeval in age, and alike
in constitution and figure." In his mind, Felix took shape as almost a hidden, unknown part of himself. This identity confusion created the ultimate

drama of the novel when the long-lost brother, completely by accident and unknown to Stephen, showed up in Philadelphia. His presence prompted several incidents of mistaken identity and entangled the already trouble-prone protagonist in further mysterious difficulties. While Stephen was a young man of "restless, changeful, and impetuous temper," his look-alike brother radiated a "benign complacency" and demonstrated a calm voice and steady character. After being informed of Felix's existence, an amazed Stephen anticipated that their meeting would recover "an essential part of myself," provide "a passage into a new state of being," and somehow make him whole. Appropriately, Sydney Carlton unraveled the mystery and set up a reunion. He prepared to lead Felix into a room to see the waiting Stephen, thereby establishing an image common to later depth psychology: a highly symbolic confrontation of Id, Superego, and lost Ego in a maelstrom of psychological confusion (pp. 88, 97, 267, 270–72).

Before describing the actual meeting, however, *Memoirs of Stephen Calvert* ended abruptly. The meeting of Stephen, Felix, and Sydney never took place as Brown was unable to formulate a resolution of individual fragmentation. In a brief postscript, the author suggested lamely that the "reader's fancy . . . will easily imagine to itself the consequences of such a meeting." Brown clearly could not bring *himself* to such an act of imagination. His protagonist would remain frozen in a state of fragmentation and frustration. As with our final glimpse of Frank Carwin desperately hanging on to his hidden power as a verbal chameleon, Stephen Calvert was last seen standing at the threshold of a solid identity structure, yearning for a coherence that would never be realized (p. 272).

IV

Charles Brockden Brown, both in his writing and his life, embodied the fluctuations and shifting alignments so characteristic of post-Revolutionary America. His fiction had captured the malleable nature of social relationships in an emerging market context, and it had gauged the pressures, both internal and external, which were descending upon its unfettered individuals. Meanwhile, Brown's personal life fueled his literary exploration of liberalizing change. His notorious preoccupation with abnormal psychology—too long this has been written off as mere bizarre Gothic excess—clearly reflected the sense of danger accompanying the disintegration of an older order and the emergence of a new one. Wandering on the new terrain of a competitive society, struggling with its unfamiliar valuations and demands, this novelist had come face to face with a fragmentation of identity and purpose in early liberal America.

A man of heightened sensitivity and exorbitant emotionalism, Brown had sensed early on the internal fluidity at the core of liberal society's confident individualism. Chameleon-like characters, drawn from the felt experiences of historical transformation, emerged from his imagination to people all of his novels. In *Memoirs of Stephen Calvert*, Brown pinpointed this sense of widespread personal volatility in early modern America: "The wisest and soberest of human beings is, in some respects, a madman; that is, he acts against his better reason, and his feet stand still, or go south, when every motive is busy in impelling him north. He cannot infer from his conduct, on one occasion, how he shall act when the same or a similar occasion hereafter occurs."[39]

Such divided instincts and motivations, of course, had plagued the writer's own life. Close observers of Brown's personality and conduct throughout his life were struck by its incoherent quality. Boon companion William Dunlap, for instance, described the young novelist as a creature of "perfect opposites." Brown, straining for success while shuffling the competing demands of reason and passion, appeared so inconsistent that Dunlap could hardly believe that "so much eccentricity, and so much regularity were the productions of one man." Another contemporary observer reacted in similar fashion when faced with the schizoid character of the novelist's private manuscripts. In Brown's journals and notebooks, this aspiring biographer noted with amazement, "to all appearances, two persons are present." Swinging wildly between "gloom and dejection" and "gay and cheerful feelings," the young author had relentlessly engaged in "a grave colloquy and examination of himself." Playing both indolent "criminal" and "inexorable judge" in an ongoing psychological trial, he had imposed moral and social demands upon himself that he could never meet. Brown himself, however, gave perhaps the clearest indication of his own splintered identity. Just a few years before his death, he provided a brief self-revelation in an interview with a British traveler. A revealing glimpse of inner turmoil appeared in this description:

> I am conscious of a double mental existence. When I am sufficiently excited to write, all my ideas flow naturally and irresistible through the medium of sympathies which steep them in shade. . . . This I term, therefore, my imaginative being. My social one has more of light than darkness upon it, because, unless I could carry into society the excitement which makes me write, I could not fall into its feelings. Perhaps . . . the difference of the two may be thus summed up:

in my literary moods I am aiming at making the world something better than I find it; in my social ones I am content to take it as it is.⁴⁰

This divided self of market society powerfully influenced Brown's life and writings from the late 1780s through the early 1800s. It was not merely a singular, peculiar, neurotic trait. The spectre of the fragmented "person-ae" haunted the roads and waterways, the libraries and parlors, the marketplaces and churches of the early American republic. Many of Brown's fellow writers snared this figure and examined it in different forms. Hugh Henry Brackenridge's huge novel *Modern Chivalry* (1792–1815), for instance, juxtaposed the conflicting psychological characters of Captain John Farrago and his servant, Teague O'Regan, across hundreds of pages and years of serialization. The latter, an ebullient Irish confidence man, engaged in one scam after another in his determined search for success. His employer, a stuffy republican gentleman of paternal habits, denounced his servant's "preposterous aiming and stretching at promotion" and demanded virtuous self-restraint. Brackenridge, the authorial presence between the irascible Teague and the repressive captain, never resolved their conflict. The novel ultimately became a sketch of the troubled inner world of the liberal self.⁴¹

Philip Freneau, the noted American poet and essayist of the late eighteenth century, commented in similar fashion on the fragmented character of his ambitious countrymen. In his view, America's "darling commerce" had created a society of manipulators where masked motives and purposeful performances predominated. If a stranger appeared before the typical man of business as a prosperous and influential individual, Freneau noted, "he smiles upon you as a bone of his bone and the flesh of his flesh; if not, he bids you adieu, and walks off with as little ceremony as possible." According to this critic, the typical American "market man"—the title of one of his essays—functioned as a lifeless "perambulating machine, till he comes to the scene of action, his counting house or his law shop," and only then did he spring to life. This eventually produced a typical "mental malady" among American social-climbing individuals: "a man, instead of apprehending he may fall, becomes anxious to go higher, until everything becomes so indistinct below . . . that he has no correct ideas, his head is full of notions—a man in this condition is mad." In a post-Revolutionary society of appearances and manipulation, Freneau seemed to conclude, a solid and dependable core of self had vanished.⁴²

This preoccupation with social flux and fragmented selves, moreover, was not peculiar to the community of American intellectuals. It reverberated throughout much of the early modern Atlantic world. In England, for example, the pathbreaking novels of the mid-eighteenth century—Daniel Defoe's *Robinson Crusoe* (1719), Samuel Richardson's *Pamela* (1740) and *Clarissa* (1748), Henry Fielding's *Joseph Andrews* (1742) and *Tom Jones* (1749)—had charted the vagaries and contingencies of individual independence. By the turn of the century, early stirrings of the romantic movement had intensified this trend. Consistently juxtaposing self and society, it trumpeted the triumph of individual creativity. On the one hand, this emergence of the "romantic artist" brought explicit criticism of laissez-faire liberalism. On the other, the persistence of a fairly rigid class system shaped a genre that examined individual autonomy within the context of hierarchical social restraints. Here the mature novel appeared most clearly, perhaps, in Jane Austen's *Pride and Prejudice* (1813) and *Emma* (1816). All in all, English literary culture in what has been described as a "decisive period" from 1750 to 1830 delineated several profound separations: the division of knowledge, the division of labor, the division of culture and aesthetics from society and production, the division of the self into role-playing fragments. As Henry Fielding had observed as early as the mid-1700s, the performative ethic of market society had made individual purpose unknowable. The world and the theater had become so alike, he wrote, that the same words were used "when we speak of life in general as when we confine ourselves to dramatic performances."[43]

Many intellectuals on the Continent pursued similar themes. Jean-Jacques Rousseau, for example, wrote widely throughout the late eighteenth century on the fragmentation and alienation that seemed to accompany commercial growth. His *Discourses on the Arts and Sciences* (1749–50) and *Discourses on the Fundamental Inequality among Men* (1753–54) argued that modern society had brought not progress but a host of artificial needs and desires. These included a frantic search for wealth and status, an ethic of competitiveness and treachery, and a personality type where greed and deception smothered the true self. His *Letter to M. D'Alembert* (1758) bitterly complained that "acting" had become a metaphor for commercial life in which one made "a traffic of oneself" and perfected "the art of counterfeiting himself, of putting on another character than his own." His novels, however, confirmed that Rousseau was no simple reactionary. Both *The New Eloisa* (1760) and *Emile* (1762) advocated liberation from paternal despotism and education of the individual based on conditioning of "natural" inclinations. This would be no easy task, however, as Rousseau acknowledged with this description of the modern individual in *Emile*: "The man of the world is entirely covered with a mask; he is so accustomed to disguise, that if, at any time he is obliged for a moment to assume his natural character his uneasiness and constraint are palpably obvious. . . . Reality is no part of his concern, he aims at nothing more than appearance."[44]

In Germany, the poet and philosopher Friedrich Schiller echoed many of the same social and psychological fears. His *Letters Concerning the Aesthetic Education of Humanity*, published in 1795, analyzed at considerable length the divided identity of the modern individual. Schiller argued that the development of profit-oriented economic structures, bureaucratic institutions, and a rationalized work ethic had created a complex, mechanical society of "innumerable but lifeless parts." Corroding the "inner unity of human nature, " this process had shaped a modern individual whose "faculties . . . [are] as separate in practice as they are distinguished by the psychologist in theory." Pressures for success had produced specialized talents while "the remaining aptitudes of the psyche are neglected in order to give undivided attention to the one which will bring honour and profit." This internal division, Schiller eloquently wrote, had seen "enjoyment divorced from labour, the means from the end, the effort from the reward. Everlastingly chained to a single little fragment of the Whole, man himself develops into nothing but a fragment; everlastingly in his ear the monotonous sound of the wheel that he turns, he never develops the harmony of his being." For this German intellectual, political reform was chimerical "as long as the split within man is not healed, and his nature so restored to wholeness that it can itself . . . guarantee the reality of this political creation of Reason."[45]

Brown's analysis of fragmenting society and selfhood thus resonated widely in the late eighteenth-century Atlantic world. His solution to the problem—a repressive bourgeois ethic of self-control—proved equally revealing. An ideal of "culture" became his means to accept yet control outbursts of social selfishness and animal instinct. Enlisting under the banner of gentility and refinement, by the early 1800s he marshaled his literary force into the cause of genteel restraint and beauty. An elevated culture of self-control, Brown hoped, would compress the individual's warring internal instincts into a whole. The writing of fiction, he once noted of himself, often "has blunted my vexations; hushed my stormy passions; turned my peevishness into soothing; my fierce revenge into heart-dissolving pity."[46]

Brown became the prototype of a new figure in nineteenth-century

American life. As a "gentleman of culture," a genteel bourgeois moralist preaching the virtues of restraint and taste, he represented a significant departure from the earlier "gentleman of letters." In the colonial era, gentlemen had dominated both intellectual life and the social structure as part of their paternal exercise of authority. Ministers, magistrates, lawyers, and the gentry, as custodians of learning, had comprised a self-conscious elite. They ritualistically displayed a culture of devotional literature and scientific treatise, classical allusion and rhetorical skill, law and history. These eighteenth-century tribunes of this "republic of letters," as one scholar has termed it, expected and received deferential respect from below. Learning was a function of the gentleman's social position. After the American Revolution, however, market expansion and popular politics increasingly transformed the cultural atmosphere. In this climate the cultural authority of an older paternal elite gradually eroded. Many gentlemen intellectuals like Brown, faced with a volatile republic of ambition and factionalism, individualism and public opinion, newspapers and novels, reshaped the traditional position. Discarding deference for persuasion, they increasingly articulated a didactic morality and a standard of genteel aesthetics as a means to influence. "Taste" and "self-control," the watchwords of new cultural arbiters, promised not only to internalize authority rather than demand crude submission to it, but to weld together fragments of society and self. These early nineteenth-century "gentlemen of culture" perceived their roles as heroic ones. As architects of stability in a tumultuous age, they shaped learning and literature as a counterweight to dominant social trends rather than, in the tradition of their paternal forefathers, displaying it as a natural product of social authority.[47]

This cultural agenda proved attractive to many others beside Brown. By the early nineteenth century, other "gentlemen of culture" were rushing to join a broad crusade promoting bourgeois values. Benjamin Rush provided a notable example. This wide-ranging American philosophe—doctor, educator, evangelical Christian essayist, and political writer—became known as the "Father of American Psychiatry" and mounted a multifront cultural campaign for self-control by the early 1800s. While firmly committed to moral free agency, Rush became convinced that avoidance of anarchy demanded the individual development of self-restraint through several techniques: a "virtuous education," "the principles and obligations of religion," the utilization of "shame and guilt" in childrearing, and a regimen of "constant labor." He sought to institutionalize these principles. Criminals, for instance, could best be reformed through a "penitentiary system" that inculcated restraint through "pain, labor, watchfulness, solitude, and silence." For the insane, Rush devised the ultimate instrument of self-control: his famous "tranquilizer chair" that restrained agitated individuals for days at a time while supposedly encouraging calm and self-regulation. Such devices seemed necessary to a man who believed that "in the United States, madness has increased since the year 1790." Social change—"an increase in the number and magnitude of the objects of ambition and avarice"—demanded cultural solutions.[48]

Others joined Rush and Brown in swelling the ranks of an American army of genteel moralists. Lyman Beecher, the New England minister and lecturer, proclaimed a consistent message throughout the early nineteenth century. There was great need for a "disciplined moral militia," he insisted, to spread the message of temperance, steady industry, and religious benevolence in a foot-loose society of "men freed from restraint." Judith Sargent Murray, in her famous collection of essays in *The Gleaner* (1798), urged American females to combine independence and self-reliance with stern "habits of industry and order." This idealized cult of "republican motherhood" established women as moral guardians, responsible for promoting virtuous conduct in their husbands and demanding it of their children. "Parson" Mason Locke Weems used his immensely popular *Life of Washington* to temper the gospel of success seeking with a message of self-restraint. The Founding Father's belief that industry was "the queen mother of all our virtues," the author maintained, went hand-in-hand with his determination to stand foremost among those who have "command over their passion." Weems' didactic pamphlets like *God's Revenge Against Gambling*, and *The Drunkard's Looking Glass* popularized the same message of internal regulation. This array of early nineteenth-century pronouncements would converge by the 1830s to create a culture of American Victorianism. Its repressive creed of firm moral character, genteel conduct, and an unrelenting work ethic would apotheosize a double-edged notion of self-control as regulator of both destiny and passion. This *mentalité*, like the concern with fragmented selfhood, also crisscrossed the Atlantic to shape nineteenth-century European bourgeois culture.[49]

Charles Brockden Brown's dual significance in post-Revolutionary America—as a barometer of psychological convulsions caused by the growth of market society and as a "gentleman of culture" urging restraint and taste—proved to be a heavy burden. At some level he sensed the enor-

mous tension between these two roles, and predicted that the liberal individual's struggle to reconcile culture and passion would be long and vexing.
Doubtless writing from a sense of his own profound divisions, Brown cau-
tioned in one of his novels that "the world is eternally producing what, to
our precipitate judgement, are prodigies, anomalies, monsters. Innate, dastardly, sordid wickedness frequently springs up where genial temperature
and wise culture had promised us the most heavenly products."[50]

This earliest of American novelists uncovered the schizoid quality of
liberal bourgeois civilization even in its formative stages. In both his writings and his life, he gauged the enormous tension generated by its dark,
hidden springs of passion desperately held in check by the moral force of a
genteel, repressive culture. More clearly than most, Brown illuminated the
"liberal ego" as the psychological type called into being by that civilization.
This early modern formulation of self featured inner-directedness, self-
control, and calculating force of will as a thin shell covering a painfully
fragmented personality structure beneath. With this Philadelphia man of
letters, the vaunted image of confident liberal individualism seemed hollow and brittle.

Brown's foreshadowing of this theme would gradually preoccupy nineteenth-century culture. In 1837, for example, Ralph Waldo Emerson would
use his "American Scholar" address to describe the United States as a society enshrining "the single individual" whose isolated "members have suffered amputation from the trunk, and strut about as so many walking
monsters—a good finger, a neck, a stomach, an elbow, but never a man."
By mid-century, popular and sensationalist Gothic novels regularly depicted human passion as a dangerous force hidden from rational view but always ready to burst to the surface. Evil, in a repressed Victorian society,
took shape as submerged deviant impulses held in check by internal mechanisms of guilt. It appeared, according to one recent description, in an
imaginative underworld of "gamblers and prostitutes, Mormons and
Catholics, slave-holders and rum-sellers, the very poor and the very rich,
the criminal and the insane," all of whom were subject to the social discipline of the penitentiary, the asylum, and the benevolence of genteel
Protestantism. This American concern with the splintering of both society
and private consciousness reached a climax with Herman Melville. In
*Moby Dick*, Captain Ahab personified the divided self as a monster of
"narrow-flowing monomania" whose massive, uncontrolled rage made him
a "formless, somnambulistic being." A few years later Melville's *The Confidence Man* presented a gloomy, biting, even surrealistic picture of a fluid

society completely filled with formless beings whose masks shifted constantly according to the demands of ambition.[51]

Across the Atlantic, a similar cultural preoccupation arose everywhere. It gave rise to popular nineteenth-century texts like Mary Shelley's *Frankenstein*, where scientific expertise summoned forth a half-human monster of libidinous instincts, or *The Strange Case of Dr. Jekyll and Mr. Hyde*, Robert Louis Stevenson's tale of the horrible double-identity of a Victorian physician. A theme of fragmentation became central to the great European critics of bourgeois liberalism. Alexis de Tocqueville argued that liberated Americans were ambitious yet seemingly never happy. The constant tension produced by success seeking and material pursuit, he argued, wearied the mind and brought on "a strange melancholy." Believing that in America "madness is commoner than anywhere else," Tocqueville concluded that within the imaginative parameters of liberal society, self-absorbed individuals "abandoning truth and reality, create monsters." Max Weber came to the gloomy belief that bourgeois culture's "most urgent task [was] the destruction of spontaneous, impulsive enjoyment" and the construction of an "iron cage" of repression. Karl Marx, castigating self-denial as a doctrine where "the less you *are* , the more you *have*," analyzed liberal capitalism as a system undermining the very notion of fixed meanings and identities. "All that is solid melts into air" in this world, Marx insisted, as relationships and beliefs "become obsolete before they can ossify." Like "the sorcerer who can no longer control the powers of the underworld," bourgeois society had created a fragmented and "partially developed individual, who is merely the bearer of one specialized social function." Sigmund Freud represented, perhaps, the culmination of this entire trend. His depth psychology of the Id, Ego, and Superego posited fragmentation as the very essence of the human condition. It further insisted that repression of instinct, with its attendant discontents, unavoidably accompanied more complex social formations. "Civilized man has exchanged a portion of his possibilities of happiness for a portion of security," Freud argued, and he insisted that little could change that.[52]

While Charles Brockden Brown stood below Melville and Marx, Weber and Freud, Tocqueville and Emerson as an observer of the society and psyche of the early modern West, he anticipated much of their criticism. He registered the historical reverberations that they would later analyze. In many ways his intellectual and emotional instincts were the same: to penetrate the ideology of liberal capitalist culture with its mask of rational, calculating self-interest, to reach the instinctual heart pulsating deep within, and to somehow reconcile the two. As this American writer and critic had suggested in a brilliantly erratic career from 1790 to 1810, American individualism had enshrined industry and artifice, gentility and manipulation as social and cultural practices. With ultimate irony, Brown demonstrated that in this new age, even bourgeois liberalism itself was not quite what it seemed to be.

# Notes

INTRODUCTION

1. On Charles Brockden Brown's nearsightedness, see Deborah Bingham, "The Identity Crisis of Charles Brockden Brown" (Ph.D. diss., Bowling Green State University, 1977), 31–32, where she quotes a recollection of Brown's close friend, William Dunlap. Brown's comment on his own name can be found in William Dunlap, *The Life of Charles Brockden Brown* (Philadelphia, 1815), 2:120.

2. Raymond Williams' metaphor is cited in E. P. Thompson, "Last Dispatches from the Border Country," *Nation* (Mar. 5, 1988): 310–11. For general discussions of recent cultural theory, see, for example, Dominick LaCapra and Steven L. Kaplan, *Modern European Intellectual History: Reappraisals and New Perspectives* (Ithaca, N.Y. 1982); Terry Eagleton, *Literary Theory: An Introduction* (Minneapolis, 1983); Michael Ryan, *Marxism and Deconstruction: A Critical Articulation* (Baltimore, 1982); H. Aram Veeser, *The New Historicism* (New York, 1989); and George Lipsitz, "Listening to Learn and Learning to Listen: Popular Culture, Cultural Theory, and American Studies," *American Quarterly* 42 (Dec. 1990): 615–36. For my own critical assessment of much of this recent theory, see Steven Watts, "The Idiocy of American Studies: Post-Structuralism, Language, and Politics in the Age of Self-Fulfillment," *American Quarterly* 43 (Dec. 1991): 625–60.

3. See Paul Allen, *The Life of Charles Brockden Brown* (1814 MS; reprint Delmar, N.Y., 1975); William Dunlap, *The Life of Charles Brockden Brown* (Philadelphia, 1815); Harry R. Warfel, *Charles Brockden Brown, American Gothic Novelist* (Gainesville, Fla., 1949); David Lee Clark, *Charles Brockden Brown: Pioneer Voice of America* (Durham, N.C., 1952).

4. See Alan Axelrod, *Charles Brockden Brown, An American Tale* (Austin, 1983); Norman S. Grabo, *The Coincidental Art of Charles Brockden Brown* (Chapel Hill, N.C., 1981); Donald A. Ringe, *Charles Brockden Brown* (New York, 1966). Broader assessments of Brown have appeared more recently as part of larger works on the literary culture of late eighteenth- and early nineteenth-century America. See, for example, Cathy N. Davidson, *Revolution and the Word: The Rise of the Novel in America* (New York, 1986), 236–53; and Michael Warner, *The Letters of the Republic: Publication and the Public Sphere in Eighteenth-Century America* (Cambridge, Mass., 1990), 152–73. For a discussion of my own assessment of the existing literature on Brown, see the Bibliographic Essay at the end of this book.

5. For recent provocative assessments of change in the early modern West, par-

ticularly with regard to cultural transformations, see Jean-Christophe Agnew, *Worlds Apart: The Market and the Theater in Anglo-American Thought, 1550–1750* (Cambridge, 1986); Jay Fliegelman, *Prodigals and Pilgrims: The American Revolution against Patriarchal Authority* (Cambridge, 1982); and Michael McKeon, *The Origins of the English Novel, 1600–1740* (Baltimore, 1987).

6. See, for instance, Joyce Appleby, *Capitalism and a New Social Order: The Republican Vision of the 1790s* (New York, 1984); Nancy F. Cott, *The Bonds of Womanhood: "Woman's Sphere" in New England, 1780–1835* (New Haven, 1977); Joseph J. Ellis, *After the Revolution: Profiles of Early American Culture* (New York, 1979); Paul E. Johnson, *A Shopkeeper's Millennium: Society and Revivals in Rochester, New York, 1815–1837* (New York, 1978); Michael Paul Rogin, *Fathers and Children: Andrew Jackson and the Subjugation of the American Indian* (New York, 1975); Sean Wilentz, *Chants Democratic: New York City and the Rise of the American Working Class, 1788–1850* (New York, 1984); and Steven Watts, *The Republic Reborn: War and the Making of Liberal America, 1790–1820* (Baltimore, 1987).

7. See Terry Eagleton, *Literary Theory: An Introduction* (Minneapolis, 1983), 115–18, for a compelling discussion of "discourse" and its theoretical implications.

8. On hegemony, see T. J. Jackson Lears, "The Concept of Cultural Hegemony: Problems and Possibilities," *American Historical Review* 90 (June 1985): 567–93. An introduction to the Frankfurt School can be found in Martin Jay, *The Dialectical Imagination* (Boston, 1973). A fuller and more precise discussion of my theoretical orientation in this book can be found in Chapter 1.

9. See Agnew, *Worlds Apart*; R. Jackson Wilson, *Figures of Speech: American Writers and the Literary Marketplace from Benjamin Franklin to Emily Dickinson* (Baltimore, 1989); Michael T. Gilmore, *American Romanticism and the Marketplace* (Chicago, 1985); Robert Shulman, *Social Criticism and Nineteenth-Century American Fictions* (Columbia, Mo., 1987); Susan Coultrap-McQuin, *Doing Literary Business: American Women Writers in the Nineteenth Century* (Chapel Hill, N.C., 1990); Michael Anesko, *"Friction with the Market": Henry James and the Profession of Authorship* (New York, 1986); and Christopher P. Wilson, *The Labor of Words: Literary Professionalism in the Progressive Era* (Athens, Ga., 1985). For a discussion of this line of analysis, see C. Deirdre Phelps' review essay, "Market Studies and Book History in American Literature," *Review* 12 (1990): 273–301.

10. The phrase "structure of feeling" has been borrowed from Raymond Williams, *Marxism and Literature* (New York, 1977), 128–35.

11. Several sources have eased the process of research for this book. Over the past decade and a half, the Kent State University Press has issued a bicentennial edition of Brown's major writings. These beautifully edited volumes, complete with historical and textual essays, have provided authoritative versions of his novels and made them wonderfully accessible. In addition, the bulk of Brown's other published writings particularly his shorter fiction, newspaper and magazine essays, and political pamphlets—has become available on microfilm. Several fat caches of private correspondence, which most of Brown's biographers have overlooked in favor of his novelistic writing, also have proved highly useful. In particular, his mid-1790s letters to close friend Joseph Bringhurst, held at the Longfellow–Hawthorne

Library at Bowdoin College, and his early nineteenth-century missives to fiancée Elizabeth Linn, on file at the Humanities Research Center at the University of Texas, have shed great light on Brown's developing cultural views.

CHAPTER I. THE NOVEL AND THE MARKET IN THE
EARLY REPUBLIC

1. Paul Allen, *The Life of Charles Brockden Brown* (1814 MS; reprint Delmar, N.Y., 1975), 11; Harry R. Warfel, *Charles Brockden Brown, American Gothic Novelist* (Gainesville, Fla., 1949), 22, 17; Thomas R. Doerflinger, *A Vigorous Spirit of Enterprise: Merchants and Economic Development in Revolutionary Philadelphia* (New York, 1986), 34–35.

2. Allen, *Charles Brockden Brown*, 10–11; the letter from Brown is quoted in David Lee Clark, *Charles Brockden Brown: Pioneer Voice of America* (Durham, N.C., 1952), 38–39, while the other quote appears on p. 60.

3. For a more extensive discussion of my interpretation of this transformation, see Steven Watts, *The Republic Reborn: War and the Making of Liberal America, 1790–1820* (Baltimore, 1987), xv–xxiii, 1–107.

4. See Raymond Williams, *Culture and Society: 1780-1950* (1958; reprint New York, 1983), for a brilliant analysis of the modern idea of "culture."

5. For various perspectives on the emergence of a market society in post-Revolutionary America, see the following works: James A. Henretta, *The Origins of American Capitalism: Collected Essays* (Boston, 1991); Christopher Clark, *The Roots of Rural Capitalism: Western Massachusetts, 1780–1860* (Ithaca, N.Y., 1990); Allan Kulikoff, "The Transition to Capitalism in Rural America," *William and Mary Quarterly* 3rd Series, 46 (Jan. 1989): 120–44; Daniel Vickers, "Competency and Competition: Economic Culture in Early America," *William and Mary Quarterly* 3rd Series, 47 (Jan. 1990): 3–29; Nancy Grey Osterund, *Bonds of Community: The Lives of Farm Women in Nineteenth-Century New York* (Ithaca, N.Y., 1991); Jeane Boydston, *Home and Work: Housework, Wages, and the Ideology of Labor in the Early Republic* (New York, 1990); Michael Merrill, "Cash Is Good to Eat: Self-Sufficiency and Exchange in the Rural Economy of the United States," *Radical History Review* 4 (Winter 1977): 42–71; and Steven Watts, *Republic Reborn*, 2–16, 64–78.

6. See Doerflinger, *Vigorous Spirit of Enterprise*, 283–364, and Watts, *Republic Reborn*, 2–9, and the extensive bibliography listings on pp. 326–27 and 336–39.

7. See, for example, Joyce Appleby, "Commercial Farming and the 'Agrarian Myth' in the Early Republic," *Journal of American History* 68 (Mar. 1982): 833–49; Diane Lindstrom, "American Economic Growth before 1840: New Evidence and New Directions," *Journal of Economic History* 39 (Mar. 1979): 289–301; and Thomas C. Cochran, "The Business Revolution," *American Historical Review* 79 (Dec. 1974): 1449–66.

8. For surveys of the vast literature on republicanism, see two articles by Robert Shalhope in the *William and Mary Quarterly*: "Toward a Republican Synthesis: The Emergence of an Understanding of Republicanism in American Historiography," 29 (Jan. 1972): 49–80, and "Republicanism and Early American Historiogra-

phy," 39 (Apr. 1982): 334–56. See also a special issue of the *American Quarterly* entitled "Republicanism in the History and Historiography of the United States," 37 (Fall 1985).

9. See the historiographical literature mentioned above, as well as the discussion in Joyce Appleby, *Capitalism and a New Social Order: The Republican Vision of the 1790s* (New York, 1984); James T. Kloppenberg, "The Virtues of Liberalism: Christianity, Republicanism, and Ethics in Early American Political Discourse," *Journal of American History* 74 (June 1987): 9–33; Rowland Berthoff, "Independence and Attachment, Virtue and Interest: From Republican Citizen to Free Enterprizer, 1787–1837," in Richard Bushman et al., *Uprooted Americans: Essays to Honor Oscar Handlin* (Boston, 1979), 99–124; and Watts, *Republic Reborn*, 11–14, 217–63.

10. Doerflinger, *Vigorous Spirit of Enterprise*, 3–5, 283–334, and Watts, *Republic Reborn*, 8–11.

11. Jay Fliegelman, *Prodigals and Pilgrims: The American Revolution against Patriarchal Authority, 1750–1800* (Cambridge, 1982), presents the best discussion of "patriarchalism" and its demise in eighteenth-century America.

12. This rhetoric of self-reliance has been discussed in Robert E. Shalhope, *The Roots of Democracy: American Thought and Culture, 1760–1800* (Boston, 1990), 139–68; Jean V. Matthews, *Toward a New Society: American Thought and Culture, 1800–1830* (Boston, 1991), 113–52; and Watts, *Republic Reborn*, 64–70.

13. On the Second Great Awakening, religion, and culture, see Nathan O. Hatch, *The Democratization of American Christianity* (New Haven, 1989); Henry F. May, *The Enlightenment in America* (New York, 1976), 337–57; Donald G. Mathews, "The Second Great Awakening as an Organizing Process, 1780–1830," *American Quarterly* 21 (Spring 1969): 23–43; and Watts, *Republic Reborn*, 113–22.

14. See May, *Enlightenment in America*, 307–62; Matthews, *Toward a New Society*, 37–39; and Emory Elliott, *Revolutionary Writers: Literature and Authority in the New Republic, 1725–1810* (New York, 1986), 30–35.

15. "The Rising Glory of America" is discussed in Joseph J. Ellis, *After the Revolution: Profiles of Early American Culture* (New York, 1979), 9–10, while much of this text discusses insightfully the tense cultural situation of the post-Revolutionary era. See also Shalhope, *Roots of Democracy*, 53–82; Elliott, *Revolutionary Writers*, 19–54; and Steven Watts, "Masks, Morals, and the Market: American Literature and Early Capitalist Culture," *Journal of the Early Republic* 6, no. 2 (1986): 127–49.

16. See the broad discussions in Elliott, *Revolutionary Writers*, and Cathy N. Davidson, *Revolution and the Word: The Rise of the Novel in America* (New York, 1986).

17. See Lewis P. Simpson, ed., *The Federalist Literary Mind* (Baton Rouge, La., 1962); and Elliott, *Revolutionary Writers*, 55–91.

18. See the essay on Parson Weems in Watts, *Republic Reborn*, 141–51.

19. See Ellis, *After the Revolution*, 73–112; David Simpson, *The Politics of American English, 1776–1850* (New York, 1986), 52–90; and Watts, *Republic Reborn*, 42–58, 112.

20. See Davidson, *Revolution and the Word*, vii, 41–44, 55–79, on the "reading revolution" in late eighteenth- and early nineteenth-century America.

21. Fine discussions of popular reading habits and the implications for culture

can be found in Bernard Bailyn et al., *The Great Republic: A History of the American People* (Lexington, Mass., 1977), 358; Russel B. Nye, *The Cultural Life of the New Nation, 1776–1830* (New York, 1930), 251–52, 240–41; Gordon S. Wood, ed., *The Rising Glory of America, 1760–1820* (New York, 1971), 253; Davidson, *Revolution and the Word*, 160, 13; and Elliott, *Revolutionary Writers*, 19–54.

22. See Davidson, *Revolution and the Word*, vii, 10; and Fliegelman, *Prodigals and Pilgrims*, 26–29, 80, 144, 240.

23. See Lionel Trilling, *The Liberal Imagination: Essays on Literature and Society* (New York, 1976), 222; Davidson, *Revolution and the Word*, 44; Dominick LaCapra, *History and Criticism* (Ithaca, N.Y., 1985), 115.

24. The dominant interpretive text in this school is Ian Watt, *The Rise of the Novel: Studies in Defoe, Richardson, and Fielding* (Berkeley, Calif., 1957), 11, 12, 13, 14–30, 49–52, 60. The block quote appears on p. 31. See also Michael McKeon, *The Origins of the English Novel, 1600–1740* (Baltimore, 1987) for a highly sophisticated revision of the Watt thesis that ties the rise of the novel to cultural, social, and epistemological instability in early modern English life.

25. See Davidson, *Revolution and the Word* (the quotation appears on p. 10) for a masterful development of this thesis.

26. On cultural hegemony, see Raymond Williams, "Base and Superstructure in Marxist Cultural Theory," *New Left Review* 82 (Nov.–Dec. 1973): 3–16; T. J. Jackson Lears, "The Concept of Cultural Hegemony: Problems and Possibilities," *American Historical Review* 90 (June 1985): 567–93; and Watts, *Republic Reborn*, xix–xxi.

27. See Watt, *Rise of the Novel*, 31–32, 34, 294; Fliegelman, *Prodigals and Pilgrims*, 26; Rhys Isaac, *The Transformation of Virginia, 1740–1790* (Chapel Hill, N.C., 1982), 121–22; Patricia Meyer Spacks, *Imagining a Self: Autobiography and Novel in Eighteenth-Century England* (Cambridge, Mass., 1976), 1.

28. See Tony Tanner, *Adultery and the Novel* (New York, 1979), 3–4.

29. Davidson, in *Revolution and the Word*, offers abundant and compelling evidence for the dissenting role of early American novels, but I offer a rather different assessment of the thrust and significance of that dissent in historical and political terms.

30. See Fliegelman, *Prodigals and Pilgrims*, 26–27; Davidson, *Revolution and the Word*, 51; Tanner, *Adultery and the Novel*, 15.

31. See Agnew, *Worlds Apart*, 14, 73, 82–83, 94–95, 97–98, 182–83, for a brilliant analysis of this twin crisis in emerging liberal culture. Carl Schorske, in his *Fin-de-Siecle Vienna: Politics and Culture* (New York, 1981), offers an interpretation of similar issues at work in late nineteenth-century liberalism.

32. See Agnew, *Worlds Apart*, 97–98, 73.

33. See McKeon, Origins of the English Novel;, 20–21, and Spacks, *Imagining a Self*, 4–6, 310.

34. See Watt, *Rise of the Novel*, 200–201, 175–76; Terry Eagleton, *Literary Theory: An Introduction* (Minneapolis, 1983), 18–19; and Agnew, *Worlds Apart*, 188–90.

35. See Fred Weinstein and Gerald M. Platt, *The Wish to Be Free: Society, Psyche, and Value Change* (Berkeley, Calif., 1969), 197–226.

36. See Spacks, *Imagining a Self*, 1, 2–3, 8, 10–11, 22, 314–15.

37. Agnew, *Worlds Apart*, 82–83, 101–2, 185–86.

38. See Max Horkheimer, "The Lessons of Fascism," in Hadley Cantril, ed., *Tensions That Cause Wars* (Urbana, Ill., 1950), 230; Philip Rieff, *The Triumph of the Therapeutic: Uses of Faith after Freud* (New York, 1966), 2–3.

39. See Spacks, *Imagining a Self*, 304–6; and Watts, *Republic Reborn*, 49–55.

40. The phrase "liberal ego" has been borrowed from two brilliant studies: Schorske, *Fin-de-Siecle Vienna*, 4–5, 22, 208–9; and Christopher Lasch, *The Minimal Self: Psychic Survival in Troubled Times* (New York, 1984), 205–23.

### CHAPTER 2. THE LAWYER AND THE RHAPSODIST

1. See David Lee Clark, *Charles Brockden Brown: Pioneer Voice of America* (Durham, N.C., 1952), 13–16; Harry R. Warfel, *Charles Brockden Brown, American Gothic Novelist* (Gainesville, Fla., 1949), 16–17; Deborah Marie Bingham, "The Identity Crisis of Charles Brockden Brown" (Ph.D. diss., Bowling Green State University, 1977), 8–11.

2. Ibid.

3. Paul Allen, *The Life of Charles Brockden Brown* (1814 MS; reprint Delmar, N.Y., 1975),10–11.

4. Clark, *Pioneer Voice*, 18–19; Warfel, *Gothic Novelist*, 22–25; Allen, *Charles Brockden Brown*, 10–11; Bingham, "Identity Crisis," 24–28.

5. Charles E. Bennett, "The Charles Brockden Brown Canon," (Ph.D. diss., University of North Carolina, 1974), 59; Allen, *Charles Brockden Brown*, 18, 23–24, 26, 25, 30, 22.

6. See Bennett, "Brown Canon," 1–3, 6–9, 11–12.

7. Ibid., 51–52, 145, 152; and Clark, *Pioneer Voice*, 17. The quotations are from two letters written by Brown to his close friend Joseph Bringhurst, Jr. A large collection of these letters is held by the Bowdoin College Library in Brunswick, Maine. Charles E. Bennett has provided an annotated census of them in his "The Letters of Charles Brockden Brown: An Annotated Census," *Resources for American Literary Study* 6 (Autumn 1976): 164–190, and citations to the Brown–Bringhurst Letters hereafter will also refer to the Bennett census. For the material in this paragraph, see Brown to Bringhurst, July 29, 1793 (Bowdoin MS), Bennett census #48; and ibid., May 20, 1792, Bennett census #21.

8. William Dunlap, *The Life of Charles Brockden Brown* (Philadelphia, 1815), 1:27; Jay Fliegelman, *Prodigals and Pilgrims: The American Revolution against Patriarchal Authority* (Cambridge, 1982), 247; Bennett, "Brown Canon," 52, 151, 60–61; and two letters from Brown to Bringhurst, May 1792 (Bowdoin MS), Bennett census #12, and Dec. 21, 1792, Bennett census #36.

9. Bingham, "Identity Crisis," 52–54; Alexander Cowie, "Historical Essay," in Charles Brockden Brown, *Wieland; or, the Transformation, An American Tale* (Kent, Ohio, 1977), 313; Allen, *Charles Brockden Brown*, 31–39; Bennett, "Brown Canon," 57; Dunlap, *Life of Brown*, 1:53–54; and Clark, *Pioneer Voice*, 33.

10. See Warfel, *Gothic Novelist*, 29–30; and Allen, *Charles Brockden Brown*, 12–13, 15–16.

11. See Bennett, "Brown Canon," 10–11, 24–25; Brown to Debby Ferris, May 28,

1795 (Bowdoin MS), Bennett census #58; Clark, *Pioneer Voice*, 195; Warfel, *Gothic Novelist*, 96.

12. See discussion in Bennett, "Brown Canon," 21–24; Brown to Bringhurst, May 1792 (Bowdoin MS), Bennett census #12, and May 20, 1792, Bennett census #21; Allen, *Charles Brockden Brown*, 52–53; Clark, *Pioneer Voice*, 26.

13. Brown to Bringhurst, Dec. 9, 1792 (Bowdoin MS), Bennett census #35; Clark, *Pioneer Voice*, 84; Brown to Bringhurst, 1793 (Bowdoin MS), Bennett census #45; Allen, *Charles Brockden Brown*, 12–13.

14. See Bingham, "Identity Crisis," 19–20, 23–24, 54–55, 7–8, 48–49; Clark, *Pioneer Voice*, 101; Warfel, *Gothic Novelist*, 19–20. On the revolt against paternalism in Revolutionary America, see Edwin G. Burrows and Michael Wallace, "The American Revolution: The Ideology and Psychology of National Liberation," *Perspectives in American History* 6 (1972): 266–303 and Fliegelman, *Prodigals and Pilgrims*.

15. See Bennett, "Brown Canon," 21; and Bennett, "Annotated Census," 164–65.

16. See several letters from Brown to Bringhurst (Bowdoin MS): July 29, 1793, Bennett census #48; May 30, 1792, Bennett census #23; and July 20, 1796, Bennett census #77.

17. Ibid.: June 11, 1793, Bennett census #46; May 30, 1792, Bennett census #23; and July 29, 1793, Bennett census #48.

18. See Allen, *Charles Brockden Brown*, 20; several letters from Brown to Bringhurst: Dec. 9, 1792, Bennett census #35; July 29, 1793, Bennett census #48; and May 20, 1792, Bennett census #21; Clark, *Pioneer Voice*, 102.

19. See Bennett, "Brown Canon," 11–12, 12–14; Clark, *Pioneer Voice*, 92; and Warfel, *Gothic Novelist*, 97.

20. See several letters from Brown to Bringhurst (Bowdoin MS): Dec. 9, 1792 , Bennett census #35; May 1792, Bennett census #12; 1793, Bennett census #42; June 11, 1793, Bennett census #46; July 25, 1793, Bennett census #47; n.d., probably 1792, Bennett census #8.

21. Ibid.: 1793, Bennett census #45; May 1792, Bennett census #14; n.d., probably 1792, Bennett census #9. For a superb discussion of the historical shaping of adolescence and identity formation in the early modern West, see Philip Aries, *Centuries of Childhood: A Social History of Family Life*, trans. Robert Baldick (New York, 1962). See Joseph Kett, *Rites of Passage: Adolescence in America, 1790 to the Present*, (New York, 1977), 14–50; and Fliegelman, *Prodigals and Pilgrims*, 3, 9–35, for equally insightful analyses of the eighteenth-century struggle with such issues in America.

22. Ibid.: July 25, 1793, Bennett census #47; Dec. 9, 1792, Bennett census #35; May 30, 1792, Bennett census #23.

23. Brown recounted this dream in a long 1793 letter to Bringhurst, Bennett census #42, while the earlier comment appeared in another letter to Bringhurst, May 30, 1792, Bennett census #23.

24. Ibid.: 1793, Bennett census #42.

25. Clark, *Pioneer Voice*, 55, for example, has argued that the "Henrietta Letters" involved a real romantic incident in Brown's life. This caused Leslie A. Fiedler to comment rather caustically that such an interpretation merely reflects how "con-

fused do sentimental life and sentimental literature become." See his *Love and Death in the American Novel* (New York, 1966), 98–99. The manuscripts of the "Henrietta Letters" are now at the Humanities Research Center at the University of Texas at Austin. Clark, however, has presented a reasonably complete reprinting of them in his *Pioneer Voice*, 55–107, and all citations to them hereafter will refer to the Clark volume.

26. "Henrietta Letters," in Clark, *Pioneer Voice*, 60–61; Bennett, "Brown Canon," 31; Brown to W. W. Wilkins, Jan. 22, 1793, quoted in Clark, *Pioneer Voice*, 35.

27. "Henrietta Letters," in Clark, *Pioneer Voice*, 58–59, 95, 89, 79–80.

28. Ibid., 64–67, 104.

29. Ibid., 87–89, 100, 101.

30. See Bennett, "Brown Canon," 68. The "Rhapsodist" essays have been reprinted in Charles Brockden Brown, *The Rhapsodist and Other Uncollected Writings*, Harry R. Warfel, ed. (New York, 1943), 1–24. Citations from the "Rhapsodist" will refer hereafter to the Warfel edition, and this particular quote appears on p. 5.

31. Warfel, ed., "Rhapsodist," 1, 1–2, 5.

32. Ibid., 13–15, 7–8, 12, 6–7.

33. Ibid., 6, 16, 11, 7.

34. See two letters from Brown to Bringhurst (Bowdoin MS): July 29, 1793, Bennett census #48; and Aug. 16, 1793, Bennett census #49. See also "Henrietta Letters," in Clark, *Pioneer Voice*, 105, 98, 71–72, 56–57.

35. Brown to Wilkins, Jan. 22, 1793, quoted in Clark, *Pioneer Voice*, 34; Brown to Wilkins, quoted in Warfel, *Gothic Novelist*, 51; Brown to Bringhurst, 1792 Bowdoin MS), Bennett census #10; Bennett, "Brown Canon," 157–158, 148; letters from Brown to Bringhurst Bowdoin MS), on Aug. 9, 1792, Bennett census #30, and May 20, 1792, Bennett census #21; Elihu Smith's comment quoted in Alan Axelrod, *Charles Brockden Brown, an American Tale* (Austin, 1983), 171; and "Henrietta Letters," in Clark, *Pioneer Voice*, 104.

36. See Bingham, "Identity Crisis."

37. See Charles Brockden Brown, "Belles-Lettres Club Address" in Allen, *Charles Brockden Brown*, 25; and "Henrietta Letters," in Clark, *Pioneer Voice*, 103.

CHAPTER 3. THE YOUNG ARTIST AS SOCIAL VISIONARY

1. The literature on early national politics is enormous. For two syntheses of the period, see Richard Buel, Jr., *Securing the Revolution: Ideology in American Politics, 1789–1815* (Ithica, N.Y., 1972), and Steven Watts, *Republic Reborn: War and the Making of Liberal America, 1790–1820* (Baltimore, 1987).

2. See Thomas M. Doerflinger, *A Vigorous Spirit of Enterprise: Merchants and Economic Development in Revolutionary Philadelphia* (New York, 1986).

3. See Russell B. Nye, *The Cultural Life of the New Nation, 1776–1830* (New York, 1930); Daniel J. Boorstin, *The Lost World of Thomas Jefferson* (Boston, 1948); Joseph J. Ellis, *After the Revolution: Profiles of Early American Culture* (New York, 1979); and Charles C. Sellers, *Mr. Peale's Museum* (New York, 1980).

4. See William Dunlap, *The Life of Charles Brockden Brown* (Philadelphia, 1815), 2: 92, and Harry R. Warfel, *Charles Brockden Brown, American Gothic Novelist* (Gainesville, Fla., 1949), 88–91.

5. See Warfel, *Gothic Novelist*, 40, 46–50; David Lee Clark, *Charles Brockden Brown: Pioneer Voice of America* (Durham, N.C., 1952), 108–10, 126–31; Charles E. Bennett, "The Charles Brockden Brown Canon," (Ph.D. diss., University of North Carolina, 1974), 183–84. The quote is from a letter reprinted in Clark, *Pioneer Voice*, 129.

6. Warfel, *Gothic Novelist*, 86–88.

7. Ibid., 54–55; Clark, *Pioneer Voice*, 157, 322–23, 325; Bennett, "Brown Canon," 175–81; Charles Brockden Brown, "A Series of Original Letters," (Feb.–Apr. 1798), reprinted in Harry R. Warfel, ed., *The Rhapsodist and Other Uncollected Writings* (New York, 1943), 104; Charles Brockden Brown, "A Lesson on Sensibility," *Weekly Magazine* 2 (May 19, 1798): 71–72.

8. Smith's letters of May 7 and May 27, 1796 are largely extracted in Warfel, *Gothic Novelist*, 56–60, 60–64. These quotes appear on pp. 58 and 62.

9. Ibid., 56–57, 60–61, 60, 63–64, 64.

10. This view of Brown's nascent "radicalism" runs contrary to the view of scholars like Jane Tompkins and Robert D. Arner, who see the author as more conservative throughout his career. Tompkins, in her *Sensational Designs: The Cultural Work of American Fiction, 1790–1860* (New York, 1985), argues that Brown developed in his writing a Federalist sensibility that insisted on the virtues of social order, commercial growth, and urban life. Arner, in his "Historical Essay" in the Kent State edition of Brown's *Alcuin: A Dialogue* (Kent, Ohio, 1987), suggests in parallel fashion that Brown's views on gender relations and women's rights were quite traditional from the beginning. While it perhaps would be a mistake to overplay the intensity of Brown's radical impulses, I believe that his fervent attacks on Christianity, his attraction to writers like Godwin and Rousseau, and his recurring critique of commercial values make it impossible to see him as a conservative cultural or political figure at this stage of his life. Later, of course, the story would be different.

11. See Clark, *Pioneer Voice*, 323, 321.

12. See several letters from Brown to Joseph Bringhurst, Jr. (Bowdoin MS): Oct. 24, 1795, Bennett census #63; 1795, Bennett census #62; Dec. 21, 1792, Bennett census #36.

13. Ibid.: June 11, 1793, Bennett census #46; 1795, Bennett census #62.

14. Ibid. Dec. 21, 1792, Bennett census #36.

15. Bennett, "Brown Canon," 164–71, has skillfully pieced together Brown's "Ellendale" novel in terms of its composition and its surviving segments.

16. See Charles Brockden Brown's "Ellendale Letters" (Humanities Research Center, University of Texas at Austin), Aug. 29 and 31, 1793; Bennett, "Brown Canon," 169–70.

17. See the "Harry Wallace" fragment reprinted in Allen, *The Life of Charles Brockden Brown* (1814 MS; reprint Delmar, N.Y., 1975), 222–42. See the "Adini" fragment reprinted in the same volume, pp. 350–87, especially pp. 382 and 369.

18. See Bennett, "Brown Canon," 27–28, 32–33; and Brown's "Devotion: An Epistle," reprinted in Clark, *Pioneer Voice*, 329.

19. See, for instance, Mary Beth Norton, *Liberty's Daughters: The Revolutionary Experience of American Women, 1750–1800* (Boston, 1980); and Linda K. Kerber,

*Women of the Republic: Intellect and Ideology in Revolutionary America* (Chapel Hill, N.C., 1980).

20. See Brown, "Henrietta Letters," in Clark, *Pioneer Voice*, 93, 94; Charles Brockden Brown, "Review" of Mary Wollstonecraft's *A Vindication of the Rights of Women*, in Philadelphia's *Ladies Magazine* (Sept. 1792): 190. On Wollstonecraft's reception in America, see Kerber, *Women of the Republic*, 222–25.

21. See Brown's comments as "The Essayist" in the Philadelphia *Ladies Magazine*: (Nov. 1792): 255; (July 1792): 60–61; (June 1792) "Address to the Ladies."

22. For insightful and informative discussions of Alcuin, see Cathy Davidson, "The Matter and Manner of Charles Brockden Brown's *Alcuin*," in Bernard Rosenthal, ed., *Critical Essays on Charles Brockden Brown* (Boston, 1981), 71–86; and Robert D. Arner, "Historical Essay," in Charles Brockden Brown, *Alcuin: A Dialogue* and *Memoirs of Stephen Calvert* (Kent, Ohio, 1987), 273–98.

23. For depictions of Brown as a radical protofeminist, see Lee Edwards, "Afterward," in Charles Brockden Brown, *Alcuin: A Dialogue* (New York, 1970), 92–104; and Clark, *Pioneer Voice*, 113–25. A more conservative portrait can be found in David O. Tomlinson, "Women in the Writings of Charles Brockden Brown: A Study in the Development of an Author's Thought" (Ph.D. diss., University of North Carolina, 1974).

24. All subsequent citations to Brown's *Alcuin* will refer to the Kent State University edition (Kent, Ohio, 1987). For "Mrs. Carter's" views, see pp. 24–33; for "Alcuin," see pp. 43, 13–14, 17, 37, 41–42, 26, 11–12.

25. "Alcuin's" views appear on pp. 44–56, while "Mrs. Carter's" can be found on pp. 66–70.

26. See, for example, Davidson, "Manner and Matter of Brown's *Alcuin*," 82–83.

27. Brown, *Alcuin*, 6–7, 7–8.

28. Ibid., 14–15, 20–21, 19–20.

29. Ibid., 61–62, 15.

30. Ibid., 68–70, 71, 75–76, 78, 82.

31. Ibid., 82–83, 71, 84–88.

32. See Dunlap, *Life of Brown*, 1:57; Brown to Bringhurst, 1795 (Bowdoin MS) Bennett census #62; Robert Arner, "Historical Essay," in *Alcuin* (Kent, Ohio, 1987), 301, ff. #16; Brown, *Alcuin*, 27–28.

33. Charles Brockden Brown, "Review" of William Robertson's *The History of America*, in *Monthly Magazine* 1 (June 1799): 131; Charles Brockden Brown, "Portrait of an Emigrant," *Monthly Magazine* 1 (June 1799): 164.

34. "The Man at Home" series has been reprinted in Warfel, ed., *Rhapsodist*, 27–98.

35. Ibid., 27–30, 43, 33–35, 94–98.

36. Brown's "Series of Original Letters" has also been reprinted in Warfel, ed., *Rhapsodist*, 101–31. The quotes in this paragraph appear on pp. 109, 114–15, 102–03.

37. See Henry May, *The Enlightenment in America* (New York, 1976), 172, 225, 234, 251; Cathy N. Davidson, *Revolution and the Word: The Rise of the Novel in America* (New York, 1986), 231; Staughton Lynd, *Intellectual Origins of American Radicalism* (New York, 1969), 114–16. On Godwin, see Peter H. Marshall, *William Godwin* (New Haven, Conn., 1984).

38. See William Dunlap, *Life of Brown*, 2:15; Allen, *Charles Brockden Brown*, 106; Warfel, *Gothic Novelist*, 54–55; Brown to Bringhurst, Oct. 30, 1795 (Bowdoin MS), Bennett census #64; Brown letter quoted in Warfel, *Gothic Novelist*, 64.

39. Brown to Bringhurst, 1795 (Bowdoin MS), Bennett census #62; Brown, "Lesson on Sensibility," 73; Charles Brockden Brown, "The Essayist," Philadelphia *Ladies Magazine* (Oct. 1792): 213 and (Aug. 1792): 159–60.

40. Charles Brockden Brown, Letter to Susan Goldophin, July 2–3, 1793 (Humanities Research Center, University of Texas at Austin), 2–3.

41. Ibid., 4.

42. Charles Brockden Brown, "On the Nature and Essential Qualities of Poetry, as Distinguised from Prose," *Ladies Magazine* 1 (Sept. 1792): 156.

43. Brown, *Alcuin*, 7–8.

CHAPTER 4. THE MAJOR NOVELS (I)

1. Brown's letter to close friend William Wood Wilkins, written sometime in the early 1790s, is quoted in David Lee Clark, *Charles Brockden Brown: Pioneer Voice of America* (Durham, N.C., 1952), 38–39.

2. See Charles E. Bennett, "The Charles Brockden Brown Canon" (Ph.D. diss., University of North Carolina, 1974), 195–208, for a clear and convincing analysis of the chronology of composition and publication for these four novels. *Carwin* and *Stephen Calvert* will be discussed in Chapter 7 of this book.

3. For a discussion of Brown's influence on nineteenth-century authors, see Alexander Cowie, "Historical Essay," in Charles Brockden Brown, *Wieland; or, the Transformation, An American Tale* and *Memoirs of Carwin, the Biloquist* (Kent, Ohio, 1977), 341–45. All subsequent citations for *Wieland* in this chapter will refer to this Kent State University Press bicentennial edition of Brown's novel. Michael Warner, in his recent book *The Letters of the Republic: Publication and the Public Sphere in Eighteenth-Century America* (Cambridge, Mass., 1990), has suggested that Brown's novels were not "novels" at all in the modern sense, but transitional texts lying halfway between a republican, public "print discourse" of the eighteenth century and a modern, privatized "literary textuality" of the nineteenth. While there is a germ of truth here, I believe that Warner exaggerates the republican qualities of this author's fictional texts. Brown's Gothic sensibility did not lend itself easily to the traditional gentleman's ethos of civic virtue, nor did his inclination from his earliest days as a writer to insist on the absolute integrity and self-reliance of the individual writer. In my view, Brown's books, although crudely structured and often bitterly critical of liberalizing society, were clearly early versions of the modern novel.

4. See Charles Brockden Brown, "On the Nature and Essential Qualities of Poetry, as Distinguished from Prose," Philadelphia *Ladies Magazine* 1 (Sept. 1792), 154, 153, 157, 155, 158, 151.

5. Brown's letter to Susan Godolphin, July 2–3, 1793 (Humanitites Research Center, University of Texas at Austin), 5–6.

6. Brown to Joseph Bringhurst, Jr., probably in 1795 (Bowdoin MS), Bennett census #62; Charles Brockden Brown, *Alcuin: A Dialogue* and *Memoirs of Stephen Calvert* (Kent, Ohio, 1987), 13; Brown, "Advertisement," in *Wieland*, 3; "Advertise-

ment" for *Sky-Walk*, Mar. 17, 1798, quoted in Harry R. Warfel, *Charles Brockden Brown, American Gothic Novelist* (Gainesville, Fla., 1949); Brown, "Henrietta Letters," in Clark, *Pioneer Voice*, 99.

7. Charles Brockden Brown, "The Essayist," *Ladies Magazine*, 1 (June 1792): 16–17; Brown, "The Man at Home" in the *Weekly Magazine*, reprinted in Harry R. Warfel, ed., *The Rhapsodist and Other Uncollected Writings* (New York, 1943), 46, 32; Brown to Bringhurst, Dec. 21, 1792 (Bowdoin MS), Bennett census #36; Brown quoted in Warfel, *Gothic Novelist*, 7.

8. See Charles Brockden Brown, "Walstein's School of History" from the Aug.–Sept. 1799 *Monthly Magazine*, reprinted in Harry Warfel, ed., *Rhapsodist*, 145–46. For useful commentaries on this text, see ibid., xi; Bennett, "Brown Canon," 228; and Deborah M. Bingham, "The Identity Crisis of Charles Brockden Brown" (Ph.D. diss., Bowling Green State University, 1977), 87.

9. Brown, "Walstein's School," 147, 150, 146–47, 152. This connection between capitalist development and sexual regulation would reach its high point in the ideology of nineteenth-century Victorian America, where market growth and erotic repression became flip sides of the same developmental coin. See, for instance, the essays in Daniel Walker Howe, ed., *Victorian America* (Philadelphia, 1976). This connection also has deep roots in theoretical interpretations of the development of Western capitalism, particularly among the Frankfurt School. For a good example, see Herbert Marcuse, *Eros and Civilization: A Philosophical Inquiry into Freud* (New York, 1955).

10. Brown, "Walstein's School," 148–49, 150, 151, 148.

11. Ibid., 153, 150, 151–52. Brown's expressed view in "Walstein's School" lends credence to a view of him as an Enlightenment reformer of radical sympathies, at least early in his career.

12. See William Dunlap, *The Life of Charles Brockden Brown* (Philadelphia, 1815), 1:54; Paul Allen, *The Life of Charles Brockden Brown* (1814 MS; reprint Delmar, N.Y., 1975); Bingham, "Identity Crisis," 111–12, 115; Dunlap, *Life of Brown*, 2:8, 10–11.

13. Dunlap, *Life of Brown*, 2:56, 94–95; Warfel, *Gothic Novelist*, 90.

14. John Bernard, *Retrospectives of America, 1797–1811* (New York, 1887), 253; Clark, *Pioneer Voice*, 160.

15. See Brown, *Wieland*.

16. Ibid., 3, 114. For discussions of Brown and sensationalist psychology, see Donald A. Ringe, *Charles Brockden Brown* (New York, 1966), 27, 31–34; Larzer Ziff, "A Reading of *Wieland*," *Publications of the Modern Language Association of America* 77 (1962): 51–57; and Arthur Kimball, *Rational Fictions: A Study of Charles Brockden Brown* (McKinnville, Oreg., 1968). For a treatment of Lockean psychology and its general cultural impact, see Henry F May, *The Enlightenment in America* (New York, 1976), 7–10. While such works correctly point out Brown's dark critique of the psychology of sensation, they also tend to overplay his skepticism about reason. Not only did Brown attempt to salvage reason by placing it on a more realistic foundation, but he also probed beyond the mere philosophical dimension of this issue. His novels like *Wieland* also contained a powerful critique of liberal individualism. For an insightful discussion of this text that parallels mine in certain ways,

see Jay Fliegelman, "Introduction," *Wieland and Memoirs of Carwin the Biloquist* (New York, 1991), vii–xlii.

17. Brown, *Wieland*, 1, 35, 87.

18. Ibid., 22, 5, 35. See the brilliant discussion of declining paternalism in Jay Fliegelman, *Prodigals and Pilgrims: The American Revolution against Patriarchal Authority, 1750–1800* (Cambridge, 1982).

19. Brown, *Wieland*, 8–9.

20. Ibid., 22, 23, 176, 224. For a provocative discussion of the religious themes in this novel, see Bernard Rosenthal, "The Voices of *Wieland*," in his *Critical Essays on Charles Brockden Brown* (Boston, 1981), 104–25.

21. Brown, *Wieland*, 14–19, describes the shocking death of Clara and Theodore's father. I would note that this focus on internal privations and pressures is not just a question of Enlightenment epistemology and sensationalist psychology, as many literary treatments of the novel have implied. It also has social, political, and material roots in the liberation of the individual in post-Revolutionary America. These issues also preoccupied Brown throughout his life.

22. Ibid., 23, 38, 25, 22, 224, 230–31.

23. Ibid., 147, 83, 233.

24. On the chronology of the composition and publication of *Carwin, the Biloquist*, see Alexander Cowie's "Historical Essay" in *Wieland*, 335, 361. This text, which is crucial for understanding Brown, will be treated in Chapter 6 of this book.

25. Brown, *Wieland*, 50–53, 90.

26. Ibid., 76, 93–94, 124.

27. Ibid., 198, 199.

28. Ibid., 224–25, 190, 211, 90–91.

29. Ibid., 3; Dunlap, *Life of Brown*, 2:93. See also Russell B. Nye's discussion in his "Historical Essay," in Charles Brockden Brown, *Ormond; or, the Secret Witness* (Kent, Ohio, 1982), 307–09. All subsequent citations for *Ormond* will refer to this bicentennial edition from the Kent State University Press.

30. *Ormond* remains the least studied of Brown's major novels. For discussions of the literary influences at work on this novel, see Nye, "Historical Essay," *Ormond*, 313–21, and Ernest Marchand, "Introduction," *Ormond* (New York, 1937), ix–xliv. Norman Grabo, *The Coincidental Art of Charles Brockden Brown* (Chapel Hill, N.C., 1981), 30–55, argues for Brown's artistry in twisting the familiar form of the sentimental romance. My interpretation veers away from these in its emphasis on Brown's exploration of individual agency and social opportunity in the post-Revolutionary republic.

31. Brown, *Ormond*, 3–4, 195–96.

32. Brown, "The Man at Home," in Warfel, ed., *Rhapsodist*, 71–72.

33. Brown, *Ormond*, 113–14, 114–15, 115–16, 177.

34. Ibid., 116, 254. See Jean-Christophe Agnew, *Worlds Apart: The Market and the Theatre in Anglo-American Thought, 1550–1750* (Cambridge, 1986) for a brilliant analysis of the connections between theatrical imagery and market social relations in the early modern West.

CHAPTER 5. THE MAJOR NOVELS (II)

1. Charles Brockden Brown, Preface, in *Arthur Mervyn; or, Memoirs of the Year 1793* (Kent, Ohio, 1980), 3. All subsequent citations to this novel will refer to this bicentennial edition from the Kent State University Press.

2. William Dunlap, *The Life of Charles Brockden Brown* (Philadelphia, 1815), 3:97; Brown, *Arthur Mervyn*, 226. The secondary literature on *Arthur Mervyn* is quite large, and much of it revolves around the key question of Arthur's sincerity and character. See, for example, James Russo, "The Chameleon of Convenient Vice: A Study of the Narrative of *Arthur Mervyn*," *Studies in the Novel* 11 (1979): 381–405, in which Arthur is pictured as an outright liar and fraud; Warner Berthoff, "Introduction," *Arthur Mervyn* (New York, 1962), which presents Arthur in more ambiguous terms as a "moral sharper"; and James H. Justus, "Arthur Mervyn, American," *American Literature* 42 (1970): 304–24, an essay that reads the young protagonist as a typical, ambitious young individual seeking self-definition and success. My own view leans toward the interpretation Justus proffers, but with two amendments. First, I would emphasize the importance of the socioeconomic context of the market revolution in the late 1700s. Second, I would stress that the very question of Arthur's character underlines the increasingly protean, malleable quality of the self in this fluid commercial setting.

3. Brown, *Arthur Mervyn*, 394. See Daniel E. Cohen, "Arthur Mervyn and His Elders: The Ambivalence of Youth in the Early Republic," *William and Mary Quarterly* 43 (1986): 362–80, for a penetrating discussion of how this novel depicts the "volatile social world" of the late eighteenth century, particularly its generational conflicts and sense of crisis accruing to individuals' search for "personal independence."

4. Ibid., 154, 46, 11, 341–42, 434, 293. Jane Tompkins, in her *Sensational Designs: The Cultural Work of American Fiction, 1790–1860* (New York, 1985), sees *Arthur Mervyn* as a Federalist political plea in behalf of "civic virtue" and an urban commercial order. This reveals only half of the picture in the novel. While Brown certainly unfolds a virtuous critique of rampant individualism, he also bitterly attacks a "diseased" urban and commercial life as part of that very problem. His alienation and uncertainty are more pervasive than Tompkins admits, and in total they do not really comprise a Federalist political agenda.

5. Brown, *Arthur Mervyn*, 10–11, 21, 214–15, 58, 57, 47, 174, 312.

6. Ibid., 14, 226, 250, 248, 232–36, 285–89, 248–49.

7. Ibid., 308, 322, 323.

8. Cathy Davidson's treatment of *Arthur Mervyn* in her *Revolution and the Word: The Rise of the Novel in America* (New York, 1986), 236–53, discusses with great insight the connection between public and private decay in this novel. Arthur, in her words, strains to probe "the limits of individualism" and posits "an intriguingly modern concept of personality." While this strikes me as accurate, I disagree with her further assertion that the novel represents a Bakhtinian "carnivalesque performance" that invites an undermining of traditional proprieties and constraints. Brown's self-consciously tragic, alienated, and intellectualist sensibility, it seems to me, do not quite fit the "carnivalesque" mode of playful, ritualistic subversion.

9. Brown, *Arthur Mervyn*, 219, 85, 107, 265.

10. Ibid., 125, 237, 119, 332, 330.

11. Arthur Mervyn as quoted in Emory Elliott, "Narrative Unity and Moral Resolution in *Arthur Mervyn*," in Bernard Rosenthal, ed., *Critical Essays on Charles Brockden Brown* (Boston, 1981), 142; Brown, *Arthur Mervyn*, 340, 436.

12. Emory Elliott, in his *Revolutionary Writers: Literature and Authority in the New Republic, 1725–1810* (New York, 1982), 234–65, provides a succinct and shrewd portrait of social and cultural disarray in the post-Revolutionary period. He correctly notes, in my opinion, that Brown's novels, particularly *Arthur Mervyn*, offer "explorations of the impact of the social and economic order on the lives of individuals."

13. Brown, *Arthur Mervyn*, 24, 195, 328. On the connection to Milton, see Alan Axelrod, *Charles Brockden Brown, An American Tale* (Austin, 1983), 142, 191.

14. Brown, *Arthur Mervyn*, 227.

15. Ibid., 18, 129. Shirley Samuels, "Plague and Politics in 1793: *Arthur Mervyn*," *Criticism* 27 (1985): 225–46, argues persuasively that this novel ties family tensions to broader social upheavals in the late eighteenth-century Atlantic world. See Cohen, "Arthur Mervyn and His Elders," for a parallel analysis; and Jay Fliegelman, *Prodigals and Pilgrims: The American Revolution against Patriarchal Authority, 1750–1800* (Cambridge, 1982), for a broader treatment of the breakup of the patriarchal model of the family.

16. Brown, *Arthur Mervyn*, 296.

17. Ibid., 432, 429–30, 428.

18. For insightful interpretations of this novel, see Dennis Berthold, "Charles Brockden Brown, *Edgar Huntly*, and the Origins of the American Picturesque," *William and Mary Quarterly* 41 (1984): 62–84, which stresses Brown's utilization of "picturesque aesthetics" from eighteenth-century landscape painting; Beverly R. Voloshin, "*Edgar Huntly* and the Coherence of the Self," *Early American Literature* 23 (1988): 262–80, which sees the novel as a reflection of an early modern questioning of "the coherence of the perceiving self"; Norman Grabo, *The Coincidental Art of Brown* (Chapel Hill, N.C., 1981), which analyzes Brown's "doubling" technique in the book as central to his fictive art; and Richard Slotkin, *Regeneration through Violence: The Mythology of the American Frontier, 1600–1860* (Middletown, Conn., 1973), 382–90, which sees this novel as an embodiment of "archetypal myth patterns" in America in which individuals seek to locate and destroy the dark side of their own nature in animal and Indian representations. My own view of the novel tends to submerge these thematic and structural tendencies within a broader context of liberalizing culture and fragmenting individualism in the post-Revolutionary American republic.

19. Charles Brockden Brown, *Edgar Huntly; or, Memoirs of a Sleepwalker* (Kent, Ohio, 1984), 3. All citations for this text will refer to this bicentennial edition from the Kent State University Press. Sydney J. Krause's "Historical Essay" in this volume shows how Brown gathered together many sources on irrational, abnormal human behavior and funneled them into this tale.

20. Ibid., 154, 155.

21. Ibid., 156, 279, 259, 292. Once again, see Fliegelman, *Prodigals and Pilgrims*;

Cohen, "Arthur Mervyn and his Elders"; and Samuels, "Plague and Politics in 1793," for skilled analyses of changing modes of family authority in late eighteenth-century America.

22. Brown, *Edgar Huntly*, 14, 74.

23. Leslie A. Fiedler, *Love and Death in the American Novel* (New York, 1975), 157; Brown, *Edgar Huntly*, 33. Other works that focus on this novel's exploration of the unconscious include Slotkin, *Regeneration through Violence*; Voloshin, "*Edgar Huntly* and the Coherence of the Self"; and David Brion Davis, *Homicide in American Fiction, 1798-1860: A Study in Social Values* (Ithaca, N.Y., 1957), 94–100.

24. Brown, *Edgar Huntly*, 23, 161–62.

25. Ibid., 192, 185, 197, 212. Slotkin, in his *Regeneration through Violence*, has made the most compelling argument for a persistent violence in American culture, a trait that is reflected in its literary expression. He has linked violence to a desire within the American individual to purge his darker instincts and get on with the business of mastering the New World. According to Slotkin, this cultural process of objectifying libidinous urges in images of Nature, particularly Indians and animals, and then eliminating them has constituted "the myth of regeneration through the violence of the bout" (p. 557).

26. Brown, *Edgar Huntly*, 94–95, 171, 15, 16, 192.

27. Ibid., 35-36, 290, 110, 278. See Grabo, *Coincidental Art of Charles Brockden Brown*, 160–85, for a sophisticated analysis of Brown's deployment of "doubling" in his fiction writing.

28. See Charles Brockden Brown, "Novel-Reading," *Literary Magazine and American Register*, 1 (Mar., 1804): 405.

### CHAPTER 6. THE WRITER AS BOURGEOIS MORALIST

1. Brown's letter of April 1800 to his brother James is quoted in David Lee Clark, *Charles Brockden Brown: Pioneer Voice of America* (Durham, N.C., 1952), 195.

2. My reading of the two novels has been influenced particularly by Sydney J. Krause, "*Clara Howard* and *Jane Talbot*: Godwin on Trial," in Bernard Rosenthal, ed., *Critical Essays on Charles Brockden Brown* (Boston, 1981), 184–211, who suggests that these novels tested and pulled back from an earlier engagement with radicalism. In general, Brown's last two completed books remain far less studied than his four "major" novels of the 1790s. A few exceptions exist. Paul Witherington's "Brockden Brown's Other Novels: *Clara Howard* and *Jane Talbot*," *Nineteenth-Century Fiction* 29 (1974): 257–72, argues that these two "domestic novels" were linked to his earlier novels in thematic terms of "chastened individualism." Both Clark, *Pioneer Voice*, 181–85, and Charles E. Bennett, "The Brown Canon" (Ph.D. diss., University of North Carolina, 1974), 98–100, 224–25, suggest that Brown knuckled under to sentimental, female, popular literary values in these novels. Norman Grabo, *The Coincidental Art of Charles Brockden Brown* (Chapel Hill, N.C. 1981), 129–57, analyzes the texts as superficial tales that, having abandoned all sense of "complexities and ambiguities," became "trivial and silly." Deborah M. Bingham, "The Identity Crisis of Charles Brockden Brown" (Ph.D. diss., Bowling Green State University, 1977), presents a convincing picture of Brown's retreat from "public" literary and intellectual life into a "private" realm of security and family-orient-

ed endeavors during this period, a process that was fed by these two domestic novels. Overall, I have tried to examine these themes and resituate them as parts of a broader process in Brown's life and, indeed, in American culture as a whole: the solidification of a bourgeois sensibility with its moral code based on restraint, gentility, and self-control. This process, I maintain, was part of a response to the dislocations accompanying rapid market growth in the post-Revolutionary decades.

3. See Donald A. Ringe, "Historical Essay," in Brown, *Clara Howard, in a Series of Letters* and *Jane Talbot, a Novel* (Kent, Ohio, 1986), 441. All subsequent references to these two novels will refer to this bicentennial edition from the Kent State University Press.

4. Brown, *Clara Howard*, 3, 38, 40, 64, 89.

5. For a persuasive account of *Jane Talbot*'s publishing history, see Ringe, "Historical Essay," 443–52.

6. Brown, *Jane Talbot*, 188–89, 314, 305, 307.

7. For several sophisticated analyses of gendered notions of virtue and self-interest as they developed in the several decades after the American Revolution, see the following works: two articles by Ruth H. Bloch, "American Feminine Ideals in Transition: The Rise of the Moral Mother, 1785–1815," *Feminist Studies* 4 (1978): 101–26, and "The Gendered Meaning of Virtue in Revolutionary America," *Signs* 13 (Autumn 1987): 37–58; Jan Lewis, "The Republican Wife: Virtue and Seduction in the Early Republic," *William and Mary Quarterly* 44 (Oct. 1987): 696–721; and Linda K. Kerber's comments on "republican motherhood" in her *Women of the Republic: Intellect and Ideology in Revolutionary America* (Chapel Hill, N.C. 1980), 269–88.

8. See Bennett, "Brown Canon," 83–84, 88–92, 98–99, 121–22.

9. Charles Brockden Brown, "Editor's Address," *Literary Magazine* (Oct. 1803): 4; "On the State of American Literature," by "M," *Monthly Magazine* 1 (Apr. 1799): 16. The latter essay has been identified as Brown's by Sydney Krause in Rosenthal, ed., *Critical Essays*, 209, n. 8.

10. Brown quoted in Bingham, "Identity Crisis," 173; William Dunlap, *The Life of Brown* (Philadelphia, 1815), 2:49; Brown, quoted in Harry R. Warfel, *Charles Brockden Brown, American Gothic Novelist* (Gainesville, Fla., 1949), 187, 201.

11. Charles Brockden Brown, "Editor's Address," *Literary Magazine* (1803): 5; "Preface," *Monthly Magazine* (Oct. 1800): 259–60, 262–63; "Student's Diary," *Literary Magazine* (1803): 327.

12. Charles Brockden Brown, "Preface" to *American Review* (1801), quoted in Robert E. Spiller, *American Literary Revolution, 1783–1837* (Garden City, N.Y., 1967), 32; "Why the Arts Are Discouraged in America," *Literary Magazine* 6 (July 1806): 77; "Alliance between Poverty and Genius," *Literary Magazine* 3 (May 1805): 333.

13. See Bingham, "Identity Crisis," 144–47; Brown's letters to Elizabeth Linn (Humanities Research Center, University of Texas at Austin): Mar. 30, 1801; May 25, 1804; and Dec. 2, 1802.

14. Charles Brockden Brown, "The Trials of Arden," *Monthly Magazine* 3 (July 1800): 19–36.

15. Ibid., 20, 24, 27–28.

16. See the insightful analysis in Bingham, "Identity Crisis," 129, 116–17, 133–34. See also Dunlap, *Life of Brown*, 2:50.

17. See Clark, *Pioneer Voice*, 197–98, 214–15, and Warfel, *Gothic Novelist*, 229.

18. Charles Brockden Brown, "A Student's Diary," *Literary Magazine* 1 (1803): 85; and Clark, *Pioneer Voice*, 197–98.

19. See Brown's letters to Elizabeth Linn (MS, University of Texas): Apr. 4, 1801; Mar. 17, 1801; Apr. 29, 1801; undated letter; Apr. 13, 1801; Mar. 30, 1801.

20. Ibid., "Tuesday afternoon" (n.d.); undated letter; "Tuesday afternoon" (n.d.); Feb. 28, 1801.

21. Ibid., Mar. 27, 1801; Dec. 15, 1800; Apr. 14, 1801. See Carroll Smith-Rosenberg, *Disorderly Conduct: Visions of Gender in Victorian America* (New York, 1985); Ann Douglas, *The Feminization of American Culture* (New York, 1977); and Karen Halttunen, *Confidence Men and Painted Women: A Study of Middle-Class Culture in America, 1830–1870* (New Haven, 1982), for discussions of gender and the development of a bourgeois code of self-control in the nineteenth century.

22. Ibid., Mar. 30, 1801. See Cathy Davidson's discussion of John Gregory in her *Revolution and the Word: The Rise of the Novel in America* (New York, 1986), 126–27. See Mary Beth Norton, *Liberty's Daughters: The Revolutionary Experience of American Women, 1750–1800* (Glenview, Ill., 1980), and Linda K. Kerber, *Women of the Republic: Intellect and Ideology in Revolutionary America* (Chapel Hill, N.C., 1980), for two superb overviews of transforming gender formulations regarding women in the early American republic.

23. Brown's letters to Elizabeth Linn (MS, University of Texas): Apr. 29, 1801; Apr. 10, 1801; Mar. 31, 1801; Apr. 1, 1801.

24. Ibid., undated (probably Mar. or Apr. 1801); Apr. 1, 1801; Apr. 9, 1801.

25. Ibid., Mar. 6, 1801; Mar. 10, 1801; Apr. 10, 1801; Mar. 27, 1801; Mar. 7, 1801. See Christopher Lasch, *Haven in a Heartless World: The Family Beseiged* (New York, 1977), and Edward Shorter, *The Making of the Modern Family* (New York, 1977), for broad treatments of the development of the bourgeois family.

26. Brown's letters to Elizabeth Linn (MS, University of Texas): Feb. 20, 1801; Mar. 10, 1801; Feb. 17, 1801; Mar. 2, 1801; Apr. 9, 1801.

27. Ibid., Mar. 23, 1801; Apr. 27, 1801; Apr. 9, 1801; Apr. 11, 1801; Apr. 29, 1801; Mar. 18, 1801.

28. On Victorian culture in America, see, in addition to other works cited in nn. for this chapter, Daniel Walker Howe, ed., *Victorian America* (Philadelphia, 1976); Mary Kelly, *Private Women, Public Stage: Literary Domesticity in Nineteenth-Century America* (New York, 1984); and John F. Kasson, *Rudeness and Civility: Manners in Nineteenth-Century America* (New York, 1990).

29. See Warfel, *Gothic Novelist*, 189, 227–29.

30. See Brown's letters in William Dunlap, *Life of Brown*, 2:111 12, 113, and his letter in Clark, *Pioneer Voice*, 213. Elizabeth Brown's obituary can be found in ibid., 292–94.

31. Charles Brockden Brown, "Editor's Address to the Public," *Literary Magazine* 1 (Oct. 1803): 5.

32. Charles Brockden Brown, " On Standards of Taste," *Literary Magazine* 6 (Oct. 1806): 294; "A Student's Diary," *Literary Magazine* 2 (1804): 85 and 1 (1803):

164; "Death of Hamilton," *Literary Magazine*, 2 (Aug. 1804): 337; "Editor's Address," *Literary Magazine* 1 (Oct. 1803): 5; and "Dialogues of the Living," *Monthly Magazine* 1 (Apr. 1799): 19–21.

33. Charles Brockden Brown, "A Miser," *Literary Magazine* 2 (July 1804): 246; "A Miser's Prayer," *Monthly Magazine* 3 (Dec. 1800): 412–13.

34. Charles Brockden Brown, "Female Clothing," *Literary Magazine* 6 (July 1806): 22–23; "On Novel Writing," *Literary Magazine* 2 (Dec. 1804): 697; "On Music as a Female Accomplishment," *Port-Folio* 2 (1802): 292, 307; "On Painting as a Female Accomplishment," *Port-Folio* 2 (1802): 332; "Thoughts on Religion as a Branch of Female Education," *Literary Magazine* 2 (June 1804): 168; Dunlap, *Life of Brown*, 2:119–20.

35. Brown, "Novels," *Literary Magazine* 3 (Jan. 1805): 16–17; "Novel Writing," *Literary Magazine* (1804): 694, 693; "A Student's Diary," *Literary Magazine* 1 (1803): 404–5.

36. "Student's Diary," 323–24; "Novel Writing," 696–97, 694; "Original Papers for the Port-Folio: The American Lounger," *Port-Folio* 2 (June 1802): 185–86.

37. Charles Brockden Brown, "Plan for the Improvement and Diffusion of the Arts, Adapted to the United States," *Literary Magazine* 3 (Mar. 1805): 181–83; "Thoughts on Religion as a Branch of Female Education," *Literary Magazine* 2 (June 1804): 166-167; Brown's final statement, made in 1807, is quoted in Bingham, "Identity Crisis," 169.

38. Brown, "Religion and Female Education," 166; "On the Scheme of an American Language," *Monthly Magazine* 3 (July 1800): 1–2; "On Classical Learning," *Literary Magazine* 3 (Apr. 1805): 256–57.

39. Brown, "On Standards of Taste," *Literary Magazine* 6 (Oct. 1806): 294–95.

40. Brown, "Student's Diary," 6, 81, 408, 328; "On a Scheme for Describing American Manners," *Monthly Magazine* 3 (July 1800): 10; "On a Taste for the Picturesque," *Monthly Magazine* 3 (July 1800): 12; "The Difference between History and Romance," *Monthly Magazine* 2 (Apr. 1800): 251, 253, 252.

41. Charles Brockden Brown, "On the Merits of the Founders of the French Revolution," *Literary Magazine* 6 (Nov. 1806): 352; "Is a Free or Despotic Government Most Friendly to Human Happiness?" *Literary Magazine* 3 (Mar. 1805): 180.

42. Brown, "Free and Despotic Governments," 178; "Of the French Revolution," 353–55, 358–59, 356, 354, 351–52.

43. Brown's comments on paternalism appeared in the 1800 *Monthly Magazine*, and they are quoted in Jay Fliegelman, *Prodigals and Pilgrims: The American Revolution against Patriarchal Authority, 1750–1800* (Cambridge, 1982), 89.

44. Charles Brockden Brown, "On the Scheme of an American Language," *Monthly Magazine* 3 (July, 1800): 1; "American Manners," 8. See Joseph J. Ellis, *After the Revolution: Profiles of Early American Culture* (New York, 1979); Ronald T. Takaki, *Iron Cages: Race and Culture in 19th-Century America* (Seattle, 1979); and Steven Watts, *Republic Reborn: War and the Making of Liberal America, 1790–1820* (Baltimore, 1987), for various treatments of the cultural campaign to confront individualism and thwart its excesses with an ethic of self-control.

45. Brown, "Student's Diary," 8. See Raymond Williams, *Culture and Society: 1780–1950* (New York, 1983) , xvi–xviii, 47, for a brilliant argument on how the very

definition of modern "culture" is rooted in the social relationships of market capitalism.

46. Brown, "Standards of Taste," 294–95. Terry Eagleton, *The Function of Criticism: From The Spectator to Post-Structuralism* (London, 1984), 10–17, 26, presents a searching theoretical analysis of the role of the "critic" in confirming developing discourses of capitalism.

CHAPTER 7. THE WRITER AND THE LIBERAL EGO

1. Charles Brockden Brown, "The Scribbler," *Port-Folio* 1 (1809): 57, 59.

2. See Charles E. Bennett, "The Charles Brockden Brown Canon" (Ph.D. diss., University of North Carolina, 1974), 113, 115–16. William Dunlap is quoted in Deborah Marie Bingham, "The Identity Crisis of Charles Brockden Brown" (Ph.D. diss., Bowling Green State University, 1977), 178.

3. See Bennett, "Brown Canon," 233, 242.

4. See Harry R. Warfel, *Brown, American Gothic Novelist* (Gainesville, Fla., 1949), 233; Davaid Lee Clark, *Brown: Pioneer Voice of America* (Durham, N.C., 1952), 215–16, 291; and William Dunlap, *The Life of Brown* (Philadelphia, 1815), 2:86.

5. On Victorian culture, see the essays in Daniel Walker Howe, ed., *Victorian America* (Philadelphia, 1976).

6. Bennett, "Brown Canon," 110–11; Clark, *Pioneer Voice*, 303; C. F. Volney (translated with occasional remarks by Brown), *A View of the Soil and Climate of the United States of America* (New York, 1968; facsimile of Philadelphia, 1804 ed.), 2, 338, 108.

7. Brown, *Volney* translation, nn. on pages 225, 402, 231, 370–71, 443, 381. For various treatments of Anglo-American attitudes about American Indian sex and violence in the late 1700s and early 1800s, see Richard Slotkin, *Regeneration through Violence: The Mythology of the American Frontier, 1600–1860* (Middletown, Conn., 1973); Richard Drinnon, *Facing West: The Metaphysics of Indian-Hating and Empire Building* (New York, 1980); Michael Paul Rogin, *Fathers and Children: Andrew Jackson and the Subjugation of the American Indian* (New York, 1975); and Ronald Takaki, *Iron Cages: Race and Culture in 19th-Century America* (Seattle, 1979), especially pp. 55–65, 80–107.

8. Ibid., nn. on pp. 194–95, 331, 259, 442.

9. Charles Brockden Brown, "Sketch of American Literature for 1806–07," *American Register* 1 (1807): 184–85; "The Scribbler," *Port- Folio* 1 (1809): 421–24.

10. Brown, "American Literature for 1806–07," 173–74; "Scribbler," *Port- Folio*, 2 (1809): 33–34, 124:26, 1 (1809): 59–60, 175, 162–63, 339–41. See Joseph J. Ellis, *After the Revolution: Profiles of Early American Culture* (New York, 1979), for a trenchant discussion of how American intellectuals struggled with their fears of cultural provincialism and their hopes for an "American Athens" in the post-Revolutionary era.

11. See Charles E. Bennett, "Charles Brockden Brown: Man of Letters," in Bernard Rosenthal, ed., *Critical Essays on Charles Brockden Brown* (Boston, 1981), 219. Bennett suggests that this collection of stories be entitled "History of the Carrils," but Warner Berthoff argues convincingly that *Historical Sketches* is a more appropriate general title for these loosely connected works. See Berthoff's "Charles

Brockden Brown's Historical 'Sketches': A Consideration," *American Literature* 28 (1956): 147–54. Bennett and Berthoff provide the fullest analysis of this fictional project.

12. Dunlap, *Life of Brown* 1:169, 258. My discussion of this novelistic project relies on the astute detective work of Charles E. Bennett. In particular, see his "Brown Canon," p. 227 *passim*, and his "Man of Letters," in *Critical Essays*, 219–20, 223, especially ff. # 32, for his convincing description of Brown's "Carril," or *Historical Sketches* project.

13. Brown, "Carrils," in Dunlap, *Life of Brown*, 1:173–74; "Specimen of Agricultural Improvement," *Literary Magazine* 3 (1805): 86–87.

14. Brown, "Carrils," in William Dunlap, *Life of Brown*, 1:170–71, 209, 207.

15. Charles Brockden Brown, "Specimen of Political Improvement," *Literary Magazine* 3 (1805): 220; "Agricultural Improvement," 87, 88–89.

16. Brown, "Agricultural Improvement," 87–90, 92–93; "Political Improvement," 203–5, 127.

17. Brown, "Political Improvement," 122–27.

18. Ibid., 120–22.

19. Brown, "Agricultural Improvement," 91–93.

20. Brown, "Agricultural Improvement," 91; "Political Improvement," 126–28. The unbounded power of Sir Arthur Carril, with its authoritarian thrust, might suggest that Brown was indeed a conservative Federalist, a reactionary republican as portrayed by scholars like Jane Tompkins. This text, however, seems to suggest a more complex situation. It helps reveal, I believe, the ambiguity of Brown's engagement with a liberalizing society, where he accepted a market society of competition, merit, and productivity while simultaneously seeking to restrain its anarchic excesses. Moreover, it is perhaps easier to see Carril as an individualist superman rather than as a premodern authority figure.

21. For a discussion of late nineteenth-century "antimodern modernism," see Jackson Lears, *No Place of Grace: Antimodernism and the Transformation of American Culture, 1880–1920* (New York, 1981), 296–97, 300–12.

22. See Charles Brockden Brown, *An Address to the Government of the United States on the Cession of Louisiana* (Philadelphia, 1803); *Monroe's Embassy; or, The Conduct of the Government in Relation to Our Claims to the Navigation of the Mississippi* (Philadelphia, 1803); *An Address to the Congress of the United States, on the Utility and Justice of Restrictions upon Foreign Commerce* (Philadelphia, 1809).

23. Charles Brockden Brown, "Annals of Europe and America," *American Register* 3 (1808): 69; "Annals of Europe and America," *American Register* 1 (1807): 3–4; *Monroe's Embassy*, 22–23.

24. Charles Brockden Brown, "Facts and Calculations Respecting the Population and Territory of the United States of America," *Weekly Magazine* 3 (Aug. 1798): 74, 75; "Annals of Europe and America," *American Register* 1 (1806–1807): 67, 66.

25. Brown, *Cession of Louisiana*, 49; *Monroe's Embassy*, 36, 27.

26. Brown, *Cession of Louisiana*, 16–17, 61, 62–63, 64–65.

27. See Brown's articles in the *American Register*: "Preface," 2 (1807): iii–iv; "Annals of Europe and America," 5 (1809): 5; "A Sketch of American Literature for

1806–07," 1 (1806–7): 182; "Annals of Europe and America," 3 (1808): 64; "Annals of Europe and America," 5 (1809): 7–8. The final quote comes from Brown, *Cession of Louisiana*, 70–71.

28. Brown, *Cession of Louisiana*, 88, 92, 80–81, 77–78; *Monroe's Embassy*, 27–28. See also his *Restrictions upon Foreign Commerce*, 74–75. Drew R. McCoy, in his *The Elusive Republic: Political Economy in Jeffersonian America* (Chapel Hill, N.C., 1980), cogently analyzes the late eighteenth-century urge for "expansion across space" as an antidote to traditional fears of "decay over time" in republican ideology. This revitalized republicanism provided an ideological accommodation to the growth of a market society in post-Revolutionary America.

29. Brown, *Restrictions upon Foreign Commerce*, 73–74, 81, 83, 84.

30. Ibid., 89–90, 85–88. For more examples of Brown's perception of American national interest and destiny, see also pp. 36, 77–78.

31. See the account in Dunlap, *Life of Brown*, 2:87–89.

32. See the discussion in Chapter 1, pp. 20–25, for a theoretical analysis of capitalist culture and psychological fragmentation.

33. Richard Henry Dana, "The Novels of Charles Brockden Brown," *United States Review and Literary Gazette* 2 (Aug. 1827): 321–22.

34. On the writing and publishing of this protonovel, see Alexander Cowie, "Historical Essay," in *Wieland; or, the Transformation, an American Tale* and *Memoirs of Carwin, the Biloquist* (Kent, Ohio, 1977), 334–37. All future references to *Carwin* are from this authoritative edition of the text.

35. Brown, *Carwin*, 247–48, 254, 262.

36. On the background and writing of this text, see Robert D. Arner, "Historical Essay," in *Alcuin* and *Memoirs of Stephen Calvert* (Kent, Ohio, 1987), 298–301; and Bennett, "Brown Canon," 198–99. All future references to this novel will be from this authoritative Kent State University Press edition.

37. Brown, *Stephen Calvert*, 71–72.

38. Ibid., 138, 141, 140. See also pp. 247–48 for another example of Carlton's demands.

39. Brown, *Stephen Calvert*, 179–80.

40. Dunlap, *Life of Brown*, 1:16; Allen, *The Life of Charles Brockden Brown* (MS; reprint Delmar, N.Y., 1975), 16, 56; John Bernard, *Retrospectives of America, 1797–1811* (New York, 1887), 252.

41. See Watts, *Republic Reborn*, 42–58, for a more extensive treatment of Brackenridge.

42. For a fuller discussion of Freneau and several other writers, see Steven Watts, "Masks, Morals, and the Market: Literature and Early Capitalist Culture," *Journal of the Early Republic* 6, no. 2 (1986): 127–49.

43. Fielding is quoted in Jean-Christophe Agnew, *Worlds Apart: The Market and the Theatre in Anglo-American Thought, 1550–1750* (Cambridge, 1986), 158–59. See also Raymond Williams, *Culture and Society: 1780–1950* (New York, [1958] 1983), 30–48; Jay Fliegelman, *Prodigals and Pilgrims: The American Revolution against Patriarchal Authority, 1750–1800* (Cambridge, 1982), 26–29; Ian Watt, *The Rise of the Novel: Studies in Defoe, Richardson, and Fielding* (Berkeley, Calif., 1957), 290,

296–99; and Michael McKeon, *The Origins of the English Novel, 1600–1740* (Baltimore, 1987), 418–20.

44. See the discussions of Rousseau in Fliegelman, *Prodigals and Pilgrims*, 29–35, 131–32, 241; Agnew, *Worlds Apart*, 190–91; and McCoy, *The Elusive Republic*, 23–25.

45. Friedrich Schiller, *On the Aesthetic Education of Man* (1795), 33, 35, 31–33, 17, 35, 45.

46. The quote appears in Charles Brockden Brown, *Arthur Mervyn; or, Memoirs of the Year 1793* (Kent, Ohio, 1980), 414.

47. See Gordon Wood, "The Democratization of Mind in the American Revolution," in Robert H. Horowitz, ed., *The Moral Foundations of the American Republic* (Charlottesville, Va., 1979), 102–28, for an insightful analysis of this process of cultural redefinition. Related discussions can be found in Davidson, *Revolution and the Word*, 42, 45, 49; Michael Warner, *The Letters of the Republic: Publication and the Public Sphere in Eighteenth-Century America* (Cambridge, Mass., 1990), 19–30, 34–72; Rhys Isaacs, "Books and the Social Authority of Learning: The Case of Mid-Eighteenth Century Virginia," in William L. Joyce et al., eds., *Printing and Society in Early America* (Worcester, Mass., 1983), 248–49; and Richard D. Brown, *Knowledge Is Power: The Diffusion of Information in Early America, 1700–1865* (New York, 1989), especially pp. 268–296.

48. See the extensive discussion of Rush in Watts, *Republic Reborn*, 131–41.

49. See Watts, *Republic Reborn*, Chapters 2–4 and Linda K. Kerber, *Women of the Republic: Intellect and Ideology in Revolutionary America* (Chapel Hill, N.C., 1980), Chapters 7–9. On American Victorianism, see two books by Daniel Walker Howe: his edited volume *Victorian America* (Philadelphia, 1975) and *The Political Culture of the American Whigs* (Chicago, 1979), especially pp. 23–42.

50. Brown, *Stephen Calvert*, 245.

51. See Ralph Waldo Emerson, "The American Scholar," in Stephen E. Whicher, ed., *Selections from Ralph Waldo Emerson* (Boston, 1960), 64; Karen Halttunen, "Gothic Mystery and the Birth of the Asylum," American Studies Association session paper, Oct. 1990, 12–15; and Herman Melville, *Moby Dick* (New York, 1972) and *The Confidence Man: His Masquerade* (New York, 1964).

52. See Alexis de Tocqueville, *Democracy in America* (New York, 1969), 536–38, 488–89; Max Weber, *The Protestant Ethic and the Spirit of Capitalism* (New York, 1958), 119, 181–82; Karl Marx, "Economic and Philosophic Manuscripts of 1844: Selections" and "Manifesto of the Communist Party," in Robert C. Tucker, ed., *The Marx-Engels Reader* (New York, 1972), 95–96, 338, 340; and Sigmund Freud, *Civilization and Its Discontents* (New York, 1961), 62.

# Bibliographic Essay

Charles Brockden Brown has been the subject of many monographs, book chapters, and articles over the years, especially during the past two decades. Many of these analyses are quite insightful and shed considerable light on this multifaceted writer and his career in the early republic. Nonetheless, from the viewpoint of the student of American culture, much of this scholarship presents distinct limitations. A variety of problems flowing from the literary emphasis of most of these studies—narrow textual analysis or old-fashioned narrative naivete in some, elitist cultural assumptions in others, abstract philosophical treatment in a few—prove troublesome to the historian of ideology and values. Thus, what follows is a critical commentary on the Brown literature. It reflects my own sense of its strengths and weaknesses, and is meant to be suggestive rather than exhaustive since a fair number of the more technical literary studies of Brown have been omitted. Most important, this essay suggests the location for my own interpretation in *The Romance of Real Life*.

Several older, full-length treatments of Charles Brockden Brown provide the basic biographical information on which subsequent studies have been based. Paul Allen's *The Life of Charles Brockden Brown* (1814 MS; reprint Delmar, N.Y.: Scholars' Facsimiles and Reprints, 1975) was originally commissioned by Brown's family shortly after his death. It was never completed and published, although one copy of a large fragment apparently found its way to print. Rediscovered in 1912 in the Historical Society of Philadelphia's archives, this crude copy consisted of a few biographical details strung together with lengthy transcribed chunks from Brown's stories, essays, and journal entries. William Dunlap, a close friend of the late novelist, was called in to complete Allen's work. After a year and a half, his *The Life of Charles Brockden Brown: Together with Selections from the Rarest of His Printed Works, from His Original Letters, and from His Manuscripts before Unpublished* (Philadelphia: James P. Parke, 1815) was produced. Long the standard account of Brown's life, Volume 1 reprinted Allen's manuscript while Volume 2 reprinted even more of Brown's letters and many of his fictional fragments. Both Dunlap and Allen are useful for gleaning basic information about Brown's life and writings, but their interpretive value is practically nil.

Shortly after World War II, the first modern biographies began to appear. Harry R. Warfel, in his *Charles Brockden Brown, American Gothic Novelist* (Gainesville: University of Florida Press, 1949), offered a solid, gracefully written narrative treatment of the author's life and times. Basically a nontheoretical analysis, the book did not dig deeply. It summarized Brown's novels, short fiction, and political pieces and focused on his Gothic techniques and status as a fledgling cultural nationalist. Shortly thereafter, David Lee Clark published *Charles Brockden Brown, Pioneer Voice of America* (Durham, N.C.: Duke University Press, 1952), a somewhat rambling study noteworthy for two things. First, it contributed additional biographical details derived from newly discovered sources, and printed a few barely known Brown stories along with large selections from the novelist's private correspondence. Second, Clark presented his subject as a disciple of the French Enlightenment and William Godwin, an advocate of democracy and women's rights who gradually became "a child of the individualistic, democratic nineteenth [century]—a romanticist." While containing a germ of truth, this overdrawn contention would later require careful modification. Donald A. Ringe's *Charles Brockden Brown* (New York: Twayne Publishers, 1966; rev. ed. 1991) comprised the last full-scale treatment of Brown's career that we have. A brief, utilitarian examination, the book displayed compact summaries of both the writer's life and his literary efforts. It presented a useful breakdown of most of Brown's major writings in terms of content, structure, and style and traced his literary influence in terms of Gothic devices and "psychological" characters. Ringe's book, like its predecessors, stressed narrative description and literary classification at the expense of critical cultural analysis.

Ironically, perhaps the fullest exploration of Brown and his work has never been published. Warner Berthoff's doctoral dissertation, "The Literary Career of Charles Brockden Brown" (Harvard University, 1954), has never found its way to print, even though it has become a staple of Brown scholarship. This "romancer" of the early republic, Berthoff argues, used narrative as a "means of exploring ideas and dramatizing ideological conflicts." Here was a liberal man of letters whose work revolved around a "testing-out of moral ideas." He demonstrated a loyalty to American "progress" and "cultural nationalism" and moved from an early attachment to "a purgative moral excitement" toward a stance of "practicable social compromise." For all of its breadth of scope, judicious judgments, and sophisticated analysis, this work nonetheless carries the burden of 1950s liberalism. Berthoff's Brown is a forerunner of the Cold War progressive intellectual, struggling for cultural stability and moral meaning in a world in flux.

In succeeding years, a growing number of studies have unfolded sophisticated new interpretations of Brown the writer. A rough indicator of this upsurge of interest can be seen in the appearance of several bibliographic efforts. "A Census of the Works of Charles Brockden Brown," *Serif* 3 (1966): 27–55, by Sydney J. Krause, reflected the desire for an authoritative knowledge of Brown's published works. A few years later Paul Witherington's "Charles Brockden Brown: A Bibliographic Essay," *Early American Literature* 9 (1974): 164–87, provided a comprehensive list of interpretive literature on the novelist to date. Around the same time, Charles E. Bennett contributed two very useful pieces. His Ph.D. dissertation, "The Charles Brockden Brown Canon" (University of North Carolina, 1974), not only surveyed the writer's literary career as the broad, multifaceted enterprise of a "man of letters" but also helped identify many of Brown's poetic and journalistic pieces. Bennett's "The Letters of Charles Brockden Brown: An Annotated Census," *Resources for American Literary Study* 6 (1976): 164–90, constructed a convenient, annotated listing of Brown's private letters and their repositories throughout the United States. Bernard Rosenthal's edited collection, *Critical Essays on Charles Brockden Brown* (Boston: G. K. Hall and Co., 1981), combined nineteenth-century reviews of Brown's novels with a number of critiques from contemporary literary scholars. These anthologies and bibliographies mirrored a heightening critical interest in the literary significance of this early national writer, an interest that had begun to crop up in several areas.

In the aftermath of Brown's full-scale biographies, considerable attention began to focus on this early national writer as a literary artist and craftsman. Warner B. Berthoff took the lead with several articles drawn from his unpublished Ph.D. dissertation. His "'A Lesson on Concealment': Brockden Brown's Method in Fiction," *Philological Quarterly* 37 (1958): 45–57, suggested that Brown improvised as he hurriedly wrote, "testing" ideas as he pursued their motivations, actions, and consequences among his characters. In "Adventures of the Young Man: An Approach to Charles Brockden Brown," *American Quarterly* 9 (1957): 421–34, Berthoff went on to argue that many of Brown's stories utilized the eighteenth-century literary trope of the young man's "initiation." Norman S. Grabo, in *The Coincidental Art of Charles Brockden Brown* (Chapel Hill: University of North Carolina Press, 1981), countered with a "New Critical close reading." He contended that Brown's obsession with doubling and coincidence was the centerpiece of his "fictive art," and portrayed this author as a sophisticated "conscious craftsman" in touch with German romanticism and sensitive to American cultural "biformity." Paul Witherington's "Brockden Brown's Other Novels: *Clara Howard* and *Jane Talbot*," *Nineteenth-Century Fiction* 29 (1974): 257–72, argued for the importance of the last two "domestic novels," linking them with the earlier "major novels" both thematically (the victory of society over the chastened individual) and stylistically (an ongoing search for narrative technique that culminated here in "comedies of manners").

More recent versions of Brown as literary craftsman have focused on language, aesthetics, and poetics. Dennis Berthold, for instance, has offered one view in his "Charles Brockden Brown, *Edgar Huntly*, and the Origins of the American Picturesque," *William and Mary Quarterly* 41 (1984): 62–84. According to Berthold, this early national author consistently and consciously utilized a "picturesque aesthetics" drawn from eighteenth-century landscape painting to promote a moral balance between civilization and the wilderness. Mark Seltzer, in his "Saying Makes It So: Language and Event in Brown's *Wieland*," *Early American Literature* 13 (1978): 81–91, argues that the inconsistencies and fluctuations in Brown's novels flowed from his uncertain attitude toward language. *Wieland*, in particular, demonstrates "an equivocation regarding the process of uttering" and presents "an uncertain causal relation between speech and response." Michael Kreyling moves this linguistic analysis into the realm of poststructuralist theory with his "Construing Brown's *Wieland*: Ambiguity and Derridean 'Freeplay,'" *Studies in the Novel* 14 (1982): 43–54. He contends that the subtitle of this novel, "The Transformation," connotes Brown's creation of a "decentered universe" that prefigured the darker work of Poe, Melville, and Hawthorne. William C. Spengemann, in a section of his *The Adventurous Muse: The Poetics of American Fiction, 1789–1900* (New Haven: Yale University Press, 1977), 98–106, sees Brown working within a tradition of "the poetics of domesticity," one of the main influences on the emergence of American romanticism. *Arthur Mervyn*, for instance, shows Brown straining to use conventions of the domestic novel to restrain an adventurous individualism. This struggle is only partly successful, Spengemann concludes, because the author's imagination constantly goes beyond the point where "he could control its moral direction."

This entire group of literary studies, while useful for considering the interior dimension of Brown's work, suffers from a central weakness. It tends to divorce that work from the social and political reality of the early American republic. While aesthetic influences are certainly important, neither literary texts nor their writers exist in a historical vacuum. The absence of a social context mars these analyses, as it does many other interpretations of Brown as well.

Both the scholarly skill and narrow scope of these literary/genre studies have been replicated in what might be termed "epistemological" studies of Brown's writing. Larzer Ziff's "A Reading of *Wieland,*" *Publications of the Modern Language Association of America* 77 (1962): 51–57, established a foundation for this approach. Brown's first novel, Ziff argued, undermined both "enlightened psychology" and the "sentimental novel" by recalling a Calvinist sensibility stressing human beings' innate depravity and deluded senses. Arthur Kimball, in *Rational Fictions: A Study of Charles Brockden Brown* (McKinnville, Ore.: Linfield Research Institute, 1968), followed with a more extensive exploration of this entire area. Brown's novels, this scholar insisted, were best understood in terms of "Lockean epistemology" and its "sensationalist psychology." Brown took Locke's notion that all knowledge could be traced to simple sensations, and, by introducing in his stories a "manipulator of the senses," subverted the process. Thus, a concern with the irrationality and savagery of the mind shaped Brown's literary assertion that "human nature has more dark corners and hidden dimensions than Enlightenment philosophy could account for." James Russo, in a brace of articles, followed this lead. His " 'The Chimeras of the Brain': Clara's Narrative in *Wieland,*" *Early American Literature* 16 (1981): 60–88, contended that the female narrator was not only the center of the tale, but also a figure who flitted between reality and insanity. This provided a dramatic illustration of the central theme of Brown's fiction: characters are "incapable of making rational judgments based on sense perceptions." In "The Chameleon of Convenient Vice: A Study of the Narrative of *Arthur Mervyn,*" *Studies in the Novel* 11 (1979): 381–405, Russo extends this analysis to argue that Arthur is neither ambiguous nor divided, but an outright seducer, fraud, liar, imposter, and criminal, and hence another manifestation of Brown's attack on the reliability of Enlightenment epistemology.

In one sense, this group of studies is useful for re-creating, at least in part, the philosophical context for Brown's thinking and correctly recognizing him as a "novelist of ideas." For these epistemological scholars, as for the literary group mentioned earlier, however, ideas themselves are construed in highly abstract and idealized terms. One gets little sense of the fluid material, social, and political environment of late eighteenth-century America in which they developed. Moreover, two other problems linger. First, this school exaggerates Brown's preoccupation with Locke and his rejection of Enlightenment psychology. In fact, this early national intellectual tried to shape a complex accommodation with "reason" both in his novels of the 1790s and in his journalistic and political essays after 1800. Second, the epistemological school attributes to Brown a clearer and more focused literary intellect than the evidence supports. Brown's encounter with Lockean psychology was at best haphazard, and it mingled with a host of other influences—Richardson's didactic novels, Godwinian radicalism, Rousseau's romanticism, republican ideology, pressures of the marketplace—in molding his eclectic fiction.

Such problems of narrow focus have prompted some scholars to broaden their scope of inquiry by relocating Brown's writings in their cultural context. One variation of this enterprise has described his literature as an expression of an eighteenth-century search for cultural "identity." Alan Axelrod, for instance, in *Charles Brockden Brown, An American Tale* (Austin: University of Texas Press, 1983), has argued that Brown's fiction represents a larger struggle between Old World "civilization" and New World "wilderness" as part of a search for an "American identity" during the early national decades. In a pair of articles that focus on one novel, A. Carl Bredahl has pursued a parallel path. His "Transformation in *Wieland*," *Early American Literature* 12 (1977): 77–91, anticipated Axelrod with an emphasis on the novel's "transformation," emerging from New World imagination and its demonic energy. "The Two Portraits in *Wieland*," *Early American Fiction* 16 (1981): 54–59, casts a wider cultural net. It suggested that this text mirrors a broad cultural shift in this period from an "allegiance to the abstract" toward "a fascination with the concrete." Drawing on Foucault's notion of the "episteme," the author contends that this shift moved away from a sense of organic kinship toward a discriminating ethos based on "identity" and "function." Two other articles underlined this cultural preoccupation with identity. Both "Arthur Mervyn, American," *American Literature* 42 (1970): 304–24, by James H. Justus, and "Studied Ambiguities: *Arthur Mervyn* and the Problem of the Unreliable Narrator," *American Literature* 42 (1970): 18–27, by Patrick Brancaccio, depict this novel as the story of a young man on the make in a competitive society. Such works, of course, are at least partly rooted in an older version of this theme found in R. W. B. Lewis, *The American Adam: Innocence, Tragedy, and Tradition in the Nineteenth Century* (Chicago: University of Chicago Press, 1955), 90–98. Brown's character Arthur Mervyn, according to Lewis, was an early prototype of "the hero in space," standing outside time in an unbounded "area of total possibility." This venturous, solitary American Adam "has no past and no inheritance to help or hinder him; he brings with him nothing but a pure and empty heart and a mind like a *tabula rasa.*" As these critics have suggested, several persistent themes in Brown's novels—suspicions about personal character, social manipulation, misappropriation of money and goods—reveal a larger cultural dilemma of the individual seeking self-definition and success in a fluid social milieu.

Within the cultural identity school, a pair of studies has focused in particular on Brown's relationship to an American proclivity for violence. Richard Slotkin's eloquent *Regeneration through Violence: The Mythology of the American Frontier, 1600–1860* (Middletown, Conn.: Wesleyan University Press, 1973), has presented Brown's *Edgar Huntly* as emerging from a long tradition of American frontier tales. As a "drama of evolving consciousness" in the early romantic era, this novel explored the "wilderness" of the human mind and its hidden impulses to evil as the protagonist searched for his identity. Edgar's quest, Slotkin argues, reflected "archetypal myth patterns" in this New World culture as Americans consistently sought the dark side of their own nature in animal and Indian representations. An earlier study of similar issues can be found in David Brion Davis, *Homicide in American Fiction, 1798-1860: A Study in Social Values* (Ithaca: Cornell University Press, 1957). Fictional deployments of homicide, Davis argues, served as a barometer of American cultural values in the period between Independence and the Civil War. Charles Brockden Brown's notoriously violent novels, depicting sensual indulgence, indolence, and seduction, demonstrate a broader concern in the post-Revolutionary republic. With liberation from traditional authority, Brown and many of his contemporaries believed, freedom might take a dark turn and lead to a triumph of the passions.

Another cultural interpretation has specifically linked Brown's literary innovations to larger cultural traits in America. Two classics in American literary criticism have led the way. Richard Chase, in his famous *The American Novel and Its Tradition* (Garden City, N.Y.: Doubleday Anchor Books, 1957), argued that "melodrama," or the depiction of "tragedy in a vacuum," characterized Brown's fiction. This trait helped initiate the "romance" tradition at the heart of the American novel. For Chase, the writings of this early national author offered a prototype for what became a typically schizoid way of looking at the world: Americans "tend to ideology and psychology; they are adept at depicting the largest public abstractions and the smallest and most elusive turn of the inner mind. But they do not have a firm sense of a social arena where ideology and psychology find a concrete representation and are seen in their fullest human significance." In *Love and Death in the American Novel* (New York: Stein and Day, 1960; rev. ed. 1966), Leslie Fiedler reads Brown in a somewhat different light. Attempting to define what is "peculiarly American" in our books and culture, this critic argues for the prominence of the "Gothic" mode, and describes Brown in terms of "The Invention of the American Gothic." By successfully shifting the focus of the genre from the ruined castles of Europe to the forests and caves of the New World, this early novelist helped shape an American sensibility that was "nonrealistic and negative, sadist and melodramatic—a literature of darkness and the grotesque in a land of light and affirmation." More recently, Michael Davitt Bell has built on the insights of Chase and Fiedler. His "'The Double-Tongued Deceiver': Sincerity and Duplicity in the Novels of Charles Brockden Brown," *Early American Literature* 9 (1974): 143–63, argues that Brown's major novels, as the epistemological interpreters insist, indeed turn on a contest between "sincerity" and "duplicity." Rather than indicating an attack on Lockean rationalism, however, this suggests the subversive force of "literary art and literary imagination" in late eighteenth-century America, an age when the novel itself is associated with a revolutionary assault on social order. In his *The Development of American Romance: The Sacrifice of Relation* (Chicago: University of Chicago Press, 1980), Bell broadens the argument to consider the development of imaginative "romance" as a manifestation of "imagination" in a culture that deified realism and facts. Brockden Brown, he believes, was a precursor of American romanticism "as the first American romancer to respond seriously and profoundly to the antifictional hysteria of his culture." As a literary champion of "imaginative power" who eventually faltered, this author embodied what would become a pattern in the lives of nineteenth-century romancers: writing as alienation from a utilitarian society of sober truth, as a "deviant career" based on a personal "sacrifice of relation" to social normalcy.

In one sense, these "cultural" readings represent a critical advance in their determination to move beyond Brown's texts with their philosophical ideas and literary techniques into a contextual analysis of his writing. This helps relocate Brown in his cultural setting and provides a much fuller understanding of his ideas and labors as a writer. In another sense, however, this interpretation disappoints because of an excessively abstract and disembodied vision of American culture. The same difficulties emerge here that once troubled the "myth and symbol" scholarship of the early American Studies movement: a habit of conflating elite culture with all culture, an eagerness to avoid the material context for ideas, a tendency to ignore the actual historical environment of texts in order to establish connection with highly generalized cultural abstractions. In other words, the Brown emerging from such studies appears in a fuller context, but is obscured by the cloud of a cosmic "American Mind."

Over the past couple of decades, some scholarship on Charles Brockden Brown has taken a happy turn for the historical. On a number of fronts, criticism has attempted to combine literary and cultural analysis with a sensitivity to the unsettled historical conditions of the late eighteenth-century American Republic. William Hedges, in "Charles Brockden Brown and the Culture of Contradictions," *Early American Literature* 9 (1974): 107–42, sounded a clarion call for this kind of research. Most studies of this author, Hedges noted, gave "no very clear sense of Brown as a person who lived in a particular time and place." The Atlantic world of the late eighteenth century was torn by numerous conflicts and "contradictions," and Brown's notorious torment and alienation as a writer need to be explained in terms of their relation to the intellectual, social, and political instability of this particular era. A number of earlier works, of course, had offered brief and oversimplified attempts at a kind of political analysis. Charles Cole's "Brockden Brown and the Jefferson Administration," *Pennsylvania Magazine of History and Biography* 72 (1948): 253–63, contended that Brown had changed from a "Jeffersonian radical" in the 1790s to a quasi-Federalist, caustic critic of the Jeffersonians by the early 1800s. Warner Berthoff offered a more sophisticated revision of this thesis in a pair of articles. This end-of-the-century author, he argued in "Brockden Brown: The Politics of the Man of Letters," *Serif* 3 (1966): 3–11, actually shifted from an early concern with "the metaphysics of spiritual transformation" to a sense of "practicable social compromise" after 1800. This shift, as Berthoff had noted in "Charles Brockden Brown's Historical 'Sketches': A Consideration," *American Literature* 28 (1956): 147–54, was especially evident in the conservatism of his major (and only partially published) attempt at fiction late in life. Much more recently, John Seelye's essay, "Charles Brockden Brown and Early American Fiction," in Emory Elliott, ed., *Columbia Literary History of the United States* (New York: Columbia University Press, 1987), 168–86, has updated this kind of analysis. Brown's literature, he writes, was not so much a precursor of romanticism as a "reflection of the political temper of his age," especially in terms of simultaneously borrowing and subverting the genre of the "Jacobin novel."

This general trend toward a historicized rendering of Brown's career has gone in several parallel directions. One group of studies has focused on the theme of cultural "identity," but not in the highly generalized terms of the "New World" or the "American Mind" of earlier mentioned texts. Instead, the emphasis has fallen on the specific dynamics of late eighteenth-century culture. Lawrence J. Friedman, for instance, has linked the evolution of Brown's writings to the consolidation of a nationalist "patriotic crusade" in America by the early nineteenth century. In a chapter of his *Inventors of the Promised Land* (New York: Alfred A. Knopf, 1975), 79–105, he argues that Brown underwent a "conversion" around 1803 by rejecting literature, philosophy, and criticism in favor of commerce, politics, and "doctrinaire patriotism." This switch, Friedman suggests, derived from Brown's unsatisfying critique in the 1790s, which was full of "abstract intellectual analysis" but little sense of real "social action." Brown ultimately gravitated toward conservative nationalism because "the dogmatic patriot was at least a vigorous social animal—much more so than the isolated dissident." Deborah M. Bingham has seen a different cultural dynamic at work. Her "The Identity Crisis of Charles Brockden Brown" (Ph.D. diss., Bowling Green State University, 1977), has drawn on the theories of Erik Erikson to assert that Brown's writing was largely a response to an adolescent "identity crisis" conditioned by the breakdown of a "patriarchal" family model in the post-Revolutionary era. In a more literary treatment, Beverly R. Voloshin, in her "*Edgar Huntly* and the Coherence of the Self," *Early American Literature* 23 (1988): 262–80, addressed Brown's work as part of an eighteenth-century cultural crisis, in which there was a growing proclivity to question "the coherence of the perceiving self." Challenging Lockean psychology by probing the "subconsciousness" of the human psyche, Brown's writings intimated that both the "linear self" and the orderly world to which it was connected constantly threatened "to elude the net of self-presence and representation."

Similar works have focused on Brown's struggle to shape his identity as a writer under adverse cultural circumstances. Maurice J. Bennett, in "A Portrait of the Artist in Eighteenth-Century America: Charles Brockden

Brown's *Memoirs of Stephen Calvert*," *William and Mary Quarterly* 39 (1982): 492–507, argues that Brown's writings, particularly this long novelistic fragment, comprised an effort to shape through literature a "productive exercise of the imagination" in a skeptical, materialistic American society. This social and cultural struggle helped produce a body of writing that became a prototype for "the romantic convention of the Divided Self." Robert A. Ferguson suggests a similar theme. His article, "Literature and Vocation in the Early Republic: The Example of Charles Brockden Brown," *Modern Philology* 78 (1980): 139–52, promotes the notion that "vocational anxiety" in the late 1700s—a period in which the traditional model of the "gentleman of letters" was falling into disrepair—beset Brown in terms of an anguished career choice between being a respectable lawyer or a dubious author. As Ferguson elaborates in his book *Law and Letters in American Culture* (Cambridge, Mass.: Harvard University Press, 1984), the author's writings became a focal point for this struggle between "the artist and republican culture." In novels that took shape as a "fantasy world for projecting occupational difficulties," characters such as Arthur Mervyn, Stephen Calvert, and Theodore Wieland were figures representing "the desire to appear useful in an age of utility."

Another recent group of historical studies of Brown has focused not so much on identity issues as "authority." In the turbulent world of post-Revolutionary America, traditional authority structures of all kinds seemed to be transforming or crumbling and the writings of this prolific author, some scholars have suggested, embodied this sea change. Jay Fliegelman, for example, in his brilliant book *Prodigals and Pilgrims: The American Revolution against Patriarchal Authority, 1750–1800* (Cambridge: Cambridge University Press, 1984), has addressed Brown in a section entitled "Ventriloquists, Counterfeiters, and the Seduction of the Mind." He suggests that Brown, especially in *Wieland*, was part and parcel of a late eighteenth-century assault on patriarchal authority. Brown's vision of liberation was not an optimistic one: in a post-Lockean world in which the "seduction" and "licentiousness" of the French Revolution seemed to be running amok, authority had become subject to wild imagination and misrepresentation. Fliegelman has embroidered upon this theme in his "Introduction" to a recent edition of *Wieland* (New York: Penguin Books, 1991), vii–xlii, where he notes that the novel explores "the conflicting claims of authority and liberty" and the "question of agency" that perplexed Americans during the 1790s.

Other scholars have explored various dimensions of this "crisis of authority." Mark R. Patterson, in a chapter of his *Authority, Autonomy, and Representation in American Literature, 1776–1865* (Princeton: Princeton University Press, 1988), 61–78, contends that the volatile, overwrought quality of Brown's fiction can be traced to a particular version of this issue. Just as the central political issue of the late 1700s and early 1800s concerned the location and character of civic authority, a central cultural issue for writers was the definition of their own authority through new forms of literary representation. Thus, Brown explored how democratization shifted public authority into the realm of "private judgment," and his characters represented the disturbing possibilities inherent in this "internalization of political issues." Robert S. Levine has moved to rehistoricize Brown's fiction by stressing its close ties to "countersubversion" in the explosive atmosphere of the late eighteenth-century Atlantic world. In *Conspiracy and Romance* (New York: Cambridge University Press, 1989), he argues that the French Revolution destabilized traditional notions of authority and community, thus creating in the infant New World republic a frightening picture of "conspiring villains and vulnerable Americans." Brown engaged this "conspiratorial discourse" in novels with plots that teemed with mysterious, nefarious reformers associated with the Bavarian Illuminati, and with structures that linked "social and narrative uncertainty." *Ormond*, Levine contends, provides the best dramatization of this cultural theme through its blending of the seduction novel's sexual anxiety and the countersubversive novel's "fear of conspiracy." Brown, as a "connoisseur of conspiracy," presents "a dark picture of America's political and social precariousness" in an age of upheaval. Jane Tompkins, in two sections of her *Sensational Designs: The Cultural Work of American Fiction, 1790–1860* (New York: Oxford University Press, 1985), 40–61, 62–93, offers yet another version of the "authority" thesis. Brown, she insists, shaped his fiction not in terms of artistic creation but as "political tracts" aimed at reining in individual licentiousness. Thus, *Wieland* was intended as a "plea for the restoration of civic authority" while *Arthur Mervyn* promoted a Federalist vision of "civic virtue" based on benevolence, urban life, and commercial growth.

Feminist scholarship over the past two decades has provided a special look at the gendered relationship between Brown's writings and fluid structures of authority in America during the late 1700s. Judith Ann Cunningham's "Charles Brockden Brown's Pursuit of a Realistic Feminism" (Ph.D. diss., Ball State University, 1971) offers a typical reading of Brown as an early advocate of women's rights and challenger of traditional male authority. Lee R. Edwards, in an "Afterword" to an edition of Brown's *Al-*

*cuin: A Dialogue* (New York: Grossman Publishers, 1970), 92–104, described this work as "the first sustained and earnest argument for the rights of women to appear in this country." Fritz Flieschman took this argument even further. In his essay "Charles Brockden Brown: Feminism in Fiction," which appeared in his edited volume *American Novelists Reconsidered: Essays in Feminist Criticism* (Boston: G. K. Hall, 1982), 6–41, Fleischman asserted that Brown's advocacy of female rights in *Alcuin* extended through all of his novels, even the domestic tales of the early nineteenth century, because of their special emphasis on "strong, independent women." Cynthia S. Jordan, in a chapter of her *Second Stories: The Politics of Language, Form, and Gender in Early American Fiction* (Chapel Hill: University of North Carolina Press, 1989), has complicated these rather simplistic renderings of Brown the protofeminist. Brown's sympathy for female equality, she argues, was shaped by a larger loyalty to "his predecessors' patriarchal world view." Thus, his feminism "consisted of the belief that women are equal to men in their capacity to experience and to act upon the full range of human passions." These essays, however, tend to exaggerate Brown's protofeminism. His views on women and social authority were highly ambiguous throughout the 1790s, before taking a bourgeois turn in the early 1800s. Moreover, he consistently struggled with, rather than confidently defined, the very notion of "feminine" and the place of women in the American social structure. This balanced view is probably best suggested by Cathy N. Davidson's "The Matter and Manner of Charles Brockden Brown's *Alcuin*," in Bernard Rosenthal, ed., *Critical Essays on Charles Brockden Brown* (Boston: G. K. Hall, 1981), 71–86.

In many ways, these various historicized studies of Charles Brockden Brown and American culture have greatly enhanced our understanding of this author and critic. Many of the essential, but previously obscured, connections between his writing and the fluid values and perceptions of his age have been clarified. Certain limitations, however, persist. These works tend to be too focused thematically and insufficiently synthetic. By isolating problems of identity, authority, or gender, one overlooks the fact that such issues were thoroughly entangled in a post-Revolutionary society in flux. In addition, this scholarship often oversimplifies the political dimension of Brown's work. He demonstrated, for instance, a complex, ambivalent, and developing attitude about patriarchal authority during his maturation from the late 1780s through the early nineteenth century. Moreover, Brown was neither a devotee of internalized political agency nor a committed Federalist upholder of civic authority in the face of individual licentiousness. He spent much of his post-adolescent life wrestling with such issues, and the life-long ambiguity of his politics surfaced clearly in the curious political pamphlets and "historical" fiction of his final years. Finally, once again, these cultural studies of Brown suffer from excessive abstraction. Their portraits of this intellectual figure, while compelling and instructive in many ways, present a picture that is removed, in certain cases, from the ongoing vicissitudes of his private life and, in many cases, from the actual socioeconomic and political transformations of this tumultuous age. In other words, while Brown's career and writings have been historicized, he still seems to be free-floating in a world of ideas removed from their material moorings.

Recent renderings of Brown have produced a handful of analyses that, in my view, present the fullest understanding we have of the writer, his texts, and his context. Their reconstruction of the connections among identity, ideology, social milieu, and cultural currents in the world of late eighteenth-century America make these pieces enormously suggestive and insightful. Emory Elliott's "Charles Brockden Brown: The Burden of the Past," in his *Revolutionary Writers: Literature and Authority in the New Republic, 1725–1810* (New York: Oxford University Press, 1982), 218–70, sketches a compelling general picture of a crisis of authority in the decades following the American Revolution. Brown the writer, he argues, was caught up in two traumatic and intertwined developments. Civic turmoil in the 1780s and 1790s created an uncertain vacillation between Federalist fears of mobocracy and Jeffersonian hopes of republican liberalism, while social upheaval in the Atlantic world had brought a collapse of faith in "reason" and Enlightenment epistemology. Brown's writings reflected this sense of political and cultural fluidity and his novels emerged as "explorations of the impact of the social and economic order on the lives of individuals." *Arthur Mervyn* particularly summarized this thematic thrust, as Arthur came to symbolize the individual struggling to survive "in the social turmoil of the post-Revolutionary age."

Three other works have followed Elliott's lead to delineate other important aspects of the social and cultural flux characterizing Brown and his world. Daniel E. Cohen, in "Arthur Mervyn and his Elders: The Ambivalence of Youth in the Early Republic," *William and Mary Quarterly* 43 (1986): 362–80, attempts to resituate Brown in the generationally riven culture of the late eighteenth-century republic. Faced with a "volatile social world," Brown struggled with the problems of his age: generational conflict over the transfer of "liquid wealth" in a commercializing economy, a shift in childrearing and education toward the ideal of "rational independence," the problematic transition from childhood dependence to adult self-reliance, the tension between "vocational subordination" and "personal independence." Brown, especially in his novel *Arthur Mervyn*, illustrated "the transition period of the Early Republic," standing midway between the patriarchal authority of traditional colonial society and the internalized moral autonomy of Jacksonian America. Shirley Samuels has identified a similar theme in terms of family authority, ideology, and the novel genre in a disconnected and threatening era. In "Plague and Politics in 1793: *Arthur Mervyn*," *Criticism* 27 (1985): 225–46, she asserts that the Philadelphia "yellow fever" plague in this novel represented fears of sickness in the American body politic: a conflation of social licentiousness, rampant sexuality, and political upheaval associated with "the contagion" of Jacobin principles. Brown, however, uses this tale to pose both the family and the novel as "restoratives" to bring order out of chaos. Drawing upon Foucault's notion of "disciplinary institutions," Samuels contends that the self-destruction of Welbeck's corrupt family, Arthur's attempts to insinuate himself with the Hadwin family, and his ultimate marriage to Ascha represent a final triumph of "family order." And the novel itself—she terms it an "educational tool"—becomes part of the solution as it teaches readers "what to fear" and "to desire home and family." In this reading Brown emerges as an important figure in making "the institution of the novel" a centerpiece of nineteenth-century bourgeois life. Larzer Ziff's treatment of this novelist in his *Writing in the New Nation: Prose, Print, and Politics in the Early United States* (New Haven: Yale University Press, 1991) parallels Cohen and Samuels. American political culture and print culture, he argues, were "twins born from the same conditions." Issues of "political representation" and "literary representation" paralleled one another and both, in turn, were wrapped up in "a shift in the economic sphere from real to personal—or represented—property." Focusing on *Arthur Mervyn*, Ziff argues that Brown depicts the United States as a mobile land of opportunity where social, and economic manipulation predominate and where there is no reality beyond representation. "Success lies in the ability to construct a reputation and capitalize on it rather than remaining within a self unaugmented by representation; personal property has greater influence than real."

Finally, a pair of brilliant books by Michael Warner and Cathy N. Davidson have utilized language theory to penetrate the cultural meaning of the novel as "discourse" in a volatile social setting. Warner has explored the emergence of a "bourgeois public sphere" in *The Letters of the Republic:*

*Publication and the Public Sphere in Eighteenth-Century America* (Cambridge, Mass.: Harvard University Press, 1990). This cultural realm, he argues, stood separate from both the state and private life, and depended on "print discourse"—newspapers, pamphlets, broadsides, coffeehouses, literary salons, magazines—to formulate a notion of "the people" as an entity reading and acting on the same information. Thus, the public sphere and republicanism "jointly made each other intelligible." By the late 1700s, Warner continues, this civic print discourse was coming into contact with "liberal values of literary textuality" that emphasized reading as a private experience. Thus, early American novels, like those of Charles Brockden Brown, became a "hinge" between an older republican model of civic print discourse and a newer one of "modernity." *Arthur Mervyn* embodied this tension as a novel that "resists being a novel." The text offered an old-fashioned republican anxiety about the possibility of "virtue" in a world of credit, capital, and fluid social relations, while at the same time it undermined the paradigm of republican literature by using a genre of "privatizing discourse." Thus, Brown's writings led a tense coexistence between a civic/republican mode and an individualist/liberal one.

Cathy Davidson's analysis of the rise of the novel in America adds yet another dimension to this portrait of discursive meaning. Her study of late eighteenth-century fiction, entitled *Revolution and the Word: The Rise of the Novel in America* (New York: Oxford University Press, 1986), posits that the novel spearheaded a "reading revolution" that undermined the "gentleman's" literary sphere. Appealing to marginalized groups in American society—women, the lower classes, the barely educated—this genre culturally and politically subverted older modes of authority by radically extending literary participation. Brown's novels, Davidson believes, appeared at just this historical moment of cultural transition and employed Gothic techniques to probe "the limits of individualism." Tales like *Arthur Mervyn* used horror to depict the outward decay of an established order, while also burrowing deep into the psyche to show a decay within from irrational urges. Such ambiguity also appeared in the character of Arthur, whom the author deployed to challenge the notion of "rational choice" and to show the vicissitudes of "modern personality" in an age of growing individualism. Overall, according to Davidson, Brown displayed in his fiction a "carnivalesque performance" in which determined ambiguities of character and plot sustain a spirit of "revolt" against social constraints and proprieties.

Even with this group of essays, there remains considerable room for interpretive addition and synthesis. We catch tantalizing glimpses of Charles

Brockden Brown and his cultural world, but a certain narrowness and fragmented quality accruing to this work—understandable given the restrictions imposed by article or chapter-length studies—suggest that several vital tasks remain. First, there is need for a study that looks at the whole of Brown's career and the entire corpus of his writing, not just bits and pieces here and there. The kind of analysis that recent historicized studies have made of *Arthur Mervyn* needs to be extended both forward and backward to gain a full picture of this author's entire career. Moreover, such analysis should branch out into the great variety of Brownian texts: fiction, non-fiction, extensive private writings. Second, there is need for a study of Brown that links the volatile and emotional literary productions of his "public" life with the notorious disarray of his "private" life. The various crises of the late eighteenth-century American republic had psychological as well as civic resonances, and recovering the links between the two is crucial. Finally, there is need for a synthetic cultural study of Brown that examines his ideas and their expression, yet firmly grounds those issues in the socioeconomic and political transformations of post-Revolutionary America. Such a study would reconnect problems of identity, ideology, discourse, and social change as they came together in one individual's experience. By recreating as fully as possible the historical context binding writer and context, text and subtext, *The Romance of Real Life* attempts to fulfill these tasks.

# Index

Adams, John Quincy, 10

Advice literature, 6

*Alcuin* (Brown), 51, 60-65, 120; and characters' shifting positions within, 62; different readings of, 61; liberalism versus collectivism in, 63-65; and male authority, 61-62; and market critique, 62-65

American Philosophical Society, 50

*American Register, or General Repository of History, Politics, and Science,* 143-44, 165, 168

American Revolution, 3, 5, 8, 12, 15, 27, 49, 61

Ames, Fisher, 10

*Arthur Mervyn* (Brown), 72, 80, 101-15, 130; and collapse of paternalism, 112-13; and the confidence man, 103, 108-9, 110-12; and critique of commercial values, 109-10, 115; and gender formulations, 113-15; and individual fragmentation, 103-4, 107-8, 112, 115; plot of, 102-3, and search for moral principles, 106-7, 115; and sexual tensions, 105, 113-14; sincerity versus deception in, 105-6, 108-10, 111-12; and success seeking, 104-5; and symbolism of the yellow fever, 102, 110, 115

Astor, John Jacob, 4

Austen, Jane, 194

Bakhtin, Mikhail, 14

Barlow, 10

Bavarian Illuminati, 94, 183

Beecher, Lyman, 7, 197

Brackenridge, Hugh Henry, 8, 11, 12 193

Brown, Charles Brockden: and abnormal psychology, 82-83, 117, 191; adolescence of, 29-30, 35, 40; as advocate of commercial

growth, 176-77; and American factionalism, 178-79; and American imperialism, 167, 179-80; and *American Register, or General Repository of History, Politics, and Science,* 143-44, 165, 168; on artistic endeavor and commercial values, 145-46; and attraction to writing, 71, 79; and Belles-Lettres Club, 29, 31, 58; career of, xi, xiii, 2, 25-26, 46-48, 50-60, 65-70, 71, 128-30, 131-32, 143-46, 148-49, 161-63, 164-66, 180, 191-93; and career retrenchment in early nineteenth century, 131-32, 146-47, 164, 165, 169, 180; and challenges to traditional social authority, 51, 54, 129; and Christianity, 54-57, 83-84, 158; and courtship of Elizabeth Linn, 148-50; as critic of paternalism, 161; as cultural critic, 155-56, 158-63, 164, 180-81, 195-96, 197-98; and cultural nationalism, 51, 117, 168; domestic life of, 143, 154-55, 165; and dream life, 41-42, 46, 122-23, 152; as editor and journalist, 132, 143-45, 169; education of, 28-30; and embrace of bourgeois morality in early nineteenth century, xvi, 133, 137, 143, 146, 150-54, 156, 158-59, 161-63, 166, 167-68, 170, 195-96; emotional crises of, 34, 36-42, 47, 52-54, 78, 153-54; and the Enlightenment, 29-30, 31, 58; failing health of, 165-66; family background of, 27-28; and French Revolution, 160-61; and friendship with Joseph Bringhurst, Jr., 33-34, 36, 40, 55-56, 83-84; and friendship with William Woods Wilkins, 33-34; and gender formulations, 58-64, 92-93, 132, 149-54, 157; on genteel taste, 159-60; and Godwin, William, 67-69, 91, 124; and

243

Library of Congress Cataloging-in-Publication Data

Watts, Steven, 1952–
    The romance of real life : Charles Brockden Brown and the origins
of American culture / Steven Watts.
        p.    cm.
    Includes bibliographical references (p.) and index.
    ISBN 0-8018-4686-2 (alk. paper)
    1. Brown, Charles Brockden, 1771-1810.  2. Authors and readers—
United States—History—18th century.  3. Novelists, American—
18th century—Biography.  4. Novelists, American—19th century—
Biography.  5. United States—Civilization—1783-1865.
6. Authorship—History—18th century.  I. Title.
PS1136.W35  1994
813'.2—dc20
[B]      93-11601